Legislating Without Experience

Legislating Without Experience

Case Studies in State Legislative Term Limits

Edited by Rick Farmer,
Christopher Z. Mooney,
Richard J. Powell, and
John C. Green

LEXINGTON BOOKS

A division of
ROWMAN & LITTLEFIELD PUBLISHERS, INC.
Lanham • Boulder • New York • Toronto • Plymouth, UK

LEXINGTON BOOKS

A division of Rowman & Littlefield Publishers, Inc.
A wholly owned subsidiary of The Rowman & Littlefield Publishing Group, Inc.
4501 Forbes Boulevard, Suite 200
Lanham, MD 20706

Estover Road
Plymouth PL6 7PY
United Kingdom

Copyright © 2007 by Lexington Books

British Library Cataloguing in Publication Information Available

Library of Congress Cataloging-in-Publication Data

Legislating without experience: case studies in state legislative term limits / edited
  by Rick Farmer . . . [et al.].
    p. cm.
  Includes bibliographical references.
  ISBN-13: 978-0-7391-1144-4 (cloth : alk. paper)
  ISBN-10: 0-7391-1144-2 (cloth : alk. paper)
  ISBN-13: 978-0-7391-1145-1 (pbk. : alk. paper)
  ISBN-10: 0-7391-1145-0 (pbk. : alk. paper)
  1. Legislation—United States—States. 2. Term limits (Public office)—United
States—States. 3. Legislators—Term of office—United States—States.
4. Legislative power—United States—States. 5. Legislative bodies—United
States—States. I. Farmer, Rick, 1958-
  KF4945.L44 2007
  328.73'073—dc22   2007031853

Printed in the United States of America

♾™ The paper used in this publication meets the minimum requirements of
American National Standard for Information Sciences—Permanence of Paper
for Printed Library Materials, ANSI/NISO Z39.48-1992.

Contents

Tables and Figures

TABLES

FIGURES

Preface

Several visionary students of state legislatures met at the Eagleton Institute of Politics at Rutgers University in 2000 to define a major national study. That conversation produced the Joint Project on Term Limits (JPTL). The project was a first of its kind collaboration between the National Conference of State Legislatures, the Council of State Governments and the State Legislative Leaders Foundation. With the national prestige of these organizations, JPTL was able to assemble a dream team of scholars for a three year, in-depth examination of the effects of term limits. The results of this effort can be found in several academic papers, reports and books. The three most prominent include: *Coping With Term Limits: A Practical Guide* (NCSL 2006), *Institutional Change in American Politics: The Case of Term Limits* (Michigan 2007), and this volume.

Our collection, produced by JPTL scholars, is unique. It is arranged in a case study format and organized by levels of legislative professionalism. In each category of professionalism a comparable control state that is not restricted by term limits appears. These control state chapters provide an analysis for each section. The strength of this approach is the ability to provide single state narratives and analytical chapters in the same volume.

As editors we were honored to work with such distinguished scholars. JPTL included additional work beyond these case studies. We would like to thank individually the scholars who contributed to the overall project, but who did not draft one of our chapters. These include Jennie Drage-Bowser, Keon Chi, Mary Lou Cooper, Brenda Erickson, Gary Moncrief, Dick Niemi, David Ogle, Lynda Powell, and Tim Storey. Considerable data in this book would not exist without their contributions.

We would like to thank our chapter contributors for their encouragement, prodding and patience with this project. Their kind offers of assistance, rapid response to request and diligent revisions brought this project to completion. They deserve all of the credit for the contents of this book and none of the blame for its flaws.

The Ray C. Bliss Institute of Applied Politics at the University of Akron played a major role in the development of this book. The Institute provided funding for a joint meeting of the JPTL research group and the 2004 State Politics and Policy conference. We would like to thank Kimberly Haverkamp for her efforts in organizing that meeting.

This volume is heavily indebted to Janet Bolois of the Bliss Institute for sorting through our various chapter manuscripts and developing the final unified document. Her work with our editors at Lexington was instrumental in bring this project to fruition.

Finally, we would like to thank Lexington Books. This book gave us the opportunity to work with them once again. They were especially patient as life and careers repeatedly distracted us from our mission. In particular, we appreciate NT Ngo's assistance in keeping this project alive and seeing it through to completion.

Rick Farmer
Chris Mooney
Rich Powell
John Green

1

Introduction: Accelerating Change with Term Limits

Rick Farmer and John C. Green

"Politicians are a lot like diapers. They should be charged frequently, and for the same reasons." This line, delivered by Robin Williams in the movie *Man of the Year* (2006), graphically depicts the voter cynicism that led to term limits for government officials. In the early 1990s citizen initiatives began imposing term limits on state legislators as a way of making certain that they were changed regularly. By 2000 term limits were forcing the retirement of legislators in ten states.

This volume examines the effects of state legislative term limits using case studies from six of the states that have experienced the restrictions. The states are grouped by level of legislative professionalism: professionalized, semi-professionalized and citizen legislatures (see Squire 1992). In each professionalism category a case study of an untermed[1] state legislature is included as a control state, creating a quasi-experiment. These comparisons provide the best opportunity to date for separating the effects of term limits from other trends in state legislative politics.

The results indicate that the effects of term limits vary by legislative professionalism. They also indicate that many of the anticipated effects of term limits by both proponents and opponents did not come to pass. While some of the predictions appear true at first glance, when compared to the control states the term limits effects disappear. This is not to say that term limits have had no effect. In many cases term limits have had a profound effect. Among the most important effects of term limits is the acceleration of trends developing before term limits were ever considered.

PREDICTED EFFECTS OF TERM LIMITS

State legislative term limits made their initial appearance on the modern public agenda in 1990 when Oklahoma and California held the first term limits referenda. Term limits were not a new idea. Aristotle wrote about "rotation in office," many colonial constitutions included them, and the Founding Fathers grappled with the concept at the Constitutional Convention. Executive term limits grew in popularity following Franklin Roosevelt's presidency and are currently active in thirty-seven states (National Governors Association 2007). But, prior to 1990, state legislative term limits were absent from the national discussion for almost two centuries.

The popular rise of term limits has rarely been examined (see Karp 1995). A major contributing factor was voter cynicism (Farmer 1993). For the average citizen the ability to limit politicians is an easy issue, requiring little thought. As a result, seventeen years later the concept remains popular with voters (University of Akron 2007).

Immediately after the modern concept of state legislative term limits emerged, scholars were called upon to project the consequences of limiting the terms of legislators. With little to work with other than legislative traditions and interview data scholars began to speculate about the likely effects (Malbin and Benjamin 1992; Moncrief and Thompson 1993; Moncrief, Thompson, and Cassie 1996; Grofman 1996). Of course, it was difficult to foresee the future, and it was impossible to predict the many different forms term limits would take in the various states. Nonetheless their work raised many of the hypotheses currently under examination.

The effects of term limits may be directly related to the specific provisions of each state's term limits law and the degree of professionalization in each state legislature. Six states have lifetime bans; nine states ban only consecutive terms. In some cases movement to the opposite chamber restarts the term limits clock. Table 1.1 provides a list of states with term limits, the limit in each chamber, and the first year the limits prevented members from seeking reelection.

The demographics of the legislature were predicted to change as a result of term limits. Removing entrenched white male incumbents was thought to create opportunities for women and minorities (Petracca 1991a). Incumbents are always difficult to defeat. By creating open seats candidates from these traditionally under-represented groups had a better chance of winning. However, these groups could take advantage of the opportunity only if experienced potential legislative candidates were well positioned in lower level offices preparing to run (Powell 2000). To be successful they needed a farm team. The removal of career politicians was expected to lead to a "new breed" of legislator, who was more independent and less career oriented (Moncrief and Thompson 1993).

Table 1.1. Term-limited States and Year of Impact

State	Year Enacted	House Limit	House Year of Impact	Senate Limit	Senate Year of Impact
Maine	1993	8	1996	8	1996
California	1990	6	1996	8	1998
Colorado	1990	8	1998	8	1998
Arkansas	1992	6	1998	8	2000
Michigan	1992	6	1998	8	2002
Arizona	1992	8	2000	8	2000
Florida	1992	8	2000	8	2000
Ohio	1992	8	2000	8	2000
Montana	1992	8	2000	8	2000
South Dakota	1992	8	2000	8	2000
Missouri	1992	8	2002	8	2002
Oklahoma	1990	12	2004	12	2004
Nebraska	2000	N/A	N/A	8	2006
Louisiana	1995	12	2007	12	2007
Nevada	1996	12	2010	12	2010

Source: National Conference of State Legislatures, current as of May 2007

The increased number of open seats and termed incumbents seeking other offices were anticipated to raise the overall level of electoral competition within a state (Petracca 1991a). Alternatively, competition could be depressed by strategic politicians waiting for term limits to force an incumbent into retirement (Rausch 1998). Also, increased competition potentially raises the cost of campaigning for the state legislature (Clucas 1994).

Scholars and legislators express particular concern about a potential shift in institutional power. The constitutional balance of power between the three branches of government is delicate. Weakening the legislative branch through term limits was likely to enhance the relative power of the governor (Rosenthal 1992, 207–8; Beyle 1992). Removing experience and institutional memory from the legislature also potentially strengthened the hand of legislative staff, administrative agencies, and lobbyists who became the repository of institutional memory and experience (Rosenthal 1992, 206; Capell 1993). Many observers feared that special interest would take over the legislature (Malbin and Benjamin 1992). Additionally with experienced leaders removed from the legislature, leadership and committee chairs likely would become less effective and power would shift to individual members or outside influences (Malbin and Benjamin 1992, 212–13).

Recent work brought some data to bear on these early predictions (see Farmer, Rausch and Green 2003; Carey, Niemi, and Powell 2000; State Politics and Policy Quarterly 2006). However, this volume offers for the first time a side-by-side comparison of term limits case studies along with comparable control states in a quasi-experimental design. These case studies not only describe the changes taking place in six termed state legislatures, they offer direct comparisons with untermed states. The results are an opportunity to disentangle the current trends in state legislatures from the effects of term limits.

METHODOLOGY

The National Conference of State Legislatures, the Council of State Governments and the State Legislative Leaders Foundation assembled a team of scholars in 2001 to examine the effects of state legislative term limits. Six term limited states were identified for study, two professionalized, two semi-professionalized, and two citizen legislatures. Three untermed states were similarly selected. State legislative scholars from each of the states were recruited to conduct the study. Cooperation of the legislative leadership was sought in each state, as a way to facilitate data collection.

A national mail survey of legislators was conducted. 2982 legislative members responded to the survey. Also, a survey of knowledgeable observers was conducted in each state. This included 614 former legislators, journalists, lobbyists, and other members of the capital community. In addition, many hours of interviews and observations were conducted in each state. Numerous official documents, news articles, and other sources were collected.

This effort produced a three-year, systematic and comprehensive examination of state legislative term limits. These data are comparable across the case studies. Apples-to-apples comparisons are possible between termed and untermed states of similar professionalism and between various degrees of professionalism.

Of course, social science datasets are rarely perfect. Each state conducts its legislative process in slightly different ways. In some cases apples-to-apples data simply do not exist. In some instances response rates were better or researchers did not have full access to the desired data. Nonetheless this study conducted as the Joint Project on Term Limits is the most comprehensive and directly comparable dataset compiled on state legislative term limits to date.

Professionalized States

California and Ohio were chosen for the two professionalized case studies. Illinois was selected as the untermed control state. The six-year limits in the California Assembly are among the most restrictive in the nation. These restrictive limits may magnify the effects. Ohio's eight-year limits per chamber are typical of term limits in many states, suggesting a pattern that may

Table 1.2. Summary of Changes in Professionalized Legislatures, 1992–2002

	California	*Ohio*	*Illinois*
House Term Limits	6 years	8 years	None
Senate Term Limits	8 years	8 years	None
Composition			
Turnover	Increased	Increased	Declined
Descriptive Representation	Increase in number of women and members of minority groups	Slight decrease for women, modest gains for minorities	Modest gains for women and members of minority groups
Elections	More caucus centered	More caucus centered	More caucus centered
Institution			
Leaders	Decreased power	No apparent change	No apparent change
Committees	Decreased power	Decreased power	Traditionally weak
Nonpartisan Staff	Decreased power	Decreased power	Decreased power
Lobbyist	Increasing power	Decreasing power	Increasing power
Legislative Process			
Partisanship	Increased	Increased	Increased
Civility	Decreased	Decreased	No change
Gubernatorial Power	Increased	Decreased	Increased

be highly generalizable. Despite these differences, data from these two states produced remarkably similar results. The effects of term limits become visible when these data are juxtaposed with data from Illinois. Table 1.2 highlights the results from these three states.

The composition of these legislatures experienced modest changes due to term limits. Limits naturally increase turnover in state legislatures. In fact, they insure an average proportional turnover based on the length of the limits. California's six-year limits insure a minimum turnover of 33 percent per election cycle. Ohio's eight-year limits guarantee a 25 percent turnover per cycle. Any legislator attrition raises turnover above these minimums. Turnover increased in California and Ohio during the study period, but remained stable in untermed Illinois. The results were mixed on demographic changes. Moderate gains were made by minorities, but the same was true for Illinois. Elections became more caucus centered in all three states, following a national trend unrelated to term limits.

The institutions appear to have been weakened by term limits. Leaders lost power in California, but not in Ohio and Illinois. Looking at the other states in the study, Ohio is an anomaly. Leadership power in Ohio is likely the result of specific circumstances within the state that caused it to buck the trend in other termed states. This suggests that leadership power is only partially related to institutional arrangements. Other factors may be more important. Committees lost power in both California and Ohio. In Illinois committees were traditionally weak, so the comparison may not be indicative of the effect. However these states fall in line with the other states in the study, suggesting that weakened committees are an effect of term limits. Non-partisan staff lost clout in all three states, indicating an overall decline in professionalized states and not necessarily an effect of term limits. Lobbyists gained influence in California and Illinois but not in Ohio, making it difficult to identify the trend. With longtime friends termed out, lobbyists in Ohio were scrambling to build new relationships. California and Illinois are likely experiencing the growth of lobbying taking place around the country.

Significant changes occurred regarding the legislative process, but these changes are difficult to attribute to term limits. In all three professionalized states partisanship was increasing. Civility decreased in the two termed states. No change was observed in the control state. This loss of civility is likely an effect of term limits given the loss of members with friends across the aisle. Gubernatorial power increased in California and Illinois. Ohio was again the anomaly. This is likely the result of the Taft administration and not a result of term limits.

Two clear trends can be attributed to term limits in the professionalized states: greater turnover in membership and less civility among the members. The other variables produced mixed results or followed a national trend developing without term limits.

Semi-Professionalized States

Arizona and Colorado were chosen for the termed case studies among the semi-professionalized states. Indiana served as the untermed control state. The eight-year limits in Arizona and Colorado fit the typical term limits model. Once again, the results within the semi-professionalized group were very similar. Table 1.3 displays the results for this group.

Increased turnover was the primary change in legislative composition. Both termed states experienced significant increases in turnover, while the control state did not. All three states saw more career oriented members. While this is the opposite of what term limits advocates sought, the fact that the control state experienced the same phenomenon reduces the likelihood that it is an effect of term limits. Term limits failed to stop careerism, but they probably did not produce it. Little change was found in electoral competition, but the cost of campaigns rose in all three states. Again, this may be perverse to term limits advocates intentions, but these effects are not necessarily caused by term limits.

Table 1.3. Summary of Changes in Semi-Professionalized Legislatures, 1992–2002

	Arizona	*Colorado*	*Indiana*
House Term Limits	8 years	8 years	None
Senate Term Limits	8 years	8 years	None
Composition			
Turnover	Significant increase	Moderate to large increase	No change
Descriptive Representation	Slight to no change in demographics; more careerist	Slight to no change in demographics; more careerist	No change in demographics, except less part-timers
Elections	No change in competition, increased campaign costs	No change in competition, increased campaign costs	Increased campaign costs
Institution			
Leaders	Decreased power	Decreased power	No change; strong
Committees	Moderate decrease in power	Decrease in power and effectiveness	No change
Nonpartisan Staff	Increased influenced	Modest increase in influence	No change; little importance
Lobbyist	Modest increase in power; working harder; insider lobbyists lost power	Increasing power; working harder; insider lobbyists lost power	Little/slow/no change
Legislative Process			
Partisanship	Increased	Increased	No change
Civility	Decreased	Decreased	No change
Gubernatorial Power	No change	Increased	No change

Institutionally these semi-professional legislatures suffered as a result of term limits. The power of legislative leaders in Arizona and Colorado declined, while their power in Indiana remained unchanged. The power of committees withered in the termed states, but not in the control state. The power of non-partisan staff increased in the two termed states. Staff power remained the same in Indiana. Lobbyists' power changed little in Indiana, but increased overall in Arizona and Colorado. Clearly, term limits had major implications for institutional strength in the semi-professional states.

The legislative process also experienced significant changes as a result of term limits. Partisanship increased in the two termed states, but not in the control state. Civility also decreased in Arizona and Colorado, but not in Indiana. Gubernatorial power increased in Colorado. It was stable in Arizona

and Indiana. Colorado's increase in gubernatorial power follows the trend
in other termed states and is likely the effect of term limits. Arizona, like
Ohio, is likely the result of specific circumstances.

The effects of term limits on the semi-professionalized states are much
clearer than in the professionalized states. This is due in part to the fact that
Ohio had strong legislative leadership which countered several of the effects
and muddled the trend line. The effects in the semi-professionalized states
were most distinct in the institution and the legislative process.

Citizen Legislatures

Arkansas and Maine were chosen as the termed case studies for the citizen
legislatures. Kansas was the untermed control state. Arkansas' six year limit
in the lower chamber is exacerbated by the sixty-day biennial sessions. Unless a special session is called, a Representative's maximum career is 180 legislative days. This lifetime ban is arguably the most restrictive in the country.
Maine's eight-year limits fit the mold of most states. Table 1.4 summarizes
the findings in these three states.

Some changes occurred in the composition of the legislature. Turnover
increased, as in all termed states. In Arkansas women grew in number in the
legislature. Republicans also made gains. These changes were not evident in
the other two states. Data were not available on electoral competition in
Maine and Kansas, but competition increased in Arkansas. Given that these
data do not agree between these specific cases and they do not match the
trends in other states it is difficult to conclude that term limits are the cause
of these changes in Arkansas. It is clear that term limits increased turnover
in all of the term limited states.

The institutional effects were more identifiable. Leadership power increased in Arkansas, but decreased in Maine. No change was observed in
Kansas. Arkansas and Ohio were the anomalies in leadership power. Traditionally, Arkansas' legislature was dominated by a powerful, seniority
driven committee system. Legislative leadership was weak. Term limits
forced changes in the leadership traditions in Arkansas. Maine's experience
matches that of other term limited states. While these trends are in opposite directions, both are the results of term limits. All three states saw a decrease in committee power. This followed the trend in other termed states.
Non-partisan staff saw an increase in power in both Arkansas and Maine.
No change occurred in Kansas. This effect is similar to the one found in the
semi-professional states. Lobbyists lost power in both term limited states,
with no change in the control state. This effect does not match the previous findings.

The effects on the legislative process were very similar to those found in
other states. Partisanship increased and civility decreased in the termed states,

Table 1.4. Summary of Changes in Citizen Legislatures, 1992–2002

	Arkansas	*Maine*	*Kansas*
House Term Limits	6 years	8 years	None
Senate Term Limits	8 years	8 years	None
Composition			
Turnover	Increased	Increased	No significant change
Descriptive Representation	Increase in number of women legislators and Republicans	No significant change	No significant change
Elections	Increased competition	No data	No data
Institution			
Leaders	Increased power	Decreased power	No change
Committees	Decreased power	Decreased power	Decrease in Senate committee power; no change in House
Nonpartisan Staff	Increased power	Slight increase in power	No change
Lobbyist	Decreased influence	Decreased influence	No change
Legislative Process			
Partisanship	Some increase	Some increase	No change; significant infighting among Republicans
Civility	Decreased	Decreased	No change
Gubernatorial Power	Increased	Increased	No change

but not in the control state. Gubernatorial power increased in Arkansas and Maine, but not in Kansas.

AGGREGATE FINDINGS

These results suggest differences in the effects of term limits based on the level of professionalism within the state legislatures. A greater number of effects were identified in the less professionalized legislatures. In seven of ten

Table 1.5. Summary of Changes in Termed States that Deviate from the Control State, 1992-2002

	Professionalized	*Semi-Professionalized*	*Citizen*
Termed States	California	Arizona	Arkansas
	Ohio	Colorado	Maine
Untermed States	Illinois	Indiana	Kansas
Composition			
Turnover	+	+	+
Descriptive Representation	×	×	×
Elections	×	×	×
Institution			
Leaders	−	−	−
Committees	−	−	×
Nonpartisan Staff	×	+	+
Lobbyist	×	+	−
Legislative Process			
Partisanship	+	+	+
Civility	−	−	−
Gubernatorial Power	+	×	+

+ indicates an increase
− indicates a decrease
× indicates no deviation from the control state

categories depicted in Table 1.5 an effect deviating from the control case was found for both the semi-professionalized and the citizen legislatures. In only six of ten categories did a similar effect occur for the professionalized states.

Many effects were common to all termed states. Increased turnover among members was consistent across all levels of professionalism. Term limits force a natural rotation of office. Demographic changes were inconsistent and deviated little from the control states. Campaigns were more caucus centered in all three professionalized states and more expensive in all three semi-professionalized states. Leadership power declined in four of the six termed states. In Ohio and Arkansas, where leadership held their own, circumstance and tradition created the anomaly. These changes did not occur in the control states, suggesting that leadership power is generally diminished by term limits at all levels of legislative professionalism. Committees experienced decreased power in all six term limited states. This also occurred in the citizen legislature control state of Kansas. Non-partisan staff lost power in all three professionalized states. However, they had an increase in power in the four less professionalized termed legislatures. This indicates a general shift away from non-partisan staff in professionalized states, and a greater reliance on non-partisan staff in termed semi-professionalized and citizen legislatures. The results for lobbyists were mixed. Clearly, they are working harder to keep up in some areas and losing ground in others. Partisanship and civility were consistent in all six termed states. Civility is decreasing as partisanship increases. The loss of relationships within the legislature and the increased caucus activity lead to these outcomes. The only consistent change in gubernatorial power was the increase found in the citizen legislatures. However, the circumstances in Ohio suggest the result there was a monetary phenomenon and the governor may gain clout in time.

OTHER TRENDS IN TERMED STATES

In addition to the systematic data described above, several other findings are apparent from the case studies in this volume. For example, the case studies demonstrate that term limits create chaos in state legislatures. This is particularly true during the transition of the first session after term limits take effect. In California, chaos emerged around the Speakership. In Ohio, chaos ensued in the leadership of both lower house caucuses. In Arkansas, the chaos occurred around the new committee chairmen. Not only did chaos develop in leadership and committees, but also with the rank and file members. Anytime 30 to 50 percent of the members are serving their first term a certain amount of chaos is inevitable.

Trends developing across the country are accelerated by term limits. When a trend is emerging a few seats at a time and term limits suddenly force a large number of open seats, the trend is realized more rapidly. States, where minorities were making gradual gains, suddenly witnessed a surge of minority representation. Similarly, where caucus centered campaigns were becoming the norm, caucus centered campaigns are now a way of life. In fact, these case studies found several trends that were occurring in both the termed and untermed states. In many cases those trends were accelerated in the termed states. It would be difficult to say that term limits caused the trend, but it is clear that term limits allowed the trend to infuse the legislative process more quickly.

The caucus has become the center of activity in term-limited legislatures. This has allowed the caucus leadership to regain some of their lost clout. The caucus is the campaign machine that recruits the candidates, raises the funds, directs the campaigns, and commands the new members' loyalties. This has given rise to greater partisanship within the legislature and less civility among the members. Partisanship creates teamwork for getting things done within the legislature. It also widens the divide, which must be bridged to maintain the integrity of the institution. Democracy depends upon cooperation as well as competition.

Many of the effects of term limits can be attributed directly to the disruption of relationships within the legislative community. Declining civility is at least partly the result of long time members with well-developed friendships on both sides of the aisle being termed. Chaos occurs in part because new members do not know whom to call when they need an answer. The rise of the caucus can be traced to the fact that new members have no friends in the capital city other than their campaign team. Where lobbying has declined it is the result of lost relationships.

The legislature is not a static body. An analysis of legislative reform must recognize that the legislature is a dynamic system of internal and external forces (Farmer 1993). Adaptations are constantly developing. One of the most important adaptations is that everyone around the Capitol complex is working harder. With old friends termed out, journalists, lobbyists, staff and legislators are all working harder to make the process work. Relationships are the grease that makes the wheels of government turn. Without that grease it takes much more effort to turn the wheels.

CONCLUSION

The chapters contained in this volume offer an unique insight into term limits. They provide a quasi-experimental study whose findings are highly generalizable. They include four termed states with limits very similar to those of other termed states. They provide multiple cases in each of three levels of legislative professionalism. These data can be cut several different ways and yield valuable comparisons.

The data are apples-to-apples comparisons whenever possible. The studies were designed to be parallel and conducted simultaneously. Rarely do such opportunities come available in state legislative studies.

The results suggest that term limits have had numerous effects on state legislatures. These effects vary by the level of professionalism in each state legislature. In many cases these effects are simply an acceleration of a trend already in place. In other cases, these effects significantly alter the legislative playing field.

It is early, yet, in the study of state legislative term limits. The full results will not be known for another eight or ten years. By then sufficient data will be available to separate the anomalies from the trend lines.

Beauty is in the eye of the beholder. Many of the effects of term limits are a two-sided coin. For example, partisanship breeds intra-party teamwork and inter-party strife. Among the general public, term limits remain popular. The prospects for easing or eliminating term limits are slim. In their cynicism about politicians average voters are likely to respond to this chapter by saying, "if term limits make politicians work harder then term limits are a good thing." Term limits are an expression of the public's distrust of power.

NOTE

1. Peery and Little (2003) suggest "termed" and "untermed" as a standard way of describing the presents or absents of term limits.

I

PROFESSIONALIZED STATE LEGISLATURES

2

Institutional Imbalance: The Effect of Six-year Limits in California

Bruce Cain, Thad Kousser and Karl T. Kurtz

California was an early laboratory of term limits. She was the second state to pass limits. In addition, the Assembly's six-year limit was among the first to take effect. California became a bellwether, depicting what subsequent states could expect from term limits.

The six- and eight-year lifetime limits are among the most restrictive term limits in the country. As a result the effects of term limits are more exaggerated in California than in most states. The ability to move between chambers eases the effects in the Senate, creating a significant disparity between the two bodies. Overall, leadership, committees, staff support and power have all diminished in measurable ways, particularly in the lower chamber.

A BRIEF HISTORY

In the 1960s, California was among the first states to convert its legislature into a full-time, professional body. Almost three decades later, it became one of the states pioneering legislative term limits. Aside from the fact that both transformations occurred through initiatives, they share little else in common. Proposition 1A, supported by leaders from both parties like Governor Pat Brown and gubernatorial candidate Ronald Reagan, was designed by Assembly Speaker Jess Unruh to modernize and strengthen the state's part-time Legislature and, not incidentally, buttress his own power. It passed in 1966 by an overwhelming 75–25 percent margin (See Bell and Price 1980, 187–92). Proposition 140, designed by a politically disenchanted Los Angeles County Supervisor and by anti-tax activists, took aim at the Democratic houses and at the self-described "Ayatollah of the Assembly," (York 1999) the powerful, flamboyant and seemingly entrenched Speaker Willie Brown. The term limits campaign quickly polarized along party lines, and anti-Sacramento sentiment fueled by a long FBI corruption sting pushed the initiative to a slim 52–48 percent victory (Price 1992). Although it did not enjoy the consensus support among the state's leaders or voters that Proposition 1A had, Proposition 140 would soon transform California's Legislature just as dramatically as the professionalization movement had a quarter century before.

Even before term limits removed legislators from office, the initiative's effects on the Legislature began to be felt. One of Proposition 140's other provisions mandated significant cuts in legislative expenditures, in order to remove "political staffers" and reduce "patronage" (according to the ballot statement of its backers). Instead of cutting the size of political staffs, the Legislature essentially subverted the initiative's stated intent by eliminating funding for many nonpartisan experts. While overall staffing levels only declined by 12.5 percent from 1988 to 1996, professional organizations such as the Legislative Analyst's Office, the Senate Office of Research, and the (now defunct) Assembly Office of Research lost between 33 and 100 percent of their positions in the immediate wake of Prop. 140.[1] Since their futures in Sacramento were guaranteed to be if not nasty and brutish then certainly short, veteran legislators began to leave voluntarily, bringing a record number of special elections from 1991 to 1995. Those who remained faced short time horizons. They reacted by neglecting some of the less glorious legislative tasks such as oversight, as evidenced by sharp declines in the number of audits that they ordered and the number of requests for information on executive branch operations that they wrote into budgets. The 1995–1996 session, held on the eve of term limits implementation, featured a chaotic series of leadership battles as Willie Brown recruited a series of puppet speakers from the other side of the aisle to help him cling to power even as Republicans won a majority of Assembly seats. It finished with an end-of-session stalemate.

The bulk of our analysis of term limits begins in 1996, the first election in which Proposition 140 prevented many Assembly members and Senators from running for reelection.[2] Term limits opened up twenty-two of eighty Assembly seats and twelve of forty Senate districts.[3] The new members who won them would only be allowed to compete for three two-year terms in the Assembly and two four-year Senate terms. They were free to move from one house to the other after completing their service, but once they reached both limits, they were banned from both houses for life. Many of the termed-out Assembly members indeed ran for the Senate, where veterans of both houses like John Burton, Ross Johnson, John Vasconcellos, and Byron Sher continued to exert great influence until November 2004. While a few Senators moved in the opposite direction, the Assembly has been dominated by new members who never served before term limits.

These divergent patterns allow us to explore not only how term limits has changed Sacramento but also why these changes occurred. One way that limiting terms can affect a legislature is by bringing in a flood of fresh but inexperienced members. Term limits can also influence legislative behavior by shifting legislators' incentives, shortening their time horizons. Senators about to be kicked out of Sacramento feel this most acutely. Differences between the two houses, as well as comparison with past legislative behavior and with trends in California's congressional delegation, provide important lessons about the impact of term limits. Using both separate and combined house analyses, we explore Proposition 140's effects on the composition of California's Legislature, its internal institutions, and the policymaking process. We conclude by reporting how the Legislature has sought to adapt to the profound changes brought by term limits.

COMPOSITION OF THE LEGISLATURE

One of the primary goals of the term limits movement was to change legislatures by repopulating them, not only with new members who brought fresh perspectives but with a new *type* of legislator. This new member would not be the typical career politician likely to be captured by bureaucrats and lobbyists, but instead would return the state to the days of the citizen legislator.[4] The new breed could also be more diverse, as old, white, male incumbents were removed from office to open up opportunities to new groups. Increased turnover is a natural effect of term limits in a state where membership was highly stable, and Figure 2.1 shows that it has indeed been high since Proposition 140 went into full effect in 1996. But more important is examining the characteristics of new members to determine whether term limits has significantly altered the composition of California's Legislature.

Representation of Women and Minorities

At first glance, the most radical change that Proposition 140 appears to have brought to Sacramento has been the rapid increase in the number of women and minority legislators elected since 1990. *Los Angeles Times* reporter Eric Bailey reflected conventional wisdom when he explained that "There is no doubt that the law . . . produced a statehouse more diverse in gender, ethnicity and professional background. The Legislature now looks 'more like California'" (Bailey 2004). It is undeniably true that today's Legislature includes more women, Latinos, and Asian-Americans (though fewer African-Americans) than the body did in 1990. Yet these changes may also be the results of demographic shifts, two rounds of redistricting, and the increasing electoral viability of female candidates.

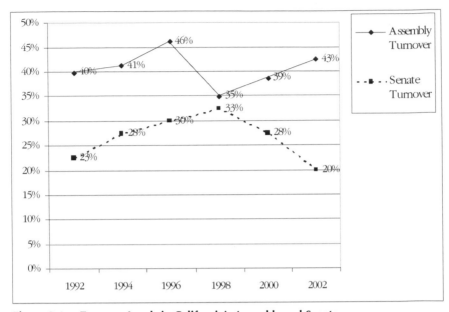

Figure 2.1.   Turnover Levels in California's Assembly and Senate
Note: Turnover levels report the percentage of new members after each election. Senate figures report
turnover as a percentage of the entire body even though only half of Senators are up for reelection in a
given election. Data taken from Moncrief, Niemi, and Powell (2004).

As a statement of cause and effect, conventional wisdom deserves a closer
look. In this section, we attempt to sort out the impact of term limits from
other explanations of the recent increase in legislative diversity. Disentan-
gling the effects of term limits from these trends is a difficult but not hope-
less task. Much can be learned about the gains that women and minorities
made by looking closely at their timing, the legislators who were replaced,
and parallel patterns in California's congressional delegation.

Unlike most other term limits states studied in this volume, California
has seen changes in the gender and ethnic composition of its Legislature
during the era of term limits passage and implementation. Figures 2.2 and
2.3 show that representation of Latinos and Asian Americans grew throughout the past decade as the number of white and black legislators declined.
In 1990, white legislators held sixty-nine of eighty Assembly seats and
thirty-four of forty Senate districts. These figures dropped to fifty-four and
twenty-seven after the 2002 elections, with the representation of minorities
groups rising from 14 percent of all legislative seats to 33 percent over this
period. Blacks held nine seats in the two houses when Proposition 140 was
passed, but hold only six today. Increases in the number of Latino legislators in both houses and Asian-Americans in the Assembly have indeed
changed the face of California's Legislature. The percentage of Sacramento

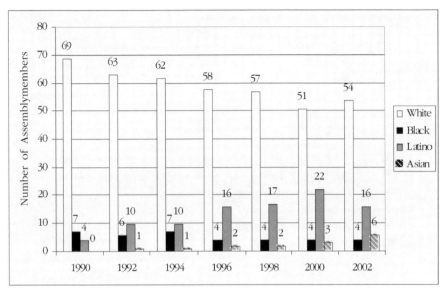

Figure 2.2. Racial and Ethnic Composition of the California Assembly, 1990–2002
Data collected from appropriate editions of the California Journal's *Roster and Government Guide.*

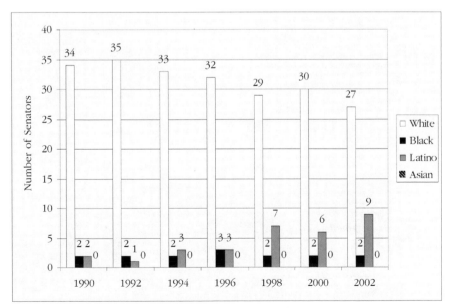

Figure 2.3. Racial and Ethnic Composition of the California Senate, 1990–2002
Data collected from appropriate editions of the California Journal's *Roster and Government Guide.*

seats held by women has also grown from 19 percent in 1990 to 29 percent in 2002.

The key question is whether term limits is responsible for these trends. In order to determine how much credit limits should get for the rise in women's representation, we present a historical look at the timing of victories by new female legislators in Figure 2.4. From 1972 to 1990, women's representation climbed slowly. An average of two new Assemblywomen were elected every two years and one new female senator every four years. Since 1990, this rate exploded to an average of eight new Assemblywomen per two-year cycle and five new women per four-year cycle in the Senate. Before attributing all of this increase to term limits, though, note the timing of the largest surge in women's representation. Figure 2.4 shows how much of this increase occurred as a result of the 1992 election, often dubbed the "Year of the Woman." Four years before Proposition 140 brought its first set of forced retirements, fifteen women were newly elected to the two houses. National events likely increased the propensity of high quality female candidates to run, and the 1991 Special Masters' redistricting gave them the opportunity by creating many open seats.

Still, after dropping in 1994, the number of new female legislators grew sharply after the implementation of term limits, bringing in twenty-eight new Assemblywomen and eleven new female senators over three elections. Whom did they replace? From 1996 to 2001, 71 percent of new Assemblywomen replaced a term-limited member, 25 percent replaced someone who ran for another office, and only one (Wilma Chan) defeated an in-

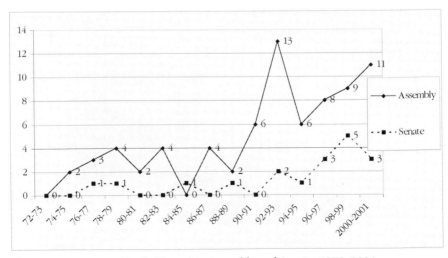

Figure 2.4.   Women Newly Elected to Assembly and Senate, 1972–2001
Data collected from Secretary of State's election records and the California Journal's *Roster and Government Guide* by Kelly Yang and reported fully in Yang (2002b).

cumbent. Contrast this to the 1990–1995 period, in which 23 percent beat an incumbent, 23 percent replaced an incumbent who retired or passed away, and 27 percent won a new seat created by redistricting. The remaining 27 percent replaced a member running for another office, probably in anticipation of term limits. Using this calculus, eighteen of the twenty-five Assemblywomen newly elected from 1990 to 1995 did not owe their victory to term limits, establishing a "natural rate" of increase in women's representation. Over the next three elections, twenty-seven Assemblywomen won seats that were directly or indirectly vacated due to term limits. Comparing these figures lets us estimate that nine Assembly seats were opened up to women by term limits over the course of three elections.[5]

A slightly different story can be told about minority representation in the Legislature. Here, the dramatic increase in minority legislators was ultimately the product of underlying demographic change. California's Latino and Asian-American populations grew dramatically in the eighties and nineties. Since much of this growth came from immigration, there was a delay in the political implications of the growth as immigrants had to become naturalized and then mobilized into the political system. In a conscientious attempt to comply with the Voting Rights Act, the 1991 Special Masters' redistricting created many more "majority-minority" districts, districts in which Latinos, especially, constituted a majority of the voting age eligible population. From 1990 to 1995, primarily because of redistricting, seventeen new minority Assembly members and four new minority State Senators were elected to office.[6] When term limits took effect from 1996 to 2001, minority gains rose to thirty-three new members in the Assembly and nine new minority Senators.

Again, we look at the veterans these new members replaced in order to make an estimate of how much of the effect can be attributed to term limits. In the early 1990s, eleven of the seventeen newly-elected minority Assembly members won their seats for reasons not linked to term limits, setting a natural rate. After term limits, 15 percent of new members beat an incumbent or replaced a retiree, but 85 percent (twenty-eight of thirty-three) took seats opened up by term limits. By this measure, Proposition 140's implementation resulted in a boost of seventeen new minority legislators. It is important to keep in mind, however, that term limits removed women and minority legislators even as they opened up seats for other women and minority candidates. During the nineties, ten women and nineteen minority legislators were termed out, and the loss of members like Willie Brown was costly for the influence and expertise of minority legislators.

The final way in which we seek to isolate the impact of term limits upon the composition of California's Legislature is by comparing trends in the Assembly and Senate to those in the state's congressional delegation. This comparison is particularly apt in California's case because of the size of its congressional delegation; currently at fifty-three members, it is in between the size of the state Senate and the Assembly. Members of Congress do not face term limits.[7] As we have noted, from 1990 to 2000, the share of state legislative seats held by women grew from 19 percent to 29 percent. Over the same period, the percentage of California's U.S. House seats occupied by women rose from 7 percent to 31 percent, an analysis that does not even count the 1992 election of Senators Barbara Boxer and Dianne Feinstein. This suggests that term limits may not be responsible for any of the increase in women's representation.

Figure 2.5 shows that the number of minority members that the state has sent to Washington has grown, though the shift has not been as great as the changes brought to Sacramento. In 1990 and 2000, we compare the composition of California's population to the breakdown of its state and federal representatives. According to the 1990 census, 26 percent of Californians were "Hispanic." Only 6.7 percent of the state's members of the U.S. House and 5 percent of its state legislators were Latino. Asian and Pacific Islanders made up 9.3 percent of the population but held 4.4 percent of U.S. House seats and no state legislative districts. With 7 percent of the state's residents, blacks held 8.9 percent of U.S. House seats and 7.5 percent of Sacramento seats (State of California, Department of Finance 1999). Minority represen-

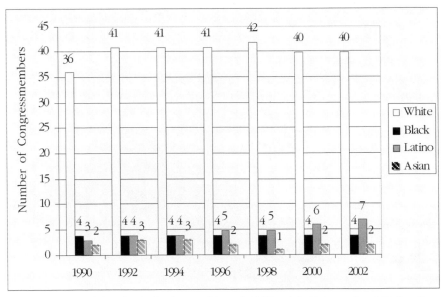

Figure 2.5.   Racial and Ethnic Composition of California's Congressional Delegation, 1996–2002

Data collected by Matt Tokeshi from the second through sixth editions of the *California Political Almanac,* Congressional Quarterly's *Who's Who in Congress* (2001), and *The Almanac of American Politics* (2004).

tatives did better competing for congressional districts than they did in state contests.

By the 2000 census, Hispanics accounted for 32.4 percent of the state's population, 11.5 percent of its congressional delegation, and 23.3 percent of its state legislators. Asian and Pacific Islanders had grown to 11.2 percent of residents, stalled at 3.8 percent of U.S. Representatives, but taken 5 percent of the seats in the Legislature. Blacks, with 6.4 percent of the population, held 7.7 percent of Congressional seats and 5 percent of state districts (State of California, Department of Finance, 2003). For Latinos and Asians, whose numbers were rapidly growing over this period, term limits seem to have made seats in Sacramento more attainable than positions in Washington. Yet for blacks, whose share of the population shrank, term limits left the gains of the 1970s and 1980s vulnerable at a time when congressional seats provided safe havens.

Overall, term limits increased the turnover rate in the California Legislature. Where there was an underlying trend amplified by redistricting, the more rapid churning of office-holders created increased opportunities for demographic shifts to manifest themselves. This point is most clearly demonstrated by the dramatic increases in the Latino legislative caucus since 1990. Where there was no consistent trend, term limits by itself did not generate one, as evidenced by the case of female representation.

Changes in Partisan Composition

One hope that may have been in the minds of some term limits supporters in California was that in addition to fundamentally altering the democratic process, limits would diminish the fortunes of the Democratic Party. Yet while Willie Brown may be gone, his party remains in firm control of Sacramento. Table 2.1 demonstrates that the only recent lapse in Democratic control came before the implementation of term limits, when a nationwide "Republican Revolution" gave California Republicans a one-seat edge in the Assembly following the 1994 elections. After struggling to consolidate their leadership of the chamber for much of the session, Republicans surrendered

Table 2.1. Democratic Seat Share in the California Legislature Following Elections

Election	Assembly Percentage	Senate Percentage	Overall Percentage
1992	60	58	59
1994	49	53	51
1996	55	60	58
1998	60	63	61
2000	63	65	64
2002	60	63	61

Table 2.2.   Seats Changing Parties in the Legislature

	Assembly				Senate			
	Untermed		Termed		Untermed		Termed	
Election	D to R	R to D	D to R	R to D	D to R	R to D	D to R	R to D
1992*	13	15	*	*	4	1	*	*
1994*	9	1	*	*	4	0	*	*
1996	0	4	1	1	0	1	2	2
1998	0	3	0	1	0	1	0	0
2000	0	0	0	2	0	0	0	0
2002	0	0	2	0	0	1	1	0

Notes: Redistricting switched Assembly seat numbers in 1992 and Senate seat numbers in 1992 and 1994. Data collected by Annette Eaton from Barone and Cohen (2003), Congressional Quarterly (2001), California Journal Press (1997), and California Senate, Assembly, and Secretary of State websites, accessed in June, 2004 at http://www.sen.ca.gov/, http://www.assembly.ca.gov, and http://www.ss.ca.gov/elections/elections.htm.

control of the Assembly when term limits took effect in 1996. Since then, they have not seriously challenged the Democratic Party's majority. During each of the first three post-term limits elections, Democrats strengthened their control of both houses of the Legislature.

Table 2.2 shows why term limits have not changed the aggregate partisanship of California's Legislature: switches in party control in any individual district are rare. In the 1992 elections, the first held after redistricting reshuffled members and districts, many seats changed hands in this game of political musical chairs. Republicans surged to capture nine Assembly seats and four Senate seats in the 1994 contests, but have captured only six districts total during the four elections of the term limits era. Democrats picked up seats over this period, too, performing better in districts where nobody was termed out than in seats opened up by limits. In general, however, the vast majority of legislative districts in California are so politically safe that incumbency status is not needed to hold onto them. Members are typically replaced by someone from their own party when they are termed out, although the impact of partisan surges may be magnified in open seats. Again, the lesson seems to be that term limits accelerate existing trends but do not create representation patterns on their own.

Other Changes in Legislator Characteristics

In order to observe how term limits changed other characteristics of California legislators, we can compare the career histories of those who entered the Assembly and Senate during the 1980s with those of members first elected in the 1990s. The first lesson is that new members are on average younger in the term limits era than rookies were before Proposition 140 passed. The mean entry age dropped from forty-seven to forty-two (Barge 2001). This understates the shift in the average age of *all* legislators, since term limits has brought in far more of these new, young members. It also obscures an emerging difference between the ages of men and women, with women more likely to enter the Legislature at an older age after raising their families. Several female legislators we spoke to suggested that this created a difference in the perspectives of male and female legislators, influencing how they worked (that is, giving women a less confrontational style) and their legislative interests (that is, female legislators take more interest in family and education issues).

Another observation may surprise those who expected that term limits would bring a new sort of citizen legislator to Sacramento: namely, limits have not halted political careerism. The good news for term limits proponents is that the number of new members who were former legislative staffers dropped from 40 percent in the 1980 to 1990 period to 16 percent from 1991 to 2000. The bad news is that there was an increase in the number of local office holders who ran for and won legislative seats in the post-term limits period. This proportion rose from 52 percent to 64 percent. In other words, local office holders as well as amateurs from the private sector were the primary beneficiaries of the new opportunities that term limits created. Given the expense of running for office in California's large legislative districts, it was difficult for large numbers of inexperienced, non-wealthy candidates to succeed in winning legislative seats.

Finally, by tracking what legislators have done after term limits removed them from office, we see that most exiting members are still responding to reelection incentives or other political motives. In the term limits era, a political career is more dynamic in the sense that it requires changing offices more frequently. The modal career path now is from a local office (that is, city council, board of supervisors, special district, school district, etc.) to the Assembly, then the Senate, and finally to higher office or to local government. While the amount who go to local government is still small, it is a more common path in the post-term limits era than before. Wherever termed legislators go, it is not back to the plow in the way that the admirers of Cincinnatus had hoped. In the first three elections after term limits were implemented, at least half of the Assembly members who were termed out in 1996 ran for another office (Yang 2002a). Fully 95 percent of Assembly members termed out in 2002 remained involved in politics, either by starting another campaign, being appointed to an administration post, or by becoming a registered lobbyist (Osborne 2004). California's Legislature has been composed of career politicians since Proposition 1A's professionalization made that type of occupation possible, and Proposition 140's term limits have done nothing to change this.

INSTITUTIONS

Leaders

A major concern of many Proposition 140 opponents was that the shortness of the imposed limits would greatly weaken legislative leadership, eventually destroying the discipline and effectiveness of the California Legislature as a whole. As it turns out, the problem has proved to be particularly acute in the Assembly. With only six years of maximum service, Assembly leaders have very little time to prepare for, and even less time to hold, key legislative positions. Since limits took effect in 1996, the end of the first term limit cycle, there have been five speakers, each serving for less than two years. Their tenure in office follows a regular cycle: it lasts for two budgets and an election. The speaker is now retired by tradition before the last election of the speaker's final term so that there is no conflict between the speaker's role as chief fundraiser for the caucus and any personal fundraising he or she must do in order to get elected to another office. The choice of Fabian Nunez as speaker in 2004 is an important departure in the sense that he was elected speaker in his first term, and thus will have a chance to serve for a longer period of time. Of course, the downside of this is that he is the least experienced speaker in recent history, serving less than one term when chosen.

The situation in the Senate is far more stable. There have only been two president pro tempores since 1996. Moreover, since most of the new senators have served for at least a term in the Assembly and typically more, the Senate leaders to come will likely continue to have much more experience than the Assembly leaders. This experience differential puts the Assembly at a disadvantage in the "Big Five" negotiations, when the governor and the four leaders of the Republican and Democratic caucuses meet to hammer out the budget framework.

We see the same patterns by extending the analysis to the set of top leaders in each house (this includes the speaker and president pro tempore, the speaker pro tempore, floor leaders, caucus leaders, and whips). Table 2.3 re-

Table 2.3. Turnover of Legislative Leaders

Election Year	Assembly Leadership Turnover	Senate Leadership Turnover
1992	2 of 6	3 of 7
1994	4 of 6	1 of 7
1996	6 of 9	5 of 7
1998	6 of 8	5 of 7
2000	6 of 8	2 of 7
2002	8 of 8	3 of 7

Note: Figures are taken from comparisons of leadership rosters reported in appropriate editions of the California Journal's Roster and Government Guide, 1992 through 2004.

veals two important facts: first, leadership turnover is higher in the Assembly than in the Senate, but second that in most years there is significant leadership turnover in both houses. This fact in and of itself would not bother term limit proponents since it was precisely the length and stability of Willie Brown's Speakership that fueled their desire for reform. But even Republicans, who had by and large supported Proposition 140, said in interviews that the inexperience and instability of leadership was a problem for both parties.

Committees

"There has been an essential evisceration of the hearing process. . . . Nothing dies anymore, and there are no rules" —Former Senator who served in the executive branch.

Although nearly every legislator and Sacramento observer has a distinct theory about how committees have changed and why, the consensus is that the committee system has broken down, especially in the Assembly. But is there really evidence that committees have become less powerful? To verify this trend, and to explore what might be driving it, records were collected on how committees have treated thousands of randomly sampled bills over the past two decades. (For a more complete discussion of these methods and findings, see Cain and Kousser (2004)). The research design in this analysis— comparing matched sessions before and after term limits, and paying attention to Assembly vs. Senate differences—uses bill histories to examine trends in committee gatekeeping. "Gatekeeping" occurs when a committee does not pass a bill that is referred to it, effectively killing the measure.[8] Because this opportunity to block the progress of legislation gives committee members the chance to control the Legislature's agenda in their policy domain, it is one of their key powers. The other significant privilege that committees are granted is the ability to shape bills by amending them. Committees do not monopolize this power, since floor amendments are in order and authors have the right to amend their own bills unilaterally at any point. Still, the most substantive amendments are usually made in California's legislative committees. Analyzing gatekeeping and amendments reveals how active committees have been in serving their traditional functions.

For four committees in each house, histories were tracked of thirty Assembly Bills assigned to the committee and thirty Senate Bills.[9] Over four sessions, the sample includes data on 1,888 randomly selected pieces of legislation.[10] The actions of all of the committees in a given house are aggregated here because they showed similar patterns. The presentation further simplified by combining findings from the two pre-term limits sessions as well as the two post-term limits sessions, since the effect of term limits is quite constant over time. Levels of gatekeeping and amendment activity are similar in the 1979–1980 and 1987–1988 sessions, but shift in nearly identical ways from these years to the post-Proposition 140 sessions with which they are matched. Comparing separate descriptions of each pair demonstrates this (see Enemark and Cross (2002), Abrams (2003), and Wong (2003)). Since the actions of California committees appear to fall into pre-term limits and post-term limits patterns, this is how the data are presented.

Table 2.4 demonstrates how often a committee's members exercise their gatekeeping powers. It combines Assembly and Senate data for each era (the 1979–1980/1987–1988 sessions before Proposition 140 passed, and the 1997–1998/1999–2000 sessions afterward), and includes bills heard in their house of origin as well as bills that have made it to the second house.

Committees killed 23.8 percent of the bills assigned to them in our pre-term limits sample, but only 16.5 percent after Proposition 140 took effect. In both eras, most of these failing bills died a silent death when supportive committee members, anticipating the preferences of their colleagues, did not ask for a vote on a bill, and a handful of bills were withdrawn by a pessimistic author. The major lesson of this table is that regardless of their methods, committees exercise their gatekeeping power less frequently after term limits than before.

One reason that term limits may have weakened gatekeeping is that inexperienced legislators do not have the expertise to identify problematic legislation, and thus kill fewer bills. An alternative explanation of reduced gatekeeping might be that term limits make legislators more likely to defer to a colleague because they feel less responsible for the long-term consequences of bad policy and more anxious to preserve their collegial relationships in the short term at any public cost. Comparing the actions of Assembly committees, whose members are inexperienced but have reasonably long time horizons, with Senate committees filled with veterans on their way out will give some insight into these competing explanations. If inexperience is to blame for the decline in gatekeeping, the sharpest decline

Table 2.4. How Often Do Committees Exercise Gatekeeping Power?

	Before Term Limits	After Term Limits
Bills Assigned to Committees	958	930
Bills Passing Committee	730	777
Bills Held in Committee or Failed Passage	213	141
Bills Withdrawn by Author	15	12
% of Bills Passing	76.2%	83.5%
% of Bills Dying	23.8%	16.5%

Figures based on bill histories listed in appropriate editions of the Senate and Assembly Final Histories, collected by Dan Enemark, Drew Cross, Matt Abrams, and Christina Wong.

should be in the rookie-filled Assembly. If deference is at work, Senators with short time horizons should account for the drop.

Table 2.5 shows that Assembly gatekeeping drastically decreased after term limits, but that the Senate gatekeeping decline, though statistically significant, was somewhat smaller. The sharpest drop in gatekeeping is for Assembly Bills heard in Assembly committees. Before term limits, Assembly members killed 36.3 percent of their colleagues' proposals, but this proportion fell to 23.3 percent after Proposition 140. The overall decline in gatekeeping is smaller for the veteran Senate (6.2 percentage points) than it is in the Assembly (8.4). Senators today are nearly as tough as they were before term limits on the bills proposed by fellow Senators (a 5.6 point drop that is not statistically significant), evidence that they are not placating their colleagues. The most dramatic drop in gatekeeping by Senate committees comes in their consideration of Assembly Bills (a 6.7 point, statistically significant decline), which did not get a very thorough screening in Assembly policy committees either. The overall lesson, though, is the nearly universal drop in gatekeeping in both houses.

Committees now screen less legislation than they did before term limits, and while the biggest change has come in the Assembly, this trend is present in nearly every one of the categories examined in Table 2.5. There has not been a similarly large increase in the percentage of introduced bills that become law. So where does gatekeeping take place? The available data suggests that policy committees have been replaced in their gatekeeping function to

Table 2.5. Gatekeeping in California's Policy Committees.

		Percentage of Bills that Fail in Committee	
When Committees from this House . . .	*Hear Bills from this House . . .*	*Before Term Limits*	*After Term Limits*
Assembly	Assembly Bills	**36.3%**	**23.3%**
	Senate Bills	16.8%	12.4%
Senate	Senate Bills	28.9%	23.3%
	Assembly Bills	**13.0%**	**6.3%**
Overall	House of Origin Bills	**32.6%**	**23.3%**
	Other House Bills	**14.9%**	**9.1%**
	Assembly Committees	**26.6%**	**18.2%**
	Senate Committees	**21.0%**	**14.8%**
	Total	**23.8%**	**16.5%**

Figures based on bill histories listed in appropriate editions of the Senate and Assembly Final Histories, collected by Dan Enemark, Drew Cross, Matt Abrams, and Christina Wong. Boldface indicates that the proportion of bills reported before term limits in any category differs from the proportion reported after term limits, at the 95% confidence level in a conventional test of significance.

some extent by appropriations committees and to a larger extent by governors wielding their veto pens.

Staff and Lobbyists

The diminished experience of the legislators would matter less if it were offset by a more stable, well-trained, and experienced staff. There is evidence that staff are more formally, and thus possibly better trained as a result of the newly formed C. A. P. I. T. O. L. Institute (discussed in the conclusion), but there is less staff stability and experience. As before, the problems seem to be more severe in the Assembly than in the Senate. The high turnover among members in office holding and on committees causes parallel staff turnover as staff follow their member to another committee and eventually to the other house.

Brokaw, Jobson, and Vercruyssen (2001) find that the average tenure of chief consultants to the Assembly's standing committees declined from 8.7 years to 4 years from 1989 to 2000, but staff tenures in the Senate rose from 5.3 years in 1990 to 7.8 years in 2000. Compounding the turnover problems, the Legislature further weakened staff expertise by choosing to cut nonpartisan and policy staff in favor of political and personal staff.

When Proposition 140 mandated staff cuts, according to lobbyist Ken Emanuels, "the Assembly took that right out of their policy staff, and fired the experienced, expensive people, hired more, very inexperienced, very inexpensive staffers, and mostly campaign people. In the Senate, the old-time staffers, who have been around a while and understood the nuances, remained. And the difference is like night and day for us" (Emanuels 2001). The Legislative Analyst's Office lost over half of its staff between 1990 and 1993, and the Assembly Office of Research was completely eliminated by 1996. By contrast, the Senate Office of Research experienced the least severe cuts among expert agencies.

The weakening of staff has forced members to be more dependent on outside groups for bill-drafting expertise. Newer members are less likely to have staff with "in the building" experience and more dependent on outside help. When asked to estimate what fraction of his bills were suggested by lobbyists and outside groups, one first-term legislator told us that he thought it was over 90 percent the first year, but then quickly added that he has since added more experienced staff and reduced the number to 70 percent.

Disparities in the tenure of staff may also allow interest groups more influence in the Assembly. A Senate committee consultant said in an interview that lobbyists are the force behind bills more often in the Assembly than in the Senate, and an Assembly consultant concurred. "For the majority of the committees, most legislation goes right over their head on the Assembly side," said lobbyist Ken Emanuels (2001). "So that gives lobbyists plenty of opportunity to move very significant legislation, which is very poorly understood, at least through one house." Interest group representatives are not uniformly thrilled with these developments, though. When healthcare lobbyist Beth Capell (2001) was asked if she works harder after term limits, she replied, "Yes, and I was one of the people that was foolhardy enough to predict that lobbyists would work harder for less results." Strategist Donna Lucas (Lucas and Novelli 2001) noted one important obstacle: "Lobbyists used to know all the players; they'd been through it before. Now, there's a whole new set of players."

LEGISLATIVE PROCESS

Partisanship and Civility

Partisanship continued to increase in the California Legislature after the passage of Proposition 140, and some have suggested that term limits is at fault. This idea is certainly plausible in the sense that since legislators do not serve together long enough to develop strong bonds, partisanship might flourish. In the words of one veteran Senator, "The single biggest effect of term limits is increased partisanship. You don't know your colleagues well, and you don't treat them as part of your future. The new members are more like staff in their partisan attitude, and staffers have always been more vitriolic."[11] Other observers believe the problem resides with leadership. "These days, there is less of a long term relationship between those two party leaders, with a much lower percentage of bills passed on consent," observed a committee consultant.

However, is term limits really to blame? We looked for evidence of this in the following way: we compared the ideological extremism (measured by AFL-CIO labor vote scores) of new and veteran members in 1997 controlling for the party registration in their respective districts. The result was that the legislators' AFL-CIO scores were closely predicted by the party registration of their districts, and moreover, that this was as true of new as it was of veteran members. So the data did not support the idea that the new members coming in at the end of the first term limit cycle were more ideological than those going out. We also tracked members of the class of 1996 over their first three sessions, comparing their voting records to those of the class of 1986. The surviving members of both groups drifted to the extremes over their careers. Term limits, by shortening careers, seems to have halted a trend that would have polarized the body even further. Of course, voting records are not the only way to measure partisanship, which may have manifested itself in other ways. But polarization in voting behavior is perhaps the most consequential expression of partisanship, and term limits did not increase it.

Balance of Power

"The governor will usually be an experienced politician and have more media exposure. Willie Brown could hold his own with [Gov. George] Deukmejian and [Gov. Pete] Wilson, but because leadership will turn over every few years, they are at a disadvantage. This adds to the power of a governor who already has constitutional powers."[12] —Legislative staff member who formerly worked in the executive branch.

"On the budget, members will be much more interested in their pork after term limits, because they don't have time there to do something tangible on the bigger scale. They are much more susceptible to getting picked off with pork."[13] —Legislative staff member.

The most powerful weapon that California's Legislature possesses in its frequent battles with governors is its ability to tighten—or to loosen—the state's purse strings. As such, budget battles provide political scientists with ideal episodes to study relations between the two branches. The question is whether term limits has sharply curtailed the Legislature's ability and/or willingness to rewrite the governor's budget proposals. Because legislators could make many consequential changes to a governor's education proposals without changing total spending in this area much, we look at budgets at the finest level of detail preserved in official documents: that is, program requirement items. An ideal research strategy would record every item in a governor's budget and compare it with the amount that the Legislature finally passed for that item. Since that was not feasible, we identified three key program areas to track over four budget cycles: health care, higher education, and business services.[14] What these areas have in common is that state officials exercise considerable discretion over their spending levels; they are not driven entirely by caseload shifts or governed by initiatives that tie the hands of policymakers. Both governors and the Legislature have the ability to set expenditures at levels that reflect their preferences. These areas reflect some of the breadth of a state government's responsibilities and are supported by different constituencies and parties.

This analysis looks at four budgets written in the four comparable sessions that we introduced in our analysis of committees. Matching up the 1980–1981 fiscal year budget with the 2000–2001 spending plan gives us the opportunity to observe legislative oversight during eras of unified government. Democratic-majority Legislatures negotiated with Democrat Jerry Brown over the second budget of his second term in 1980 and with Democrat Gray Davis over the second budget of his first term in 2000. Both were written during years of significant fiscal expansion. General Fund spending in 1980–1981 was 13.3 percent higher than in the previous fiscal year, whereas expenditures grew by 17.4 percent between the 1999–2000 and the 2000–2001 budgets.[15] Democrats also controlled both houses of the Legislature when budgets for the 1987–1988 and 1997–1998 fiscal years were written. California government was divided, though, in each of these sessions. Republican Governor George Deukmejian was beginning his second term in 1987 and Republican Pete Wilson neared the end of his second term in 1997. Spending growth was sluggish in both periods, with state spending rising by 4.8 percent in the first of these budgets and 7.7 percent in the second. These four cases give us two pairs of pre- and post-term limits budgets constructed under roughly similar political and fiscal circumstances.

Focusing on our three selected portions of the budget, we began by recording how much a governor proposed spending on a given budget item in January, and then noted how much the final appropriation deviated from this figure. Looking through appropriate editions of the Governor's Budget for each cycle, we recorded General Fund spending levels from many "Program Requirements" tables. For instance, Gov. Jerry Brown recommended spending $1,781,724 in General Fund[16] money on the Hastings College of Law's "Instruction Program" during the 1980–1981 fiscal year. By examining the funding history for this item in the next fiscal year's budget, we see that the final deal between the executive and legislative branches set spending on this item at $1,997,594. This change altered the executive proposal by 10.8 percent of its final value. It was added to all of the other changes made to the

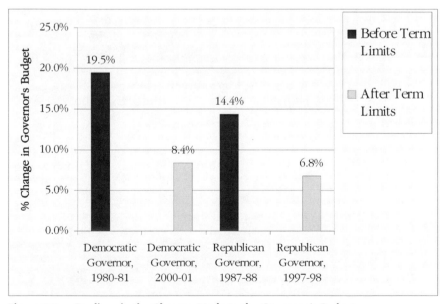

Figure 2.6. Declines in the Changes Made to the Governor's Budget
"% Changes" represents the ratio of the total line-by-line changes made by the Legislature to the total final appropriation levels in health care, higher education, and business services. Figures are taken from appropriate editions of the *Governor's Budget.*

Governor's Higher Education, Health Care, and Business Services budgets in order to compute the totals reported in Figure 2.6.

The effect of term limits on the Legislature's budgeting power is stark. In both pairs of comparable cases, the Legislature changes half as much of the governor's budget after term limits as it did before. The magnitude of this trend is the same under divided and unified government,[17] and represents billions of dollars in legislative discretion that is no longer exercised.

CONCLUSION: ADAPTING TO TERM LIMITS

Given the high level of professionalism in the California Legislature and the drastic nature of the term limits imposed on it (that is, comparatively short terms and lifetime bans), term limits should have had an effect in California if it had an effect anywhere. Clearly, that proved to be true. Leadership, the committee system, staff support and power vis-à-vis the Governor have all diminished in measurable ways. But for better or worse?

Very few state legislators and staff we spoke to, including those who succeeded termed out incumbents and Republicans who had supported Proposition 140, believe that term limits has improved the Legislature. Moreover, no one who cares about California government can be comforted by the fact that terms limits have weakened legislative effectiveness. Our assumption in this discussion is that voters did not seek to destroy legislative capacity when they approved Proposition 140 (though some pro-term limits activists explicitly sought to weaken legislatures). Rather, we think that they hoped for more turnover and for greater legislative competence at the same time.

To some extent, the Legislature has naturally adapted to term limits. But for these adaptations, things might have been a lot worse. Consider, for instance, bicameralism's role in the post-term limits era. During the constitutional revision deliberations of the mid-nineties, there was serious discussion of reducing the Legislature to one house. Bicameralism made sense, some argued, prior to the "one person, one vote" decisions in the sixties, because one house was based on equal population and the other on geographical units like counties in the so-called "federal model." But when the State Senate seats were changed to the same equal population standard used for Assembly districts, and especially when two Assembly seats were "nested" into one Senate seat under the two Special Masters' plans, there was little difference in the interests represented by the two houses. A study by David Brady and Brian Gaines found little difference in the voting patterns in the two California legislative houses after the reapportionment revolution (Brady and Gaines 1995). Moreover, conference committees that were assigned the task of reconciling different versions of bills passed in the two houses often became arenas for last minute legislative skullduggery.

This led experienced legislators such as Lucy Killea and Barry Keene to conclude that either a unicameral legislature on the model of Nebraska or a parliamentary system such as in Britain would be preferable.

But term limits has given bicameralism a new reason for existence. The lower house is the entry point and the training ground for most new legislators, while the upper house serves as the more experienced counter-balance. Evidence of this can be found in the comparative experience levels of committee chairs and senior staff, and amendment activities in the two houses. This compensation (that is, Senate experience offsetting Assembly turnover) was not planned or mandated by Proposition 140. It happened naturally as legislators pursued a logical career path from the Assembly to the Senate. When the last of the holdover legislators (those who were in office before term limits was enacted) move out of the Senate in 2004, the experience gap between the two houses should diminish somewhat, possibly also decreasing Senate-Assembly differences in the future.

Another natural adaptation is that legislators have learned that they need to mix experienced (that is, inside the building) staff with campaign loyalists. Those who filled their Sacramento offices with novices quickly found themselves at a disadvantage, relying heavily on lobbyists for expertise and guidance. But conventional wisdom soon corrected this flaw. Other staff compensations occurred by accident. For instance, we discovered evidence that inexperienced Senate committee chairs were often paired with more experienced committee staff. When we inquired as to whether this was a strategy of intentional compensation, we discovered that it was instead the artifact of less prestigious committees often having more stable staff (that is, because there was less competition for these positions); hence when the newer Senators got the less prestigious committees, they inherited more experienced staff.

But aside from these natural adaptations, what more can the Legislature do to make itself effective under term limits? There are two possibilities: improved staff and member training, and alterations to California's term limit law.

There is no doubt that member turnover has led to greater staff turnover. Most staff in California are personally hired by the legislators and committee chairs whom they serve. As new members replace termed out incumbents, they bring new staff into the process. As they move from the Assembly to the Senate, legislators take their experienced staff with them, perpetuating the imbalance in experience between the two houses. This then results in a tendency for the Senate to override the Assembly on legislative matters (for example, the asymmetry of amendment activity and the doubling of high-jacked Assembly Bills in the Senate noted in Cain and Kousser 2004) and causes unnecessary tension between them. One solution is to mix more experienced staff with new staff as we have discussed. The Assembly might accomplish this through changes in personnel policies or salary levels. In recent years, this has also meant retaining a stable of experienced staff in the Assembly speaker's office or in the Assembly majority staff. These experienced staff apparently shadow and monitor the less experienced committee and personal staffs.

The model of experienced staff advising less experienced legislators is one that many new legislators will be familiar with from their experience in local government. In the Unruh era, the concept of a professionalized staff meant non-partisan policy staff, similar to the city manager model in local government. In the modern era, legislative staffers have become more partisan after the bipartisan legislative tradition broke down with the tax revolt of 1978. Short of some new consensus being forged, the Legislature will likely continue building its experienced staff corps within the party caucuses. Still, the need for neutral expertise is apparent. Almost all of those we spoke to felt that the bill drafters in the Legislative Counsel and the policy specialists in the Legislative Analyst's Office had important functions in the term limits era.

However, the reality is that even with a determined effort to keep experienced staff, there will always be a lot of staff turnover. Hence, there needs to be an effective way to train new staff. Under Speaker Robert Hertzberg, the Assembly took steps in this direction by establishing its C.A.P.I.T.O.L. Training Institute (the California Assembly Program for Innovative Training and Orientation for the Legislature). Along with this program, Speaker Hertzberg developed manuals and documents that would make a permanent record of received legislative wisdom and practices. All of the staff and legislators we interviewed believed that this program was a welcome addition.

Legislators for the most part only attended the first couple of C.A.P.I.T.O.L. sessions. In those sessions, they learned the basics about how to set up a staff and deal with travel, facilities, and Assembly publications and resources. They got some process and ethics training, and heard presentations about the committees. The sessions also served as an opportunity for legislators to introduce themselves to one another. There were subsequent training sessions on bill writing and the budget, but it appears that legislators have a limited appetite for formal training sessions. For the most part, they would prefer to pick things up more informally from peer mentors.

A few of the legislators told us that they only attended the first few days of the C.A.P.I.T.O.L. Institute. One felt that the really valuable information about legislative tactics and how to deal with other members came from conversations with more senior members. Another, a Republican, felt that the Institute did nothing to overcome the forces of partisanship since "partisanship results from the issues not the presence or absence of personal bonds."

For staff, formal training is clearly very important and should be continued. Some of the current topics in the C. A. P. I. T. O. L. training include:

the budget process, how to staff legislation, training to be a Chief of Staff, practical management issues, scheduling tips, constituent casework and techniques for field representatives. The legislative and budgetary training are critical on the Assembly side. The more training staff have on these matters, the less the legislator's office as a whole must depend upon lobbyists and outsiders to provide expertise and knowledge.

One clear weakness in the training is in the area of oversight. As our earlier findings show, term limits have reduced the amount of oversight activity as measured by the number of budgetary supplemental requests for information from state agencies and by requests for Bureau of State Audit reports. The failure of the Legislature to do effective oversight could result in more agency waste and less compliance with the intent of laws passed. One way to improve the Legislature's oversight capacity would be to add more staff training in this area.

Finally, it is quite possible that California may need to consider some amendment to its term limits law in the future. The most promising proposal politically would be to define an overall legislative term limit equivalent to or slightly less than the effective overall limit that is currently fourteen years, but allow members to serve it in one or both houses. This would allow some members to stay in the Assembly and assume leadership positions or develop policy expertise. If only a few of the members do this, it could help redress the current bicameral imbalance. Term limits are for the foreseeable future permanent, but they can be adjusted to improve legislative effectiveness.

NOTES

1. The overall staffing figures come from two surveys conducted by the National Conference of State Legislatures, and the numbers for California's three expert staffing organizations were obtained by our research assistant, Kelly Yang. This analysis and all of those that follow in the case study are explained in greater detail in our 2004 report prepared for the Public Policy Institute of California, titled *Adapting to Term Limits: Recent Experiences and New Directions*.

2. Due to a renumbering of Senate seats after the 1990 redistricting and a seat switch with a political ally, Senate President Pro Tempore David Roberti earned himself the distinction of being the first legislator in the nation to be removed from office by term limits, in 1994. It was in 1996, though, that term limits took full effect.

3. Assembly information taken from National Conference of State Legislatures (1999) and Senate figures taken from documents provided to us by the Secretary of the Senate's office.

4. See Petracca (1991b) for an example of this justification in the debate over term limits, and Cain and Levin (1999) for a review of the literature supporting and opposing term limits before their implementation.

5. Data for our analysis of newly-elected women and minority legislators was published initially in Yang (2002b).

6. To count minority legislators, we first relied on directories that included photographs. While this was sufficient to count the number of black and Asian American officials, gauging Latino representation is often difficult. We used supplemental information such as Latino caucus membership, official biographies, lists provided by ethnic organizations, and press coverage to make final determinations, and did not count those with Portuguese heritage as Latinos.

7. Although Proposition 140 was intended to apply to California's Congressional delegation, the U.S. Supreme court rules in its 1995 *U.S. Term Limits, Inc. v. Thornton* decision that states could not limit the terms of their federal representatives.

8. Although there are procedures to discharge bills from California committees, they are used only in the rarest of cases.

9. We took these histories from the appropriate editions of the printed *Assembly Final History* and *Senate Final History*, published by the California Legislature (California Legislature 2001). Since the beginning of our analysis, these histories have been constructed from a uniform set of forms that committee staff fill out reporting the actions taken by committees, giving us confidence that figures are comparable across committees and over time.

10. Over four sessions, four committees in two houses hearing at least thirty bills from each house might have combined to hear 1,920 bills. Our sample only includes 1,888 because some committees were assigned fewer than thirty bills from the other house in some sessions.

11. Interview by authors, Sacramento, California, 25 February 2002.

12. Interview by authors, by telephone, August 2001.

13. Interview by authors, by telephone, August 2001.

14. We define higher education programs as the University of California, Hastings College of Law, the California State University, the California Maritime Academy, California Community Colleges, and the Student Aid Commission. Health Care funding in California, under our definition, went toward the Emergency Medical Services Authority, the Office of Statewide Health Planning and Development, and the many programs of the Department of Health Services. Business Services covers the Department of Alcoholic Beverage Control, the Department of Corporations, and the Department of Economic and Business Development (which later became the Department of Commerce and then the Trade and Commerce Agency).

15. Expenditure data is drawn from the Department of Finance's "Historical Data: General Fund Budget Summary" chart from www.dof.ca.gov. Note that although spending growth was strong in 1980–1981, the state at this time was establishing a new fiscal relationship with local governments to counteract their revenue losses from Proposition 13. This led Gov. Brown to begin his budget message with "Today I submit a budget for difficult times." Tighter finances during this pre-term limits budget should result in the Legislature making fewer changes in 1980–1981 than during the flush year of 2000–2001, biasing our results against finding that term limits has led to less legislative oversight of the budget.

16. "General fund" refers to the portion of a state's coffers that does not come from federal grants or from specialized state funds that are often dedicated to spe-

cific purposes. Since it is the source of funding over which California officials exercise unfettered control, we generally analyze General Fund spending exclusively in this analysis. In order to study some policy areas over time, however, we did not differentiate when General Funds were replaced by discretionary sources such as university general-purpose funds, the Alcohol Beverage Control Fund, or the State Corporations Fund.

17. We should note that, counter to our intuition, changes made to the executive proposals are greater in eras of unified than divided government. This may be because these were also years of greater fiscal growth, giving the Legislature a larger surplus to play with. It may also be yet another piece of evidence that the constitutional provision that requires a two-thirds vote in each house to pass a budget gives the legislative minority a remarkably powerful voice. Democratic leaders most likely wished to alter dramatically the spending plans proposed by Republican governors Deukmejian and Wilson, but this inclination was tempered by the requirement that they compromise with their Republican counterparts in the Legislature.

3

Legislative Power in the Buckeye State: The Revenge of Term Limits

Rick Farmer and Thomas H. Little

Legislatures, like other institutions that depend on the art of persuasion, flourish when personal relationships grease the wheels of the legislative process. State legislative term limits dissolve these personal relationships. Without this grease, the machinery of government functions less smoothly.

Inexperienced members enter the legislature knowing little about the process and not knowing who to call for answers. Early predictions about term limits claimed that less experienced legislators would become subservient to the governor, the bureaucracy, lobbyists and even their own staff. Evidence from Ohio indicates that despite term limits the legislature remains a powerful force. Certainly, the legislature is functioning differently than it was before term limits. In the absence of long-term members and long-held relationships, new relationships are being formed and reshaped every two years, the informal lines of authority are shifting, and the legislative process is more chaotic. Nonetheless, power has not dissipated and the legislature has not ground to a halt.

A BRIEF HISTORY

Like most state legislatures, the Ohio General Assembly prior to the 1970s was a part-time, semi-professional institution. Legislators were not paid well, did not serve for extended periods of time and held jobs outside of the legislature. The legislature met only a few months each year and had very limited staff support.

However, all of that changed in the early 1970s as Ohio, like many other states, began to rethink the level of support provided to its policymakers and their institutions. Building on the recommendations of the Citizens Conference of State Legislatures (1971), leaders in Ohio made a conscious effort to upgrade their membership, their institution and their support. Legislative salaries were dramatically increased. Legislators were provided with more individual staff and institutional staff offices were created and adequately funded. The legislature began meeting full time and a growing number of legislators began to consider their service to be a full time occupation. By the 1990s, the Ohio General Assembly was ranked among the five or six most professional state legislatures in America.

In 1992 the people of Ohio imposed a decidedly anti-professionalism reform. They passed a constitutional amendment imposing term limits on state legislators. The limits are eight years of consecutive service in each chamber. Members are allowed to run for the other chamber or sit out four years and return to the same body. House members were first termed out of the Ohio Legislature at the November 2000 general election. Because of staggered terms in the Senate some senior members survived through 2002. As the legislature convened in January 2003 none of the ninety-nine Representative or thirty-three Senators in the Ohio General Assembly had held their seat for more than six years.

Term limits remain relatively popular in Ohio. In November 1992 the initiative passed with 68 percent of the vote. A 2005 University of Akron Buckeye Poll found that 76 percent preferred to keep term limits "as is." Another 11 percent preferred lengthening the limit to twelve years. Only 12 percent preferred to "allow unlimited years" of service in the legislature.

Some groups and news organizations have expressed regret for supporting the original term limits proposal. In addition some current and former legislators have openly discussed lengthening or repealing the limits. Several bills have been introduced in the state legislature seeking repeal. However, an organized statewide movement has not emerged and public opinion appears to have changed very little.

The consequences of term limits are discussed below beginning with the composition of the legislature and the effect on representation. Elections give rise to representation and the effects of term limits on the election process are discussed next. Term limits alter more than membership and elections. They have consequences for legislative institutions like leadership, committees, staff and lobbyists. They also impact the legislative process including partisanship, norms and power relations. The legislature is a dynamic living organism. All of the actors in and around the legislature adjust their actions to the environmental constraints. This chapter will explore those adaptations. Finally, a few conclusions about term limits in the Buckeye state will be presented.

THE CONSEQUENCES OF TERM LIMITS

The effects of term limits in Ohio are examined specifically in three areas: composition and representation, institutional actors, and the legislative process. Data for this analysis were developed using surveys, interviews, observations and documents.

Composition and Representation

Sophomore members and long-term observers agree that it takes about one full legislative session for new members to become acclimated to the legislative process. Generally, after one year and certainly after one two-year cycle members have a good gasp of how to pass legislation and serve their district's interest in the capitol. One of the effects of term limits is to bring more freshmen members into the legislature. As Figure 3.1 shows about 20 percent of Representatives and 25 percent of Senators were freshmen each session prior to 2000.

Legislative term limits had a dramatic effect on the Ohio House in 2000. Over half (55 percent) of the House members were newcomers when the legislature convened in 2001. This created a substantial amount of chaos, as several freshmen became committee chairs. Turnover at the 2002 election remained high at near 30 percent. On the Senate side turnover climbed to 30 percent following the 1998 election. This was due in part to anticipatory effects. Because they were being termed out, some members sought other

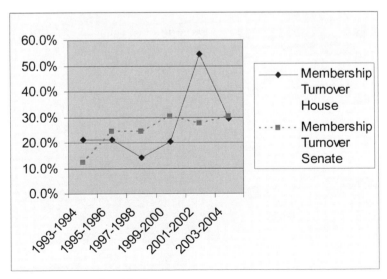

Figure 3.1. Membership Turnover

opportunities and left the Senate before their terms expired. Since the implementation of term limits, 30 percent turnover seems to be the new norm in both chambers. Eight-year limits guarantee 25 percent turnover. With voluntary retirements and election losses, 30 percent turnover is likely to continue.

The high legislative turnover has produced only minor shifts in the demographics of the legislature as shown in Table 3.1. Since the Republican revolution in 1994 the number of Republicans has steadily increased. There was no change immediately after term limits took effect in 2000, despite over half of the House members being new. However, Republicans made additional gains after redistricting in 2002.

Representation of racial minorities has increased from 11 percent immediately following the passage of term limits to 15 percent after 2002. However, there was no change in the percentage of minorities in the first year of term limits implementation. In fact, there was a slight decline in minority representation after the 1998 election because of termed members seeking other opportunities. The percentage of women in the Ohio legislature has varied little since the enactment of term limits. Women have been over 20 percent of the membership since term limits were adopted. As a result a large number of women were termed out of office in 2000. However, this did not affect their overall membership in the legislature. The average age of members increased by approximately one year after term limits were enacted. This may be due to members serving out their time rather than leaving. When term limits took effect the average age declined by over two years. Of course, the elimination of long-term members would be expected to decrease the average age.

It is widely reported that the demographics of candidates running for office has changed very little as a result of term limits (Caress 2001). These data support that conclusion. The face of the Ohio General Assembly has changed very little as a result of term limits.

In the U.S. Congress junior members generally pay close attention to their districts (Hibbing 1991). The removal of senior "safe" members would sug-

Table 3.1.   Demographic Composition of the Ohio Legislature

Year	% Democratic	% Non-White	% Women	Ave. Age*
1993-1994	50.00%	11.36%	21.97%	48.85
1995-1996	42.42%	12.87%	24.24%	49.06
1997-1998	39.39%	14.39%	21.97%	49.37
1999-2000	39.39%	13.63%	21.21%	49.98
2001-2002	39.39%	13.63%	21.97%	47.19
2003-2004	36.36%	15.15%	20.45%	47.81

*Based on reported ages to the Ohio Trucking Association (does not include all members).

gest that legislators would focus more attention on district service. However, a survey of 210 knowledgeable observers in Ohio indicated that district service was about the same in 2003 as it was ten years earlier. This is in contrast to Illinois, a comparable but untermed legislature, where constituency service was higher. Term limits have not increased or decreased representation as measured by constituency service in Ohio.

Elections

Even before the onset of legislative term limits, legislative elections in Ohio were increasingly a caucus-centered activity. That trend has continued and perhaps accelerated. Each veteran member is given a fundraising goal. These assessments vary based on the member's responsibility within the chamber. Funds are then strategically distributed to targeted races based on competitiveness. Candidates are recruited and trained, campaign professionals are hired, and costs are soaring in targeted races. This reflects a trend that has been growing across the country for a couple of decades in states with and without term limits (White and Shea 2000; Morehouse and Jewel 2003). However, the replacement of safe incumbents with open seats has accelerated the caucus activity.

Open seats often produce primaries and in some cases in Ohio these primaries have resulted in showdowns between competing groups, each of whom have recruited a candidate. However, because of Ohio's vacancy appointment law an increasing number of members leave their post in midsession. This allows the caucus to appoint an incumbent and prevent the open seat challenge.

These electoral circumstances have strengthened the hand of the majority and demoralized the minority. Democratic caucus leaders and staff express frustration at recruitment and fundraising. The minority always has trouble competing financially and in Ohio prior to the 2006 elections Republicans controlled both legislative chambers, all three branches of government, and almost every statewide office. In addition the minority finds it difficult to recruit candidates to a limited career. As one staffer put it, "Why would anyone want to come to Columbus if you know you can only serve eight years and have no hope of ever being in the majority?"

Institutions: Leaders, Committees, Staff and Lobbyists

Both the majority and minority leadership have been greatly affected by term limits in Ohio. Some of the effects are accelerations of previous trends. For example, the leadership has used the increasing caucus role in elections to strengthen the leadership's control over the caucus.

Ohio has had a long succession of strong majority leaders. As shown in Table 3.2, Vern Riffe served as Speaker from 1975–1994. In the Republican revolution of 1994 Jo Ann Davidson became Speaker. When Davidson left with the first term limited class, Larry Householder became speaker with only four years of legislative experience. Yet, Householder used his campaign prowess, negotiating skill and prerogatives of the Chair to dominate the House. Majority leadership in the Senate has also been strong. Stan Aronoff served as leader from 1989 to 1996. His assistant majority leader, Dick Finan, succeeded him. And when Finan was term limited, his assistant succeeded him.

On the minority side things were very different. Several minority leaders left the legislature just before they were termed in search of other opportunities. Since the 1996 election, as term limits were approaching, both the House and Senate had three minority leaders. Most of these transitions took place mid-term. This left the minority struggling internally to find its voice while the majority marched forward under strong leadership.

While turnover was high for the top minority leader position, the number of new members entering the leadership has been stable at about nine of eighteen for the legislature as a whole. As shown in Table 3.3, leadership turnover has declined slightly in the House. It has increased slightly in the Senate.

According to knowledgeable observers in Ohio, legislative leaders are spending more time fundraising than they did ten years ago. As a result, leaders are largely selected on the basis of their fundraising ability, and they tend to plan their path to leadership early in their careers. Something similar occurred in Michigan when term limits first took effect (Bratton and Haynie 2001a). There is no succession ladder, formal or informal in the Ohio House. Senators, have followed a more obvious succession ladder with a period of apprenticeship, but with each new class, those trends may change.

A major source of chaos within the Ohio legislature since term limits has been committees. One observer notes, "It is easy to tell which chairmen know how to run a committee and which don't." Because of the influx of new members in 2000 several freshmen legislators became committee chairs. A survey of knowledgeable observers found members in committees to be: less knowledgeable about the issues, less willing to amend or substitute language, less willing to compromise and less courteous to colleagues.

Much of the committee business has shifted to the caucus room. Members hash out their policy differences in caucus, relegating the committee process to a mere formality. This has shifted deliberation from the public committee room to the private caucus room. Deliberation occurs in the Ohio legislature, but very little of it occurs in public. It is difficult to assess whether this situation is a result of term limits, caucus centered campaigns or strong leadership. It is likely the result of the confluence of all three.

Table 3.2. Majority and Minority Leader Turnover

House				Senate			
Majority		Minority		Majority		Minority	
Vern Riffe-D	1975–1994	Corwin Nixon-R	1991–1992	Stanley Aronoff-R	1989–1996	Robert Boggs-D	1991–1996
		Jo Ann Davidson-R	1993–1994	Richard Finan-R	1997–2002	Ben Espy-D	1997–2000
Jo Ann Davidson-R	1995–2000	Patrick Sweeny-D	1995–1996			Rhine McLin-D	2000–2000
		Ross Boggs-D	1997–1998			Leigh Herrington-D	2001–2002
Larry Householder-R	2001–2004	Jack Ford-D	1999–2002	Doug White-R	2003–2004	Greg DiDinato-D	2003–2004
		Dean DePiero-D	2002–2002				
		Chris Redfern-D	2003–2004				

Table 3.3. Leadership Turnover

Year	House	Senate
1993-1994	4 of 10	1 of 8
1995-1996	6 of 10	3 of 8
1997-1998	6 of 10	3 of 8
1999-2000	5 of 10	4 of 8
2001-2002	5 of 10	4 of 8
2003-2004	4 of 10	4 of 8

Ohio has three distinct types of staff. First, each member of the House has one legislative aide. That single staffer is responsible for all functions of the office. Committee chairs get a second aide. Each Senator gets one administrative assistant and one legislative aide. Second, each caucus has a sizable staff. When Speaker Householder took charge of the House after the 2000 election, he significantly increased the Speaker's staff by reducing the number of staffers individual members had. Finally, the Legislative Service Commission is non-partisan staff, who oversees bill processing.

Lack of job security is the most important issue facing personal staff as a result of term limits. Rapid turnover is nothing new for legislative staff. However, under term limits staffers know that their boss will be leaving at a fixed date and the staffer needs an exit strategy. Some staffers have cited term limits as a reason to leave the legislature. In many cases the new member keeps the experienced staffer. Sometimes staffers find another member for whom to work. In 2001 when more than half of the House turned over, every staff member who wanted to stay with the House found a position.

The turnover in personal staff, like the turnover in members, has contributed to the loss of relationships. Staffers know each other and depend on those relationships to navigate the legislative process. With friends retiring, leaving for other jobs, or moving to new offices, everyone begins rebuilding relationships every session. Freshmen members tend to depend on their personal staff for procedural advice. They tend to depend on caucus staff for policy and political advice. As a result the power of the caucus staff has increased significantly.

Freshmen legislators, like ordinary citizens, tend to view lobbyists with suspicion. Most tend to overcome their fears as relationships begin to develop. However, in 2001 some House members refused to meet with any lobbyists until the Speaker called and asked them to accept the meeting. The biggest problem lobbyists face under term limits is the large influx of new members. Many lobbying firms hired new staff, so they would be able to meet all of the new members and build essential relationships. The number of registered lobbyists has steadily increased since 1996 from 1,138 to 1,316. Almost half of those new lobbyists came in with the 2000 term limits freshmen class. One longtime capitol reporter recently lamented that the House Education Committee used to be run by a longtime lobbyist who knew what he was doing, now the Education Committee is run by a legislator who knows little about the issues.

A survey of knowledge observers suggests that the influence of lobbyists has increased in Ohio over the past decade. But, this increase is comparable to the increase in Illinois, suggesting that term limits may not be the reason for the increase. Lobbyists are certainly powerful in Ohio, but they must work very hard to build and maintain the relationships that are the currency of their trade. They have found term limits to be a challenge in Ohio.

The Legislative Process: Partisanship, Norms and Power

The legislative process in Ohio is much more partisan and that it was before term limits. However, according to knowledgeable observers a similar situation exists in the untermed legislature of Illinois. There is also evidence that the Ohio Senate was becoming more partisan in the 1980s, well before term limits were adopted. Ohio's partisanship likely arises from its caucus centered elections. The caucus is the central organizing body, leading to an "us versus them mentality." A second contributing factor to the staunch partisanship was the size of the Republican majority. When Republicans could keep their members together they could easily pass major legislation, including the state budget, without any Democratic input. As a result, the minority party felt neglected and ignored. This situation eased a bit in 2003 when the Speaker made a special effort to involve some members of the minority party. Some observers speculate he was having trouble with his own members and needed the minority votes.

Civility has also declined in the Ohio legislature. Increased partisanship has contributed to the loss of civility, but the lack of relationships across the aisle is another important reason. Before term limits members got to know one another in committee, on the floor and at social events. These relationships grew over time. When those relationships were severed by term limits civility was affected.

A large number of freshmen enter the legislature each year. Many of these freshmen do not know anyone in Columbus except the caucus leaders and staff, who helped them get elected. They spend much of their time with caucus colleagues plotting how to defeat the other party. The relationships that would lead to civility are never developed.

Another important factor in the loss of civility is Ohio's gift law. Several observers noted that before the gift limit was lowered one or two lobbyists would take several legislators to dinner in a group. Usually this involved members of both parties. One result of these informal occasions was relationship building across the aisle. Because of the new gift limit those occasions have shifted to a group of lobbyists taking one or two legislators to dinner, so the lobbyists can split the check and keep the tab under the gift cap.

The balance of power in Ohio has shifted to the caucus and the leadership. The Speaker and the Senate President Pro-Temp have taken charge of the legislative process and the state capital. A survey of knowledgeable observers indicated that the power of the governor had declined while the power of legislative leaders and leadership staff had increased. Observers who were interviewed agree that in Ohio, personality has proven more important than institutional arrangements in determining the balance of power. The effect of term limits will be to keep the personalities in flux.

ADJUSTING TO THE NEW WORLD

A variety of adaptations have occurred in Ohio. Through these adaptations the legislature has been able to continue to function. However, it requires more work by everyone concerned to keep the process flowing.

The most important adaptation was the Speaker's efforts to recruit and train candidates. Once his people were elected he was in firm control of the House. Another major adaptation was the Speaker's new member training session conducted with presumptive members before the election. The Legislative Service Commission also expended its new member training. The use of the caucus as a forum for deliberation rather than committees was another important adaptation. The hiring of additional lobbyists is also a noteworthy occurrence.

CONCLUSION

The Ohio legislature has changed a great deal since term limits were passed in 1992. Some of the changes were related to term limits directly, others indirectly and yet others not at all. Many of the changes in Ohio are similar to those occurring in other comparable non-term limits states. Campaigns are getting more costly and more partisan. Leaders are taking a more active role in campaign fundraising, candidate recruitment and message development. Floor debates and discussion are becoming increasingly partisan. These changes are mirrored in other professional legislatures that do not have term limits.

Other changes can be attributed to the change in partisan control, increasingly caucus centered campaigns, or personalities and ingenuity, each of which may be, at least indirectly, related to legislative term limits. The large number of open seats has provided an opportunity for caucus leaders to coordinate freshmen election activity. To a great extent, the new personalities and ingenuity present in the Ohio legislature are there because of term limits. Most of the new members would have neither sought nor gained entrance into the legislature apart from the forced exodus of the senior members.

Finally, some effects are traceable directly to term limits. The loss of relationships long associated with successful legislative activity can be directly attributed to the rapid turnover of members who are either forced out by term limits or leave early to take advantage of a timely opportunity. The constant flow of new members, inexperienced committee chairs and revolving door leaders has created a much more chaotic and unpredictable process. Further, the relative inexperience of many of the members has significantly increased the workload of everyone associated with the legislature.

In the end, the Ohio legislature is functioning and functioning rather well. Perhaps it is in spite of term limits. Perhaps it is because of term limits. Our guess is that it is a little of both. While making the process chaotic and unpredictable, term limits has created the opportunity for innovative and aggressive leaders like Speaker Larry Householder to make his mark and move the House to the pinnacle of power on Capitol Square. Although increased turnover has made the learning curve much more steep, that same rapid turnover has opened the door to a coordinated legislative caucus that has passed the most ambitious policy agenda in years.

4

Truncated Careers in Professionalized State Legislatures[1]

Christopher Z. Mooney

The basic normative assumptions behind the legislative professionalism and term limits movements are at odds, or at least emphasize different values. One values competence, information, expertise, and experience, the other values rotation in office, limited government, common sense, and practical experience in the private sector. Thus, if term limits are going to have an impact anywhere, they should have an impact on professionalized state legislatures (Everson 1992; Cain and Levin 1999).

By all accounts, California, Ohio, and Illinois had among the most professional state legislatures in the country over the past quarter century (Mooney 1994). While each is organized and operates differently, these bodies each have copious staff, meet for many months each year, and pay their members a fulltime salary. This chapter assesses the impact of the state legislative term limits in California, Ohio, and Illinois, using the General Assembly as a control.

I find that many of the effects of term limits are similar to the effects of redistricting. Both increase member turnover and accelerate demographic shifts already in progress. Additional effects of term limits arise from the loss of experience and relationships caused by the truncating of legislative careers. Generally, however, term limits have not produced a new breed of legislators or legislative candidates in professionalized legislatures.

A BRIEF HISTORY

While term limits have been the most significant state legislative reform in the 1990s and 2000s, the effort to professionalize state legislatures was the most significant reform movement in the 1960s and 1970s. In response to derision by pundits and scholars that state government, and particularly state legislatures, were archaic, dysfunctional, "horse-and-buggy institutions in a jet age" (Miller 1965, 178; see also Hyneman 1938; Burns 1971; and Herzberg and Rosenthal 1972), the states consciously set about upgrading their institutions to meet the challenges of the late 20th century (Bowman and Kearney 1986). With the United States Congress as the model, the state legislatures increased their staff, time in session, and pay for its members (Squire 1992). By the 1970s, being a lawmaker in a professionalized state legislature had become a fulltime job.

Of course, not all state legislatures became fulltime, professional institutions, but several did, while most others moved in the direction of professionalism. The most professional legislatures tend to be in the most urban, heavily populated, and diverse states (King 2000; Mooney 1995). These states have significant public challenges and resources, giving them both the need for and the capacity to afford the services of a professional state government.

While term limits do not directly affect the three pillars of state legislative professionalism—staff, session length, and salary—there is a strong connection between the arguments for a citizen (that is, nonprofessional) legislature and legislative term limits. Indeed, disapproval of professionalized state legislatures and Congress helped prompt the original call for term limits in the early 1990s (Petracca 1991a, 1992; Will 1993; Ehrenhalt 1991).

Hypotheses of term limits' impacts on state legislatures typically derive from either of two general processes. First, term limits might affect state legislatures by changing their members' incentive structure, leading to the recruitment of a new type of legislator. Without the potential for unlimited tenure, those who enter and win state legislative races might have new attitudes and ideas. These "citizen legislators" would have fresh ideas and broader views, wanting to serve in government for a time and then return to the private sector (Malbin 1992; Fund 1992; Olson 1992; Elhauge, Lott, and Manning 1997). These new legislators would behave differently than those attracted to a non-term-limited legislature, and they might change the institution and politics of the legislative process accordingly. Second, term limits might affect state legislatures simply through the mechanical process of truncating legislative careers. Term-limited legislatures would have no long-serving members and the informational and attitudinal baggage these members might carry (Moncrief et al. 1992; Farmer 2002; Everson 1992). The impacts of term limits through this process would not be based on a new breed of term-limited members who behave or think differently, but rather, it would be a function solely of their truncated careers.

There is undoubtedly an overlap in the effects that these general processes might cause for state legislatures, but the distinction between them may help us understand term limits better. In the pro-term limits advocacy literature, emphasis has been placed on the change in the attitudes and recruitment of new types of legislators (Petracca 1991a, 1992; Will 1993; Ehrenhalt 1991), while the political science literature has focused on negative consequences that follow from truncating legislative careers (Mondak 1995; Francis and Kenny 1997; Opheim 1994; Lopez 2003; but see Meinke and Hasecke 2003). By assessing the impact of term limits on the most professional state legislatures, we can begin to assess which of these processes is dominant, at least at this early stage of the states' experience with this reform.

THE ILLINOIS GENERAL ASSEMBLY—
A NON-TERM-LIMITED STATE LEGISLATURE

The Illinois General Assembly is an excellent control case for helping assess the impact of term limits in professionalized state legislatures. First, it ranks consistently among the five or six most professional state legislatures on various indices and scales, along with the Ohio and California legislatures (King 2000; Mooney 1994). But more important, throughout the study period, it was characterized by stability or gradual change in a wide range of its characteristics and processes, as both interviews with observers of, and participants in, the legislative process in Illinois and the documentary data make clear. Since the 1980s, the most important characteristics of the General Assembly have been its strong, chamber-based, party leadership and a pervasive partisanship (Gove and Nowlan 1996). Two major institutional disruptions defined the body in recent years: the substantial changes in the size and electoral rules for the Illinois House of Representatives in 1982 (Everson et al. 1982; Van der Slik and Redfield 1989; Wheeler 2000) and the 1992 round of legislative redistricting (Gove 2001). Fortunately, the changes in the House took place long before the study period and both Ohio and California redistricted their legislatures at the same time as Illinois.

RESEARCH PLAN

This comparative, interrupted time-series design will help isolate the effects of term limits from those trends and changes that occurred in state legislatures as a result of other forces. This chapter compares the experiences from 1992–2002 of Ohio and California, states with term limits, to those of Illinois. Of course, with only three cases and many potential forces at work in addition to term limits, it will be impossible to draw strong cause-and-effect conclusions from these data.

In the previous two chapters, both Cain, Kousser, and Kurtz (California) and Farmer and Little (Ohio) have used comparisons in a single state over time to draw conclusions about the impacts of term limits; those insights are referenced here. A variety of data gathered through the Joint Project on Term Limits (JPTL) are also referenced. They include documentary data drawn from public sources. These data are quite comparable across states and time, but they are limited in scope. They also include several dozen interviews with state legislators and long-time observers of lawmaking in these states, including journalists, legislative staff, lobbyists, and executive agency officials. This qualitative information is less directly comparable than the documentary data, but it shows many of the more subtle impacts of term limits, such as those on the balance of power and legislative behavior. Third, a survey of state legislators nationwide (Carey et al. 2003) and a survey of knowledgeable observers in the nine JPTL states are examined.

The chapter first examines the composition of the legislature and representational issues. It considers the changing demographics of professionalized legislatures. Then, attention is turned to the effects on institutional players. The actions of leaders, committees, staff and other participants in the legislative arena are examined. Next, partisanship, civility, balance of power and adaptations are considered in the legislative process. Finally, I draw some conclusions about term limits effects from this comparison of three professionalized state legislatures.

COMPOSITION, REPRESENTATION, AND ELECTIONS

Term limits have not affected the demographics of the membership of professionalized state legislatures. As Cain, Kousser, and Kurtz showed through careful comparisons over time and with other officials in California, and as Farmer and Little found in Ohio, the basic demographic patterns and trends of the state legislatures in this study have not been affected by term limits. Figure 4.1 shows that the female membership in the Illinois General Assembly increased slowly in the study period, while it was stable in Ohio and made a big jump in California between 1994 and 1998. Figure 4.2 shows a slow, steady increase in the non-white membership of the Ohio and Illinois legislatures, with a somewhat larger increase in California. Figure 4.3 shows that the average age of legislators in Ohio and Illinois changed little during the study period, and what change there was had little pattern to it.[2] None of these demographic trends or changes appears to be related to term limits, in that Ohio's and California's patterns do not appear to be systematically different than Illinois's, nor is there a marked change in California and Ohio when their term limits became effective. This conclusion of no demographic effect of term limits matches the one drawn by Carey et al. (2003)

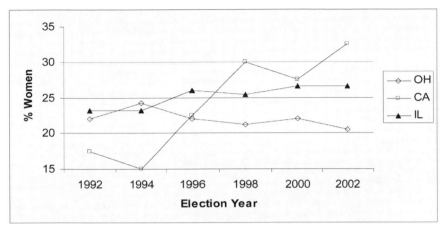

Figure 4.1.   Percentage of the State Legislature That is Female, 1992–2002

from their national survey of state legislators (see also Caress 1999 and Carroll and Jenkins 2001).

On the other hand, there is evidence that suggests that term limits, like redistricting, serve to accelerate ongoing trends whose causes lay elsewhere. Cain, Kousser, and Kurtz draw this conclusion from their California study based on the acceleration of female and racial minority representation after term limits took effect. Similarly, minority representation in Illinois took a jump after the 2001 redistricting. Term limits and redistricting may reduce incumbents' electoral advantages, whether by forcing some of them out of office or by changing their relationship with their constituents. Like friction

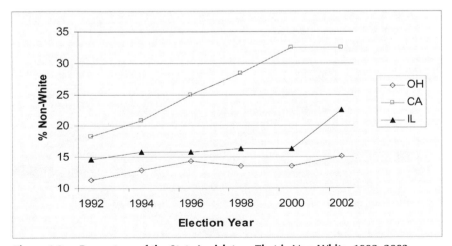

Figure 4.2.   Percentage of the State Legislature That is Non-White, 1992–2002

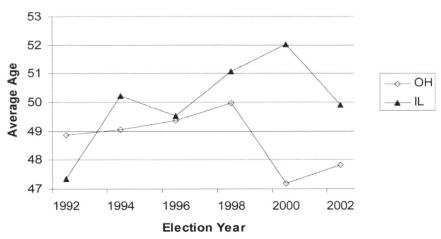

Figure 4.3. Average Age at Election of State Legislators, 1992–2002

keeps tectonic pressure from being released, the pressure of long-term social and demographic change in a state builds as incumbency advantage
blocks a representational adjustment. Then, like an earthquake, term limits
or redistricting allows these forces to be expressed fully in legislative elections. In this sense, both term limits and redistricting may enhance legislative responsiveness, as term limits advocates had hoped (Petracca 1991a;
Will 1993; Ehrenhalt 1991). And while demographic responsiveness is easy
to track, responsiveness to less obvious forces, such as changing policy ideas
and values, may also be enhanced by term limits.

A central tenet of the argument for term limits was that they would increase membership turnover in state legislatures, thereby infusing these bodies with new ideas and energy (Petracca 1992; Fund 1992). Figure 4.4 shows
that, indeed, turnover was higher in California and Ohio than in Illinois in
most of the study period, especially after term limits began to take effect.
Turnover in Illinois was generally below 20 percent in each election, while
in California and Ohio under term limits, turnover was usually greater than
30 percent, at least in their houses. Note that, again, the effect of redistricting in Illinois very much parallels that of term limits in Ohio and California.
In those elections immediately after redistricting (1992 and 2002), membership turnover jumps dramatically in Illinois, especially in the senate.

However, the percentage of new members each election does not tell the
whole story of term limits' impact on tenure in the statehouse. Also important to many areas of the state legislative process is the number of long-
serving members. Turnover may be high each election, even 50 percent or
more, but if a relatively few "old bulls" return term after term, they can
provide the institutional and policy knowledge and political power to run

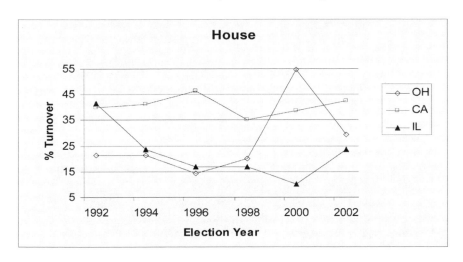

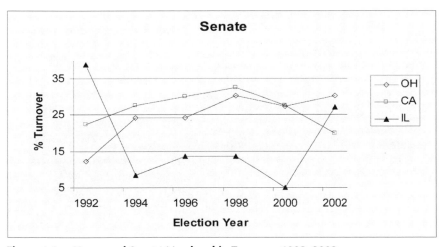

Figure 4.4.   House and Senate Membership Turnover, 1992–2002

the legislature and maintain its status as a co-equal branch of state government. This is a typical pattern in many citizen legislatures, like those in Arkansas and West Virginia. Term limits, by definition, culls these old bulls from the herd. At the start of each session, no member of the Ohio legislature will have more than six years experience in his or her chamber; in the California Assembly, that number is only four years. This is a long way from the situation in those states before term limits, and in Illinois today, when it was not unusual for some members to have served ten, fifteen, or even twenty years in a chamber.

Beyond overall membership turnover, term limits were expected to increase partisan competition in state legislative elections (Petracca 1992; Fund 1992). Term limits would reduce the advantages of incumbency, allowing more competition in a district and making both major parties more competitive. Party competition did rise, but in all three states it followed the national trend. Nationally, state legislative elections are being more directed by the party leadership of each chamber (Jewell and Morehouse 2001). This centralization of campaign finance, strategy, and staff in the office of the chamber caucus (whether formally or informally) continues unabated in Ohio and Illinois; in California, Cain, Kousser, and Kurtz report no change in the distribution of campaign money since term limits took effect.

Farmer and Little report that midterm resignations increased in Ohio during the study period, thus allowing more party leadership control of successors through appointments. However, this tactic is also commonly used in Illinois for the same reason, especially in elections before and after redistricting. By both of these measures term limits had little impact on key aspects of campaigns and elections.

On the other hand, term limits may have had some other important impacts on campaigns and elections. There is evidence from Ohio and California that term limits have led to more legislative candidates having experience in local government, while at the same time leading those who leave the legislature to be more likely to seek another elective office. Observers did not notice these trends in Illinois during the study period. These trends suggest that term limits may cause a churning effect in elections, at the local, state, and federal level, through two forces: pushing and pulling. First, legislators may be pushed out of office by term limits before they have satisfied their political ambition (Powell 2000). In non-term-limited state legislatures, a member who enjoys politics and policymaking may stay in office (assuming electoral success) until he or she wants to change, perhaps by moving into the private sector, an executive branch position, or retirement. Of course, there are those whose ambitions are not satisfied by service in the state legislature and who will, therefore, voluntarily leave that body to seek other office. But by forcing legislators out of office before they are ready to leave politics, term limits develop a cadre of experienced, successful, and perhaps desperate candidates for other offices each election. Contrary to the hopes of term limits advocates, evidence gathered in a variety of states for the JPTL indicates that legislators in term-limited states are no more likely to leave public life after six or eight years of service in the statehouse than those in non-term-limited states (Garrett 1996).

The second force at work churning up elections in term limits states is a pulling effect. That is, because term limits cause so many open seat races each election, there is more opportunity for those in local offices to move to the legislature than in non-term-limit states. Strategic politicians are hes-

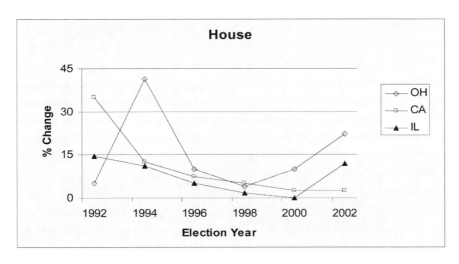

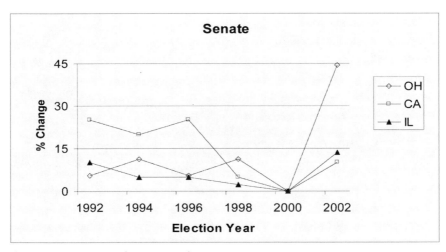

Figure 4.5.   House and Senate Partisan Turnover, 1992–2002
Note: Partisan turnover is the percentage of seats up for election in which the party of the winner was not the party of the incumbent.

itant to risk a relatively safe position they hold to challenge an incumbent for another office (Jacobson 2000). Open seats are less risky, and therefore more seated, successful, high quality candidates should leave their offices and run for the legislature in term limits states, as the qualitative data suggest is happening in Ohio and California.

Beyond overall membership turnover, term limits were expected to increase partisan competition and turnover in state legislative elections (Petracca

1992; Fund 1992). Term limits would reduce the advantages of incumbency, allowing more competition in a district, including allowing both major parties to be more competitive. The most direct way to assess the effect of term limits on the level of district-level party competition is by comparing the percentage of seats up for election in which the party of the winner was different than that of the incumbent, that is, partisan turnover. Figure 4.5 shows that there was little difference in partisan turnover in these states, either before or after term limits. Partisan turnover is generally quite low in all states, except in elections following redistricting. The California senate stands out here, with relatively high partisan turnover early in the study period, but a distinct drop in it after term limits took effect. This may be due to the very large size of these senate districts and, thus, the potential for more heterogeneity in their electorates. Why partisan turnover should decrease with term limits is unclear. The fact that the California house had consistently low partisan turnover (except after the 1992 redistricting) suggests that neither California, per se, nor term limits led to this high partisan turnover early in the study period. The major exception in Figure 4.5 is Ohio, where the effects of redistricting produced high levels of turnover in 1994 and 2002.

Thus, between the pulling of local government officials into term-limits-induced open seats and the pushing of not-yet-politics-satiated state legislators into races for other offices, term limits appear to be churning the political waters of states with professionalized legislatures. The political and policy implications of this process remain to be seen.

INSTITUTIONS:
LEADERS, COMMITTEES, STAFF, AND LOBBYISTS

Each of the three professionalized state legislatures in this study has a history of strong, long-serving party leaders. Some of the most storied state house speakers and senate presidents in the past forty years have come from Ohio, Illinois, and California, with names like Riffe, Madigan, and Brown being well known throughout the country by those in and around state governments. These leaders controlled the legislative process and shaped their institutions. These were old bull leaders who served for decades in a chamber, serving apprenticeships on substantive committees and in lesser leadership positions, often learning their skills from other old bull leaders under whom they served. By the end of their careers, they had served years in the top leadership positions in their respective chambers. Typically, such leaders were known for guarding the prerogatives of their chamber (and their own party's majority), and taking the long view of policy and politics in their states. While it has been argued that legislative professionalism reduced the power of such leaders (Rosenthal 1996), there is no doubt that these three professionalized legislatures each had strong leaders.

That is, they each had such leaders before term limits. By definition, term limits eliminates this sort of old bull legislative leader. It has even been argued that term limits advocates in California began their movement in order to rid the Assembly of its long-time speaker (Cain and Kousser 2004). On the other hand, Illinois still retains leaders of this type. During the entire study period, none of the four party caucuses in the Illinois General Assembly changed its top leader. With term limits, even the speaker and the president in California and Ohio have limited tenure in the legislature and in leadership. It is likely that this has led to reduced power for these leaders, for a number of reasons. First, top legislative leaders in term limits states have less experience in, expertise about, and knowledge of state government and policy and, therefore, less of the moral authority that these bring. Second, these leaders have less time in leadership to generate goodwill and return the favors that allowed them to be elected by their peers in the first place (Malbin and Benjamin 1992). Leaders typically consolidate power in office and grow stronger over time (Jewell and Whicker 1994), something these term-limited leaders cannot do for long. Third, term limits make these leaders lame ducks as soon as they take office. Their opponents know exactly how long they have to wait for a new leader. Potential successors begin jockeying for a future leadership bid immediately upon the current leader's election.

Fundraising skill is an important qualification for top state legislative leadership posts across the country (Jewell and Morehouse 2001). But in non-term-limit states, legislators typically also use other criteria to select their leaders, since they have more time to watch one another in office and decide who would be their best representative. In professionalized term-limited state legislatures, fundraising ability may now be the primary, if not the only, leadership selection criteria (Bratton and Haynie 2001b; Little and Farmer 2007).

Future studies will need to test these effects with more precision, but several implications for legislative leadership are suggested by the data from Illinois, California, and Ohio. First, not only does the top legislative leadership turn over more quickly in term limits states, the chambers' parties' leadership teams are also less stable (Figure 4.6), at least in non-redistricting years. We again see that redistricting in Illinois (reflected in the 1992 and 2002 elections) generated about as much instability in its legislative leadership team as term limits seem to have done in Ohio and California. Second, leaders with shorter terms will likely be weaker, leading to instability in the legislature. Carey et al. (2003) found that leaders in term limits states are generally perceived as weaker than those in non-term-limit states, as did the survey of knowledge observers in the nine JPTL study states. This could lead to less emphasis on policy (as opposed to institutional and electoral politics), a weaker position for the legislature relative to the executive branch, and other potential effects that need further study.

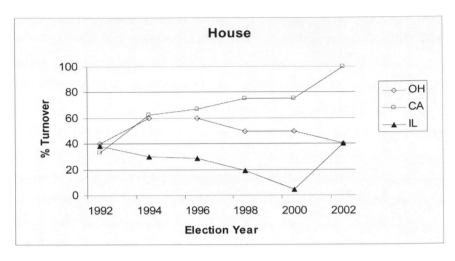

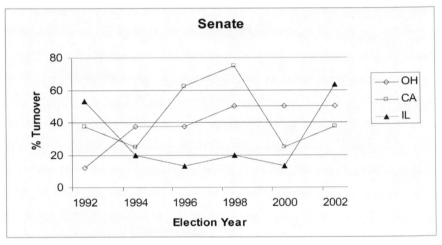

Figure 4.6. House and Senate Leadership Team Turnover, 1992–2002
Note: Leadership team turnover is the percentage of legislators who are new to the leadership teams of both parties after each election.

Along with party leadership, substantive standing committees are the principal way American-style legislatures organize themselves to accomplish their policymaking tasks. These institutions can be thought of as being in a zero-sum power game (Jewell and Whicker 1994; Clucas 2001); when leaders are strong (as in many state legislatures, such as Illinois), committees are weak, and when committees are strong (as in Congress), leaders are weak. So if term limits have reduced the power of leaders, committees may have risen in power.

However, evidence from the three professionalized legislatures in this study does not support this hypothesis. Cain, Kousser, and Kurtz found that California state legislative committees declined markedly in their gatekeeping function as a result of term limits. Farmer and Little argued that weak committees were a major source of chaos in Ohio's post-term limits legislature. The decline of committee effectiveness and power in these states is attributed to their chairs' and members' inexperience and lack of procedural and substantive expertise. In Illinois, legislative committees have long been weak (Van der Slik and Redfield 1989), largely due to their subservience to the strong party leadership. But more important, informants in Illinois indicated that legislative committee power was constant throughout the study period, supporting the argument that term limits was the cause of the decline of committees in Ohio and California. Furthermore, Carey et al. (2003) found that across the country, legislators in term limits states believed their committees to be less powerful than did their peers in non-term-limit states.

If these institutions have a zero-sum power relationship and the power of both a state legislature's leadership and committees are reduced artificially by term limits then a power vacuum may develop. It will take several more years of experience with term limits to sort out these power relationships. Time is needed both to gather more data to test various hypotheses and to allow for the power relationships in and around these term-limited state legislatures to be worked out and settle into equilibrium.

Term limits have also been hypothesized to affect the power and influence of two other groups of people working with and around the state legislature: legislative staff and lobbyists. These political actors were predicted to gain power in a term-limited legislature, with inexperienced and unknowledgeable lawmakers turning to staff and lobbyists for information and advice (Rosenthal 1992; Malbin and Benjamin 1992; Carey, Niemi, and Powell 2000; Moncrief and Thompson 2001).

This study sheds minimal light on the effect of term limits on legislative staff power or activities in professionalized legislatures. In Ohio, Farmer and Little reported that staff felt less job security since term limits were implemented and that the power of party caucus staff increased along with the influence of the caucuses themselves. In California, Cain, Kousser, and Kurtz found that the professional, nonpartisan staff was cut the most in the staff reductions that came with term limits there. In Illinois, informants saw no change in the position or activities of the staff except perhaps a gradual increase in the control of most key staff by the party caucuses. Thus, the rise of partisan staff at the expense of nonpartisan staff seems to be a secular trend across these legislatures and unrelated to term limits. There is no evidence to support the hypothesis that term limits have increased the general power of legislative staff.

While there is no evidence that lobbyists have gained influence generally under term limits in professionalized state legislatures either, there appears to be a more complex change in their role. First, consider that lobbyists have two basic resources: substantive and political information and relationships with policymakers. Every lobbyist has these resources, but in varying balances. For example, contract lobbyists, who represent a variety of clients for a fee, typically rely more on relationships, while in-house, single-association lobbyists rely more on their substantive policy knowledge and political information about their associations' membership (Rosenthal 1993; Thomas and Hrebenar 2004). Term limits may reduce the power of contract lobbyists, since limits break up the relationships with legislators, especially the old bulls and other leaders, on which much of their power rests. On the other hand, association lobbyists may gain power with term limits as inexperienced legislators need the policy information and access to constituents they have not yet been able to cultivate themselves. If both these processes were at work, their countervailing effects might lead to the observation that, overall, lobbyists' influence has not been affected by term limits. Indeed, Carey et al.'s (2003) national survey found that state legislators in term limits states felt that lobbyists were no more influential than did legislators in non-term-limits states.[3]

This study provides evidence that contract lobbyists are, in fact, losing power in term limits states. In Ohio, Farmer and Little found that new legislators viewed all lobbyists with suspicion. Some freshmen legislators would not even meet with lobbyists until their leaders forced them to do so. This is indicative of a significant diminution of the quality and quantity of the relationships with legislators that contract lobbyists, in particular, need to ply their trade. In Ohio after term limits, many new lobbyists were registered, further indicating lobbyists' and groups' need to establish new relationships with the many new legislators. In California, since term limits, legislators appear to be turning to lobbyists for more information (Cain and Kousser 2004). On the other hand, the Illinois informants consistently reported that the power of contract lobbyists had increased during the study period, while the general influence of non-contract lobbyists and groups had not changed significantly. While more research is needed to map out these relationships more precisely, this evidence suggests that term limits affect the power of lobbyists differentially depending on the type of lobbyist and the source of his or her power.

LEGISLATIVE PROCESS: PARTISANSHIP, CIVILITY, AND THE BALANCE OF POWER

Contrary to expectations, term limits appear to have had no effect on partisanship and polarization in these three state legislatures. Term limits have not decreased partisanship by banning professional politicians from state legislatures (Petracca 1991a), nor have they increased it by breaking up long-time, cross-aisle relationships among old bulls (Rosenthal 1998). In fact, informants' reports suggest an increasing partisanship in all three of the state legislatures in this study, regardless of term limits status.

On the other hand, Cain, Kousser, and Kurtz note an interesting phenomenon that suggests that the impact of term limits may have a subtle impact on partisanship through the truncation of legislative careers. They found that new California legislators were typically moderate in their partisanship and ideology (both before and after term limits), but that they diverged toward the extremes as their legislative careers progressed. Term limits stops this process before it can progress to the fullest extent, perhaps leading to less extremism and partisanship than in the absence of term limits. More research on this process is needed to sort out this relationship.

Civility in state legislatures has been decreasing for some years (Rosenthal 1998; Moncrief, Thompson, and Kurtz 1996). The shaking up of relationships through rapid turnover, the lack of long-term relationships among old bulls, and the increasingly chaotic and hectic life of state legislators under term limits suggest that civility would be even more at risk in bodies with these limits. What little evidence this study provides supports this hypothesis. In Ohio, Farmer and Little's informants reported that civility declined after term limits, while the Illinois informants did not believe that civility declined there during the study period. In California, there is no evidence either way on civility.

The knowledgeable informant survey of the nine JPTL states identifies several other attitudes on which legislators serving in professionalized bodies in term limits states differ from those in non-term-limit states. As one might expect from more junior members, the term-limited lawmakers in Ohio and California were seen as being less knowledgeable on issues and procedures, offering more amendments in committee and on the floor, caring less about the precision of their own bills and about statewide issues, and spending less time specializing in a policy area than did members of the non-term-limited Illinois General Assembly. Cain, Kousser, and Kurtz's and Farmer and Little's reports echo some of these sentiments. The negative implications for the quality of both the legislative process and public policy were not lost on the Ohio and California informants, either.

Term limits were predicted to reduce the power of the state legislature relative to the executive branch for the same reasons of information and institutional stability that led to the hypothesis that lobbyists and staff would be more powerful in a term-limited legislature (Moncrief and Thompson 2001; Malbin and Benjamin 1992). Such an effect might be especially strong in a professionalized state legislature, since a major goal of the professionalism movement was to balance the power of the branches (Burns

1971; Herzberg and Rosenthal 1972). However, the evidence from this study is not clear on this hypothesis. In Illinois, the legislature was unconcerned with executive branch oversight during the study period, and the governor was strong institutionally, used his veto frequently (and was rarely overridden), and got virtually his entire proposed budget passed each year. In Ohio, Farmer and Little's informants reported that the speaker was strong in the policymaking process throughout the study period, both before and after term limits. They attributed the speaker's power to personality rather than institutional arrangements. On the other hand, in California, Cain, Kousser, and Kurtz found a significant decline in legislative power relative to the executive branch. The inexperience of its members reduced the ability of the California legislature to rewrite executive proposals, oversight of executive agencies through post-budget information requests declined sharply, and fewer legislative audits were performed after term limits. Thus, more research needs to be done to understand the full effect of term limits on the balance of power between professionalized state legislatures and their governors.

CONCLUSION

The impact of term limits on professionalized state legislatures appears to be more the result of the mechanical process of truncating legislative careers than the recruitment of a new type of state legislator. Consider the effects for which we have the strongest evidence:

- The elimination of old bull leaders and legislators has contributed to weakening legislative leadership and reducing civility,
- The lack of experience and information about policy and procedure among legislators, has reduced the effectiveness and influence of committees,
- Power has shifted among lobbyists due to the break-up of long-standing relationships, and
- Political careers and elections for local, state, and federal offices have been destabilized by the churning effect of state legislative term limits.

These can be explained simply by the artificial truncation of legislative careers that term limits cause by definition. There is no evidence of term limits effects where a change in recruitment and election patterns would be required. For example, there were no changes in the demographics, partisanship, or ideology of these state legislatures that could be attributed to term limits. However, term limits' effects on recruitment may take longer to materialize, as potential candidates learn to adjust their career ambitions to this new institution. Therefore, scholars should watch for evidence of these effects in the future.

In several ways, the effects of term limits on these state legislatures parallel those of redistricting. For example, both term limits and redistricting increased membership and leadership turnover and accelerated demographic shifts already in progress in these bodies. The mechanism behind both of these effects is the shaking up of the constituency-legislator relationship and the concomitant reduction in incumbents' electoral advantage. Whether this enhances or detracts from representation and the quality of the legislative process remains to be seen.

At root, this is what term limits advocates foresaw for this reform. By mandating rotation in office and by discouraging careerism in politics, term limits would bring fresh ideas and values to state policymaking. This could be accomplished by recruiting a new type of member or simply by cycling many different people through the legislature. In either case, the tension between the desire for a professional, capable, co-equal state legislature and the desire not to have professional politicians serve in that legislature is one that the large, urban, resource-rich states like Ohio and California (along with Michigan, Florida, and Missouri) will need to resolve. Both scholars and reformers need to monitor closely how these states resolve this tension through recruitment, institutional, and electoral changes over the next decade.

NOTES

1. I would like to thank Tim Storey of the National Conference of State Legislatures and Brad Bonnette for their help on this project.

2. Comparable data are not available for California state legislators in the study period. Cain, Kousser, and Kurtz report that California legislators' average age when first elected dropped from forty-seven in the 1980s to forty-two in the 1990s.

3. On the other hand, in a five-state survey, Moncrief and Thompson (2001) found that lobbyists believed that interest group power increased after term limits, especially in professionalized state legislatures.

II

SEMI-PROFESSIONALIZED STATE LEGISLATURES

5

The Effects of Legislative Term Limits in Arizona: More Churning, More Chaos, and a Diminished Institutional Role for Legislators[1]

David R. Berman

In 1992, Arizona voters approved a constitutional amendment limiting individuals to four consecutive two-year terms in either the Arizona House or Senate. The limits are allowed to restart if a member of one chamber moves to the other chamber. In this chapter, I draw upon a wide range of materials including dozens of interviews with legislators, lobbyists, and knowledgeable observers, two national surveys, and copious documentary information to draw some early conclusions about the consequences of this reform, both intended and unintended.[2] But first, I discuss the nature and adoption of the reform in Arizona and how, in general terms, it has blended with other developments surrounding legislative elections and the operation of the Arizona Legislature in the 1990s and 2000s. Following this largely historical account, I examine the electoral and institutional effects of term limits in the state. On the plus side, I find while term limits had some positive effects in terms of electoral competition, they also generally reduced the power of legislative leaders and increased the influence of lobbyists and staff in the legislative process. These developments have occurred in both legislative bodies but have been more noticeable in the House than the Senate. Overall, recent newcomers to the Arizona Legislature are probably not any less knowledgeable than previous classes of newcomers, but under term limits there are more newcomers and members have less time to learn their jobs. For many, the limit to four two-year terms (eight years total) provides less of an incentive to focus on the job and too little time to learn how to do the job and do it well.

A BRIEF HISTORY

In the 1992 general election, 74 percent of Arizonans who cast a vote on Proposition 107, which enacted term limits, approved of the measure. Some of this vote may well have reflected citizen unhappiness with Congress, whose members' terms were also limited by the proposal.[3] Much of the feeling behind the vote also reflected a discontent with Arizona politicians, especially with the state's legislators. Arizona's term limits law was approved at a time when, because of events discussed below, public confidence in the state's legislature had sunk to what was perceived by many to be an all time low (Berman 2001, 17–32).

Adoption of Proposition 107

Arizona politicians in the late 1980s and early 1990s had more than their share of political embarrassments. In the late 1980s, then-Governor Evan Mecham was attacked on various grounds: a recall campaign, criminal court action, and impeachment proceedings. In 1988, after a long and bitter battle, the Arizona House impeached Mecham and the Senate ousted him from office for misusing public funds and obstructing justice. Three years later, a Phoenix Police Department sting operation, later known as AzScam, led to the indictment of seven sitting state legislators for accepting bribes from an undercover agent posing as a lobbyist trying to enlist support for casino gambling in the state. Not surprisingly, surveys following AzScam showed more than 70 percent of the Arizonans polled agreeing with the statements that Arizona lawmakers were too close to special-interest groups and that many legislators would accept a bribe if they thought they could get away with it (Yozwiak 1991).

Following AzScam, legislators attempted to restore the image of their institution by making a series of reforms. In a special session in November 1991, they even toyed with the idea of putting a term limits measure on the ballot, but failed to do so. However, a citizen's organization known as the Arizona Coalition for Limited Terms (ACLT) took up the cause through an initiative campaign. Business and anti-tax groups subsequently played prominent roles in ACLT, and a citizen's group formed earlier to push for congressional term limits also joined the coalition. ACLT's drive led to the term limit proposition approved by the voters in 1992. Reflecting their broader distrust of the legislature, voters in 1992 also approved a measure requiring a two-thirds vote of the legislature to pass any increase in taxes or other state revenue. Some effects of term limits were felt even before 2000, when the law prevented the first group of legislators from running for re-election. After the 2000 general elections, the impacts of the reform were magnified.

Developments: 1993–2000

Republicans generally dominated the 1992 general election. They retained control of the Arizona House with a 35–25 edge and won back the Senate, which they had lost two years earlier, with an 18–12 margin. At the beginning of the 1993 state legislative session, legislative leaders claimed that voter approval of the term limits measure reflected strong public support for the idea of a citizen's legislature. In this spirit, these leaders vowed to complete the work of the legislature in one hundred days so that lawmakers could return to their homes and businesses as soon as possible (Reinhart 1993).

Over the following several years, legislators from the Republican Party's right wing held most of the leadership positions and, working with a like-minded Republican governor, worked to adopt a conservative agenda, highlighted by a series of tax cuts. For much of this period, moderate Republicans and Democrats in the legislature were simply shut out of the process. There were, however, several instances of rebellion within the Republican legislative caucuses that some attributed to term limits, at least in part. For example, during a special session in 2000, five Republican senators—three of whom were term-limited from running in the following election and one of whom was retiring voluntarily—defied their leaders and signed a discharge petition to bring an education spending measure out of a committee and onto the floor for a vote (Robb 2000).

But perhaps the most publicized of these rebellions was the 1999 Mushroom Coalition revolt, so called because the sixteen revolting moderate House Republicans claimed that they were being treated like mushrooms—kept in the dark and covered with manure. Coalition members, including a number of freshmen, were especially unhappy about having had no input into the budget, which they charged was made behind closed doors by a few legislative leaders and the governor. One of the movement's leaders credited term limits with making these first-term lawmakers more aggressive; because they had only eight years in the House, they did not want to be left out of legislative business (Moeser 1999). Another coalition member added: "Because of term limits, we know we have to act sooner and take risks . . . They have liberated us. The speaker will be gone in a year. He can't put me in the doghouse for the next ten years."[4] Still another rebel commented: "I was pleased to see the overall freshman class take an active role in the legislative process, especially on the budget. I believe this will become the norm because term limits compel members to 'make their mark' on public policy from the first day they are in office."[5] Also even before 2000, when the first set of term limits "expulsions" was due to occur, the reform had effects on elections and legislators' career decisions. In some cases, long-serving legislators reluctantly took opportunities to leave their chambers prior to reaching their limited number of terms. For example, long-time House Minority Leader Art Hamilton, who could have served until 2000, decided to run for secretary of state in 1998—a race that he lost (Kiefer 1998). And as detailed below, term limits appears to have reduced competition for legislative seats in 1998 by encouraging potential candidates to wait to run until 2000 when there would be more open seats.

Term Limits Take Hold

By the 2000 general election, the Arizona legislature had experienced yet another embarrassment, this one came to be known popularly in the media as the "alternative fuels fiasco." This "fiasco" involved legislation hastily passed at the insistence of House Speaker Jeff Groscost in the spring of 2000 that provided large tax rebates to purchasers of alternative fuel vehicles. As originally passed, the law set up a rebate for the entire cost of converting any car to run on natural gas or propane and one-third of the vehicle's purchase price. But lawmakers had acted hastily and without full information, and they severely underestimated how many people would take advantage of the program and how much it would cost. The original cost estimate had been $3–5 million, but as more than twenty thousand Arizonans sought the rebate, the actual costs rose to over $500 million before the legislature repealed the law late in 2000. A poll taken in the wake of this debacle showed strong public dissatisfaction with the legislature, with 52 percent of those surveyed thinking that legislators were incompetent, 70 percent saying they acted on impulse rather than deep reflection, and 68 percent feeling that they were an embarrassment to the state (Ruelas 2000). Influenced by the alternative fuels fiasco, the election of 2000 produced a turnover of 45 percent in the House (the largest since the 48 percent turnover following the AzScam scandal in 1992) and 33 percent in the Senate.

Term limits directly contributed to the turnover in 2000 by preventing twenty-two legislators (seven in the Senate and fifteen in the House) from running for reelection. Several of these term-limited lawmakers publicly voiced their unhappiness with the law. One such senator told reporters explicitly that he would have run for his old seat again and wished that term limits did not exist. In 2000, he considered a run for Congress but decided to take the unusual, but a far safer, step of running for a seat in the Arizona House, which he won (Lucas 2000). Matters did not turn out so well for a term-limited House member who, declaring "I'm not willing to give up my career," challenged an incumbent senator from his own party; he wound up losing to the incumbent in a primary battle.[6]

Throughout the state, term limits produced some spirited primary fights for the legislature and Congress. In one Republican primary, nine candidates fought it out for two open Arizona House seats. In three cases, members forced out by term limits were replaced on the ballot by a relative—a wife, brother, and son. Voters elected all three, keeping the offices in the family. Republicans retained control of the House after the 2000 election, but a 15–15 party split in the Senate led to an unusual governing coalition, with a power-sharing arrangement of moderate Republicans and Democrats under which Republican Randall Gnant of Scottsdale became Senate president and Republicans and Democrats split committee chairs. Conservative Republicans were shut out, leading one such member to declare that he would not run again because the Senate was no longer a good place to work, having become a place lacking in courtesy and mutual respect (Lucas 2001). The 2001 House was initially more chaotic than in the past because of all the newcomers. One veteran legislator noted that the new lawmakers were unprepared to do the work of the veterans they replaced: "They're lost, quite frankly" (Kullman 2001). In the 2002 election, term limits combined with redistricting to result in historic levels of legislative turnover—close to 60 percent in both chambers. Term limits directly ousted fifteen members, six in the Senate and nine in the House, including the Senate president, the House speaker, the House majority and minority floor leaders, and the chairs of the Appropriations Committees in both chambers. The chair of the House Appropriations Committee later remarked: "I wanted to stay, but I didn't have a choice" (Scutari and Sherwood 2002). Ousted by term limits, she challenged a popular incumbent senator and lost.

Republicans retained control of the House and recaptured the Senate in 2002, ending the coalition that had governed the latter body in 2001–2002. The leadership of both chambers became more conservative. However, the 2003 legislative session once again brought unrest in the Republican caucuses. In particular, a group of about twenty Republican newcomers—both conservatives and moderates—staged an uprising in the House. The rebels were initially inclined to go follow the party leadership, but as the session progressed, they increasingly resented being shut out, especially of the budget making process. One participant remarked: "The budget is the most important thing we do at the legislature . . . We can't just sit back and let it happen without having an impact."[7] This group of rebellious Republicans called themselves the "Cellar Dwellers" because they met in the House basement.

Republican House leaders had given several of their party's freshmen what appeared to be important committee assignments, in part because there was a shortage of experienced members to fill them. But some of these newcomers later complained that their positions gave them little actual power. The Cellar Dwellers became especially assertive on the budget, demanding and securing more information. One Democratic House member noted at the time: "This group is more in a hurry, wants to influence the action, and is not willing to blindly follow leaders or vote for something they don't understand simply because leaders want it." A longtime observer added that while freshmen in the Arizona legislature had always complained about being left out of the process, the Cellar Dwellers were unusually anxious to get involved in a meaningful way. The observer felt that legislative leaders were not prepared for freshmen to be so assertive, and they blamed the rebellion, in part, on term limits.

While the Cellar Dwellers ultimately made only a minimal impact on the budget in 2003, the rebellion loosened up the budgeting process the following year, as leaders brought more rank-and-file Republicans into the process through the formation of study groups. The majority leader announced that this step resulted from calls from Republicans for more involvement, which he attributed, at least in part, to term limits (Davenport 2004). On the other hand, House leaders also demonstrated a get-tough stance with dissidents. For example, in February 2004, House Speaker Jake Flake took the unusual step of stripping two moderate Republicans of their committee chairmanships for defying leadership on a policy measure.

As the above discussion suggests, term limits have prompted Arizona legislators to make difficult decisions regarding their political careers and have both directly and indirectly contributed to legislative turnover. Term limits have also played a role in how legislators have shaped their legislative careers and in how rank-and-file members relate to leadership. In the following sections, I draw upon interview, survey, and statistical information to assess the electoral and institutional effects of term limits in Arizona more systematically.

ELECTORAL EFFECTS

First, consider term limits' various effects on elections and the electoral process, specifically their effects on legislative turnover, electoral competition, the composition of the legislature, and constituent relations.

Turnover

As Figure 5.1 illustrates, Arizona has long been characterized by relatively high legislative turnover, typically from 20 to 30 percent. Following a jump in 1992 that coincided with the adoption of Proposition 107, turnover slowly returned to historic levels by 1998. But since term limits were implemented in the 2000 election, turnover has again spiked (Figure 5.1). In the first two election cycles (2000 and 2002), term limits contributed directly to turnover by forcing thirty-seven Arizona legislators out of office, with twenty-two being forbidden from re-election in 2000 and fifteen being termed out in 2002. Public statements, some of which were noted above, and interviews

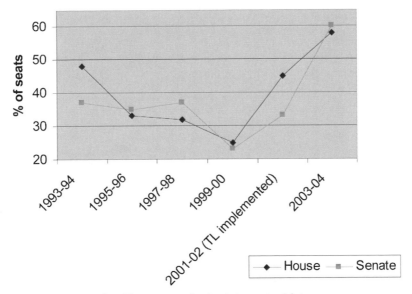

Figure 5.1. Membership Turnover in the Arizona Legislature
Source: Gary Moncrief, Richard Niemi, and Lynda Powell. 2004. "Time, Term Limits, and Turnover."
Legislative Studies Quarterly 29: 357-81.

conducted for this study suggest that most of the term-limited legislators would have been eager to run for re-election had they been allowed to do so. In addition, term limits increased turnover indirectly by encouraging some legislators to leave office prior to the expiration of their terms in order to take advantage of political opportunities presented elsewhere (Lucas 2000; Anderson 1995; Lazarus 2006).

In the first two elections after their implementation, term limits directly termed-out about 30 percent of legislators subject to the law; that is, 37 of 122 legislators in the combined freshman classes of 1992 and 1994 served four two-year terms in either the Senate or the House and were unable to stand for re-election to the legislative body in which they had served. Term limits may have also had something to do with the decision of legislators elected in those years to seek a different office prior to the expiration of their terms. Perhaps encouraged by the knowledge that their time in the House was limited, fourteen members of the House freshman classes of 1992 and 1994 sought and were able to secure election to the Senate prior to the expiration of their House term.

The Arizona experience with term limits reflects that of other states in that the reform succeeded not so much in pushing more legislators out of politics altogether as in prompting them to seek other elected positions (Lazarus 2006; Steen 2006; Powell 2000; Tothero 2003). As Table 5.1 indicates, twenty-seven of the thirty-seven termed-out legislators—over 70

Table 5.1. Actions of Legislators in the Election Following Their Being Termed-Out: Freshman Classes of 1992 and 1994

Item	Number	Percent
Term-limited legislators	37	100
House Members	24	65
Senate Members	13	35
Those who ran for office	27	73
House members who ran for Senate	15	41
Senate members who ran for House	2	5
Those who ran for other offices	10	27
Those who won any office	16	43
Those elected to other legislative body	11	30
Those who lost to another term-limited legislator	3	8

Source: Material gathered by the author.

percent—tried to continue their political careers in an uninterrupted fashion by immediately running for the other chamber or some other office. Sixteen of these twenty-seven—59 percent—were successful; indeed, three termed-out legislators actually lost to other term-out legislators. Thus, termed-out legislators demonstrate a strong desire to stay in elected office and, by and large, have been able to do so. Ambitious termed-out Arizona legislators are especially fortunate in this regard since the state has an extensive political opportunity structure, with many elected positions on the local and state level for termed-out legislators to seek (Copeland 1992).

Competition and Voter Choice

One of the benefits anticipated by term limits advocates was that as the reform threw out incumbents and created more open-seat races, greater competition for legislative offices would ensue, thus giving voters greater real choice in elections. The actual net effect of term limits on competition in Arizona state legislative races is difficult to establish. On one hand, the number of legislative candidates increased with the implementation of term limits in 2000, both in total and as the average number of candidates per seats (Table 5.2). Although these figures dipped slightly in 2002, they remained higher than at any time in the 1990s. On the other hand, term limits had several other impacts that should be taken into account in interpreting these findings. First, the anticipation of the implementation of term limits itself may have contributed to the reduced number of candidates in the 1990s, with some potential candidates passing up the opportunity to run so that they could contend in one of the many open-seat races in the 2000 election. In particular, the very low number of candidates in 1998 may have been the result of this anticipatory effect. Indeed, one legislator ex-

Table 5.2.   Candidates for Legislative Seats

Election Year	Total Candidates	Candidates Per Seat
1990	189	2.1
1992	207	2.3
1994	180	2.0
1996	211	2.3
1998	162	1.8
2000	223	2.5
2002	217	2.4
2004	192	2.1

Note: These are the number of candidates filling pre-primary nominating petitions for a seat in the 90-member Arizona Legislature, not including write-ins or post-primary filers.
Source: "Legislative Candidates," *Arizona Capital Times* (September 8, 2006): 34.

plained the lack of competition in legislative races in 1998 this way: "Why compete for something that will be an open seat in two years?" (Burchell 1998). Another difficulty in interpreting the effects of term limits on electoral competition is that a state program providing public financing for state legislative candidates was passed by Arizona voters in 1998 and implemented at the same time as term limits—2000. Survey research leads us to believe that both were important in increasing competition in 2000 and 2002, but which of the two was most important is uncertain.[8]

The effect of term limits on potential candidates' perceptions of the office may also have influenced the resulting level of competition in these races. Some interviewees suggested that term limits may have discouraged competition by making the state legislature a less attractive place for those pursuing a career in politics. This view, however, was not prevalent in our interviews. Many interviewees felt that the fact that legislators could now serve only so many years had little to do with decisions to run for the office—that prospective candidates either didn't think about it or saw it as far less important than other factors influencing their candidacy decisions, such as the amount of competition and the availability of campaign funds.[9]

Taken together, our interviewees suggested that by creating more open-seat races, term limits had indeed encouraged greater competition for state legislative seats and more choices for voters. As they saw it, people ran for seats in the Arizona Legislature who would not have done so if they would have had to face an incumbent. Furthermore, term limits have also increased electoral competition in general by encouraging or forcing legislators to run for other offices to continue their careers. Even within the legislature, term limits have frequently prompted legislators in one chamber to run for seats in the other chamber, thus increasing the competitive pool for those positions. Movement of this type has been encouraged and facilitated by the fact that Arizona senators and representatives are elected from the same districts; a switch means no change in the electoral base. By forcing out legislators anxious to continue their careers, the term limits in Arizona have also indirectly increased electoral competition in general by providing additional candidates for all types and levels of races, from Congress, to statewide offices, to local offices.

Legislative Composition

Some term limits supporters argued that the reform would bring greater representation to racial and ethnic minorities, women, members of the minority party, and, more generally, bring people with new ideas and outlooks into office. In particular, supporters expected that term limits would replace career politicians with citizen legislators who would bring their skills and experiences from the private sector to the legislature. In general, however, term limits do not appear to have caused such changes in the composition of the Arizona Legislature.

Term limits, for example, appear to have made little difference in the representation of racial and ethnic minorities. As prior to term limits, there have been one or two Native Americans and African Americans in the legislature. The most significant gains have been in the number of Latino legislators. The number of Latinos has steadily grown since term limits—moving from nine in 1997 to thirteen in 2003, to seventeen in 2005. Much of this gain, however, has been to district changes. Under a districting plan adopted in 2000, the number of minority-majority legislative districts increased from seven to nine, reflecting the growth of the minority population, particularly Latinos.

Changes in the composition of the legislature in regard to gender, party, and age are shown in Table 5.3. Compared to other states, women have always been relatively well represented in the Arizona Legislature (Berman 1998). In the first post-term-limit election, there was virtually no change in the representation of women in the legislature, with only a minor drop from

Table 5.3. Demographic Composition of the Arizona Legislature

Year	% Democratic	% Women	Ave. Age
1993–94	41.1	35.6	49.4
1995–96	36.7	30.0	49.7
1997–98	37.8	36.7	49.6
1999–00	37.8	35.6	49.9
2001–02	43.3	34.4	50.5
2003–04	37.8	26.7	51.2

Source: This information comes from various sources examined by the author including Legislators' biographies and "Women in the Arizona Legislature," *Arizona Capitol Times* (October 21, 2005): 29.

35.6 percent before the 2000 election to 34.4 percent after it. However, after the 2002 election, there were only 26.7 percent women in the Arizona Legislature, the lowest level in more than a decade. The representation of women recovered, up to about 33 percent following the 2004 election. These fluctuations appear to have been heavily influenced by national trends.[10]

Although there have been some partisan changes since 2000, these are difficult to attribute to term limits. The thirty-seven legislators who were prevented from running in 2000 and 2002 due to term limits were largely replaced by members of the same party. The underlying issue with party representation is that the redistricting process—whether conducted by the legislature or, more recently, an independent commission—has created districts that overwhelmingly favor one party over the other. Still, even within these parameters, partisan change can be affected by national trends. For example, following national trends Arizona Democrats made major strides in the 2006 election and the party picked up seven legislative seats.

Post-term-limit elections may have brought some demographic changes. Age wise, for example, the Senate appears to be getting a bit older, in part, perhaps, because term limits have encouraged old and more experienced House members to move to the Senate. Contrary to the hopes of term limits supporters, however, the reform has not filled the Arizona Legislature with citizen legislators who lack long-term political ambition and who are willing to return to their private lives after a few years of service to the state. As we saw in Table 5.1, 73 percent of the termed-out legislators in 2000 and 2002 ran for another office immediately following their final terms, and 59 percent of these won their races. A 2002 general survey of Arizona legislators to which forty-four of the ninety members responded gives us more detail on legislators' thoughts about their post-legislature careers. As Table 5.4 indicates, only 27 percent said they planned to pass up further runs for office (20 percent said they were going to retire or pursue a non-political career, while an additional 7 percent simply declared they were not going to run for any office). Most legislators in the term-limited Arizona Legislature apparently think of an elective office other than the one they are currently holding. Term limits have not purged the body of career politicians. Indeed, our interviews revealed that many legislators facing term limits spend much of their time preparing their next political move, a preoccupation that some interviewees felt distracted them from their legislative duties.

Representation

Our interviews suggested that term limits have had little impact in the way lawmakers relate to their constituents. The principal exception to this may be when lawmakers become lame ducks in their last two years in office. We heard several stories of lame ducks taking actions that they thought would

Table 5.4. Post-Legislative Career Plans of Arizona Legislators, 2002

Item	Number	%
Run for other chamber*	21	48
Run for statewide office	9	21
Run for U.S. House or Senate	9	21
Run for local office	7	16
Retire	5	11
Take appointive government position	4	9
Return to non-political career	4	9
Engage in lobbying/consulting	4	9
Seek no further office	3	7

*Nineteen of the 21 legislators who planned to run for the other chamber were serving in the House.
Source: 2002 survey of Arizona legislators (44 of 90 legislators responded) by John M. Carey, Gary F. Moncrief, Richard G. Niemi, and Lynda W. Powell, in Cooperation with the Joint Project on Term Limits, supported by the Smith-Richardson Foundation and a grant from the National Science Foundation.

be unpopular among their constituents because they felt free of any fear of being punished at the polls. On the other hand, many legislators seemed to continue to cater to their constituents right up until the end of their eight-year terms, whether because they hoped to regain their seat after sitting out one term or to represent the same people as a member of the other chamber. Even though many legislators became more future-directed in thinking about their political careers as they approached their limits, their future ambitions often centered on appealing to the same set of constituents.

SOCIAL AND BEHAVIORAL CHANGES IN THE LEGISLATIVE CORPUS

Term limits in Arizona have made three general social and behavioral changes in the legislative corpus that have had wide-ranging impacts on the legislative institution: 1) enlarging the proportion of legislators who are politically and legislatively inexperienced, 2) shortening legislators' time horizons, and 3) decreasing the amount of time available to accomplish legislative duties due to inefficiencies caused by the first two of these changes.

Legislative Inexperience

Term limits contributed to a marked decline in the level of legislative experience in the Arizona Legislature. As Table 5.5 shows, following the 1990 election, the average representative had 6.3 years of legislative service and the average senator had 6.8 years of legislative service. After term limits

Table 5.5.   **Average Years of State**
Legislative Experience for Legislators at the
Beginning of the Term and During Different
Periods

Year/Period	House	Senate
1991	6.3	6.8
1993	4.4	6.6
1995	3.6	6.2
1997	3.8	6.2
1999	3.3	7.4
2001	2.7	7.0
2003	2.0	5.9
1983–1992	6.5	9.4
1992–2003	3.5	7.0

Source: Based on information supplied by The Arizona
Legislative Council, State of Arizona.

went into effect in the 2002 election, the average years of service for representatives fell to 2.0 and for senators, it went down to 5.9. In the ten-year period prior to the adoption of term limits (1983–1992), the average service was 6.5 for representatives and 9.1 for senators; in the decade after term limits' adoption (1983–2003), the average dropped to 3.5 for the House and 7.0 for the Senate. Legislative experience in the Senate was less severely reduced than in the House because, as we have seen, many termed-out representatives moved to the Senate.

Term limits led to the departure of several legislators with decades of service and with these members was lost considerable institutional memory regarding programs, policies, procedures, and norms. These old-timers had the knowledge and experience to hold their own in political and policy discussions with lobbyists, executive agency heads, legislative staff, and the governor. Conversely, the increase in the number of inexperienced legislators with term limits has produced a body with more legislators who are uncertain about how to do their jobs and who are much less informed about the issues facing the state. Interviewees also suggested that inexperienced legislators are more vulnerable to manipulation and control by lobbyists, staff, and executive agency heads and more likely to make mistakes. Some interviewees contended that inexperience had already figured in policy mistakes, such as the alternative fuels fiasco, because newcomers failed to pick up on the subtle danger signals that more experienced lawmakers regularly catch. Interviewees felt that the problems associated with inexperience have been compounded in the term-limited legislature because legislators are more likely to move to positions of leadership before they were ready to hold them.

Reduced Time Horizons

Along with the inexperience problem, our interviewees suggested that term limits have created difficulties by reducing legislators' time horizons. Knowing that they can serve only a limited period, lawmakers are in a hurry to make their mark and move on. As one interviewee noted: "When you realize you only have eight years at the most, everything has to happen much quicker." Being in a hurry may manifest itself in legislators trying to have a quick impact by introducing bills that are not well thought out or pushing to move up quickly into important committee or leadership positions. Such short-timer thinking was also equated by interviewees with chilling the legislative climate by reducing members' efforts to get to know one another, to get along with one another, to compromise, to listen to leadership, to be respectful of the process, and to care about the welfare of the institution as a whole. All these things take time, which is in short supply in a term-limited legislature. Term limits were also seen as undermining what had been a highly functional mellowing process in the Arizona legislature, one where long years of service tended to moderate ideologically driven legislators and members got to know each other on a personal basis, making it easier to form bipartisan coalitions. On policy issues, the short-timer orientation was felt to have encouraged legislators to focus on issues that have immediate payoffs, to ignore the long-term implications of their decisions, and to be less concerned with solving long-range problems or undertaking multiyear projects.

Too Little Time

The third general social and behavioral change attributed to term limits in Arizona by many of our interviewees is that the reform strips the legislature of the time needed to adequately deal with the problems of the state. In particular, the lack of old-timers and the general inexperience of the legislative corpus have caused considerable inefficiency in the process. In addition, the crucial duties of leaders and policy experts simply take more years of on-the-job training than allowed by the law. While there was considerable disagreement among those interviewed on just how long it takes to learn the legislative job, several remarked that for most serious legislators, especially legislative leaders, at least six years is required. Thus, with an eight-year limit, legislators are forced out of office just as they begin to understand the issues and the process. The lack of time was also blamed for preventing legislators from focusing on long-term problems facing the state, even if they were predisposed to do so. As one interviewee noted: "There's no time to see things through."

THE EFFECTS OF TERM LIMITS ON
LEGISLATIVE INSTITUTIONS

Inexperience, short time horizons, and time limitations have perhaps had their most profound impact on legislative leaders, and nearly all of this impact has been to reduce the influence of these leaders. Legislative committees also experienced several problems. On the other hand, our observers felt staffers and lobbyists have generally gained influence from term limits in Arizona.

Leadership

Power in the Arizona Legislature was concentrated in its leaders before term limits, and it continued to be so after the reform was implemented. The difference has been that leaders' rule is more frequently questioned within the chambers, they are less influential with non-legislative actors, and leaders themselves are less experienced and less skilled. The Senate president and House speaker continue to appoint committee chairs and members, assign bills to committees, and generally control the fate of proposed measures. Still, interviewees suggested, term limits have made it far more difficult for legislative leaders to control members. Indeed, some have gone so far as to suggest that term limits have had a "devastating effect" on leadership power. The "Mushroom" and "Cellar Dweller" rebellions were very visible illustrations of the difficulties Arizona's legislative leaders have had in pulling their caucuses together since term limits, but they are by no means the only ones.

Under term limits, legislative leaders must rise to the top more quickly. In addition, they stay there for a briefer period and have reduced influence. Term limits has moved the legislature away from a system where a leadership position was typically an award for long, conscientious service. The reform has also led to more frequent leadership turnover and more frequent and intense competition for these positions. Table 5.6 shows the changes in leadership turnover from the pre-term-limits period to the first two term-limits sessions. Changes have been particularly apparent in the House. Following the 2000 election, five out of six House leaders were new to leadership; the only person carried over moved from majority whip to speaker. Following the 2002 election, another five new people joined the leadership ranks, the only holdover moved from minority whip to assistant minority leader. While leadership turnover was as great in the Senate after term limits were implemented, competition for these positions became more intense as former House members swelled the ranks of contenders after the 2000 and 2002 elections. For example, in 2002, the term-limited speaker of

Table 5.6. Leadership Turnover of the Arizona General Assembly

Year	House	Senate
1993–94	3 of 6	4 of 6
1995–96	3 of 6	3 of 6
1997–98	3 of 6	6 of 6
1999–00	2 of 6	3 of 6
2001–02	5 of 6	3 of 6
2003–04	5 of 6	4 of 6

Note: This table compares the number of members in leadership who were not in leadership the previous year to the total number of leaders. Leadership includes the entire formal list of majority and minority leadership.
Source: Based on various materials collected by the author.

the House was elected to the Senate and made a serious, although ultimately unsuccessful, campaign to become president of that chamber.

Our interviewees thought legislative leaders were less effective under term limits because they take their positions without the benefit of the years of training and experience that pre-term-limits leaders had and because their status as lame ducks strips them of significant power and prestige the moment they take office. Term-limited leaders were also believed to be less effective because term-limited legislators, as short-timers, are less inclined to go along with leaders' demands and, indeed, are more inclined to challenge leaders' decisions directly. As a House leader put it: "Because of term limits, the place runs like a mob, without any sense of discipline, adherence to protocol, or respect for leadership." Overall, our interviews and analyses suggest that term limits have had their most noticeable impact in Arizona on the ability of legislative majority party leaders to control their caucuses, as illustrated most vividly in the "Mushroom" and "Cellar Dweller" revolts.

Committees

Term limits also appear to have had an impact on the nature and significance of committee work. According to the 2003 knowledgeable observers survey conducted for this study, compared to a decade ago, Arizona legislators were far less collegial and courteous while doing their committee work and far less knowledgeable about issues before their committees. There was also a decline, though not as severe, in the willingness to compromise and seek public input on legislation (see Table 5.7).

Term limits have created a situation in which committees that were once dominated by long-time chairs are now being operated by relatively inex-

Table 5.7.   Committee Behavior: Arizona Legislators in 2003
Compared to a Decade Ago*

Item	Ranking
Willing to compromise in committee	2.5
Collegial and courteous in committee	2.1
Willing to amend/substitute bills in committee	2.8
Knowledge about issues before the committee	2.1
Likely to seek public input on legislation	2.6

*Scale 1 to 5, from quite a bit less to quite a bit more, 3 indicates no change.
Source: Knowledgeable Observers Survey conducted for this study.

perienced people who are less knowledgeable about the subject areas of the committees. Looking for experienced leaders to head committees, legislative leaders have sometimes turned to people returning to a legislative chamber where they had served for several years or to people with long years of service and leadership in the other house. Legislators with backgrounds as elected municipal officials have also had the type of experience that has given them an advantage in moving into committee leadership positions. Leaders too have made some reductions in the number of committees to make up for the lack of qualified chairs, but in some cases, still have turned positions over to junior people. When it comes to committee members, some committee chairs have sought to overcome the inexperience problem by bringing in specialists for briefing sessions. Often they have given newcomers vice chair positions for training purposes. In general, the lack of experience and knowledge and the increased turnover of committee members and their chairs have, as noted below, led to committees being perceived of as being far less influential than they once were in the Arizona legislative process.

Legislative Staff

Since term limits, legislative staff assistance has been of particular importance in helping newcomers to the Arizona Legislature learn how to do their job. Indeed, our interviewees stated time and again that term limits have increased the importance and influence of the legislative staff. The nonpartisan staff has increased its role of providing basic information and training newcomers, and the partisan staff (controlled the legislative majority and minority leadership) has become more influential in providing policy direction. Some interviewees felt that the partisan staff had gained considerably more influence than the nonpartisan staff and, indeed, that the partisan staff had gained too much influence. But this observation came primarily from nonpartisan staffers, members of the minority Democratic Party, and moderate

Republicans, each of whom could be seen as having a bias against increased partisan staff influence. An indicator of their influence was that, at least in the House, some interviewees noted that lobbyists first try to win over the leadership's partisan staff, believing that if they can convince these influential staffers, the leaders will follow. Since senators tend to be more experienced than House members, they are seen as less dependent on staff. As of 2004, Senate staffers are probably more important to Republicans than Democrats because the former have fewer experienced senators in office.[11]

Interest Groups and Lobbyists

While interviewees saw interest groups as generally benefiting from the lack of institutional memory and experience in the legislative corpus, they differed in their assessment of the impact of lobbyists on legislative newcomers after term limits. In particular, the assessment of lobbyist influence depended on who was asked. One view, commonly expressed by veteran legislators and other long-time observers, is that since term limits, new legislators have not only increasingly relied on lobbyists for information, but they have been more likely to be manipulated or misled because they lack both experience in dealing with lobbyists and the advantages of mentoring once done by veteran legislators. One veteran legislator reported: "I've observed new legislators listening to experienced lobbyists. My orientation is that the biases in these conversations are huge. After a certain amount of time in this institution, you recognize this bias but the inexperienced representatives don't understand just how flawed this information can be." Another veteran added: "New legislators sometimes don't realize that they are not getting all sides of a story from a lobbyist."

On the other hand, our newcomer-legislator interviewees reported that they were quite suspicious of lobbyists. Not knowing whom to trust, they shied away from lobbyists in general or took their information with a grain of salt. Indeed, one newcomer reported that she and her freshman colleagues felt that lobbyists tried to take advantage of them, conspiring among themselves to "get them [freshman legislators] before they know too much." This freshman legislator claimed to be very hard on lobbyists during their interactions, demanding to know their qualifications and wanting them to get to the point quickly. Other newcomers indicated that they were far from being entirely dependent on lobbyists, some saying that they turned to legislative staff, their legislative colleagues, and people outside the legislature, such as university researchers, for information and guidance. Likewise, lobbyists themselves gave us diverse messages in our interviews with them. Some lobbyists reported happily that legislators were increasingly relying on them for information since term limits took effect, while others complained that the newcomers didn't rely on them enough.

Overall, it is likely that due to their lack of knowledge about the issues and process and the lack of mentoring from long-serving colleagues, post-term limit legislators rely on lobbyists more than their pre-term limit peers, and, no doubt, more of these legislators are misled as a result. Lobbyists have also taken advantage of legislator, committee, and leadership turnover by bringing back bills rejected in previous years, in the hope that no one would remember the policy idea's history. This increase in lobbyist influence is probably less severe in the Senate because many of the members of that body (for example, nineteen of thirty in 2004) have served in the House, learning there whom to trust and whom not to trust. More generally, an important constraint on lobbyists of non-term-limited legislatures is that their influence is based on building a relationship of trust with legislators. Violating this trust has severe consequences, so it is infrequently done. But in a term-limited legislature, the chances that lobbyist bias or other affronts will yield retribution are much lower, due to the shorter time horizon and memory of legislators as a group. Thus, the incentive for honest and ethical lobbyist behavior is reduced, and this, indeed, appears to be yielding somewhat less honest and ethical lobbyist behavior in post-term-limit Arizona.

On the other hand, the turnover stimulated by term limits has generally made the work of lobbyists much more difficult in that they now have to make contact with and educate a large stream of freshman legislators at regular intervals. It is also clear that this turnover has hurt some groups and lobbyists far more than others. In particular, many old-time Arizona lobbyists who had built up long-term relations with long-serving legislators have found their stock-in-trade severely curtailed. Many of their legislator-contacts are now gone, having been replaced by newcomers who have no idea who these old-time lobbyists are. These one-time powerhouses are now in the same boat as every other lobbyist as they scramble to introduce themselves to the new legislators.

In summary, term limits have not, as its proponents predicted, reduced the overall influence of interest groups and lobbyists. Interest groups have always been important in the Arizona policymaking and legislative process, and they continue to be so. However, they have to operate somewhat differently since the implementation of term limits. Many lobbyists have adapted to the new conditions by investing more resources and working harder to establish contact with the parade of new legislators every two years, and those who once relied on long-standing contacts with influential senior members have lost their advantage. Under term limits, lobbyists will succeed if they are willing and able to win over transitory leaders and work harder to ingratiate themselves with the continuous parade of new members. Thus, interest groups with significant resources—whether they be money or membership—will not likely be disadvantaged by term limits. But groups without such a stock of resources may find themselves in a weaker position in the post-term-limit Arizona Legislature.

EFFECTS ON CLIMATE, PROCESS, OUTCOMES, AND STATUS

Finally, we turn to the question of how term limits have affected the civility of the legislative work climate, the legislative process, legislative outcomes, and the influence and power of the legislature relative to other institutions.

Civility and Conflict

The lack of civility in the Arizona Legislature was a problem long before the voters adopted term limits, and it remains so after the implementation of the reform. The quality of legislative life started to deteriorate during the 1988 gubernatorial impeachment of Evan Mecham, and it got worse following the AzScam scandal. One legislator who decided to retire in 1992 explained: "It's been very hectic, the tensions, the divisiveness. I wake up in the morning and I tell my wife, 'I don't want to go to work.' It's not fun anymore" (Harris 1992).

As discussed above, the Arizona Legislature has a long history of bitter conflict, not only between Democrats and Republicans, but perhaps even more detrimental to civility and comity, ideological intra-party splits.

Interviewees suggested that term limits has certainly not improved civility in the legislature, and it may have made the bickering and problems with consensus building even worse. Term limits has added to the conflict by exacerbating intra-party squabbling in the Republican Party on the basis of time served in the legislature, as seen in the Mushroom and Cellar Dweller revolts. In general, term limits has fomented division by making it easier for members to defy party leaders and limiting the amount of time legislators have to get to know each other on a personal basis, making it more difficult to find common ground on which to work out partisan or ideological differences.

The Legislative Process

Term limits has produced little change in the basic rule-based procedures by which the legislature operates, although some reforms, such as the formal commitment to the one hundred-day session, have reflected the desire to define the body as a citizen legislature, at least publicly. In one sense, the pressures generated by term limits have made the informal legislative process more inclusive. The biennial appearance of a large group of freshmen who are more anxious than ever to make a mark for themselves quickly has

Table 5.8. Annual Legislative Activity

Year	Number of Bills Introduced			Bills Passed	
	Senate	House	Total	Number	%
1990	559	692	1251	417	33.3
1991	476	503	979	335	34.2
1992	545	597	1142	369	32.3
1993	433	393	826	261	31.6
1994	565	598	1163	380	32.7
1995	407	550	957	309	32.3
1996	425	571	996	385	38.7
1997	468	577	1045	307	29.4
1998	431	698	1129	315	27.9
1999	419	706	1125	374	33.2
2000	559	721	1280	420	32.8
2001	584	637	1221	416	34.1
2002	470	712	1182	353	29.9
2003	367	541	908	285	31.4
2004	421	706	1127	351	31.1

Source: "Legislative Bill Totals," *Arizona Capitol Times,* (June 18, 2004), 5.

opened up the budgeting process, at least for the rank-and-file members of the majority party. Thus far, term limits has not brought an increase in the volume of legislation; the number of bills introduced and passed in the chambers combined has decreased steadily since 2000, but this figure varied considerably from year to year since 1990 (Table 5.8).

However, some interviewees suggested that term limits increased the number of thoughtless and frivolous bills being introduced. Some argued that more post-term-limit legislators were introducing legislation on which they were uniformed just to make a legislative record quickly or to please an interest group. Furthermore, with the weakening of legislative leadership and the committee system, some observers believed that bills were being passed with less vetting. More broadly, the constant turnover in members and leaders caused by term limits has been blamed for a general feeling of increasing chaos in the legislative process, more emotional decision-making by legislators, and more unpredictable policymaking.

Legislative Outcomes

Of course, the most important part of the legislative process is the public policy that results from it. But assessing the impacts of any reform on legislative outcomes is an iffy proposition at best, especially when that reform is of so recent a vintage. But our interviewees offered some informed, general speculation along these lines. First, many of these observers believed that term limits had hindered legislative efforts to deal with long-range problems, such as air and water pollution, and with very complicated matters, such as the budget. Term-limited legislators may have to make decisions with a more superficial understanding of such big issues. These observers felt that term limits encourage legislators to concentrate on "littler" issues and short-term problems for which there is an immediate payoff and to ignore the long-term consequences of their decisions. Beyond this, some interviewees representing rural interests worried that term limits would adversely affect these interests. Prior to term limits, these rural areas of the state had earned greater influence in the legislature than their populations merited by taking advantage of the power of seniority by sending the same people to the legislature election after election. Term limits makes such a strategy impossible.

Relative Power and Influence

Over the last few decades, the public has held the Arizona Legislature in low esteem due to a variety of criticisms. The legislature was thought to be out of touch with the voters, overrun with lobbyists, and bogged down in a decision-making style characterized by behind-the-scene manipulations, intimidation, deal-making, and procedural tricks (Berman 2001).

This low opinion of the legislature has led to a growing impatience with the body and an increased willingness by all types of groups to use the courts to prod the legislature into action and to use the initiative to circumvent the body whenever needed. Proposition 107 reflected this broad discontent with the legislature. However, it is not clear that term limits has done much, if anything, to improve citizen evaluations of the legislature or improve its power and prestige relative to other institutions in the state.

Table 5.9.   Influences of Various Forces Relative to the Arizona Legislature in 2003 Compared to a Decade Ago

Influence of	Ranking*
The Governor	3.2
Administrative Agencies	3.0
Majority and Minority Party Leaders	2.5
Partisan Staff	3.8
Personal Staff	3.4
Legislative Committees	2.7
Legislative Party Caucuses	2.8
Lobbyists	3.9

*Scale 1 to 5, from quite a bit less to quite a bit more, 3 indicates no change.
Source: Knowledgeable Observers Survey.

The knowledgeable observers tended to see lobbyists on the whole as gaining considerable influence, followed by staff (particularly the partisan staff). As they saw it majority and minority party leaders were among the principal losers (Table 5.9). While many of our interviewees claimed to see a gradual shift of power away from the legislature to the governor in recent years, most did not credit this change to term limits. They felt these were largely the result of the personal qualities and inclinations of recent governors. Some did believe that term limits gave agency heads an advantage in dealing with legislators on the budget and, by default, greater responsibility for coping with long-term problems.

CONCLUSION

If they could, many Arizona legislators would eliminate or modify the state's term limits law. Term limits has caused their lives to be more complicated and in some ways less satisfying than the lives of their pre-term-limit peers. Because of term limits, legislators have to think more strategically about running for another elective office (most commonly the other legislative chamber), swapping legislative seats (in Arizona, two term-limited rural legislators, one in the House, one in the Senate, one a Democrat and the other a Republican, decided to run for the seat being left open by the other fellow), and even keeping the seat in the family by having a relative fill in for a term or so. Living with term limits has also forced some legislators out of office just at the peak of their power and influence in a legislative body. Overall, though, the effects of term limits in Arizona have been somewhat mitigated by the ability of legislators to move from chamber to chamber.

It is probably true that term limits has increased Arizonans' opportunities to hold legislative office, encouraged greater competition for offices at all three levels of government, and given voters a greater choice among candidates. In this way, term limits has been a force toward a more inclusive governing process. At the same time, term limits has generally weakened legislative leadership and the committee system and generally increased the influence of others in the process, particularly lobbyists and staff, though not all lobbyists and staff have gained equally. While the policymaking process is more open, term limits has set in motion forces that make that process more chaotic.

NOTES

1. This chapter was originally presented at the Life with Term Limits Conference, Ray C. Bliss Institute, University of Akron, April 29–30, 2004.

2. The interviews were conducted between April 2003 and March 2004, mostly in person but sometimes by telephone and e-mail, by the author and/or Mary Lou Cooper, Program Manager, Council of State Governments, whose help on this project has been indispensable. Interviews were considered confidential, and unattributed quotes in this chapter are drawn from these interviews. In addition to the interviews, the author conducted an extensive review of newspaper files and public records. For predictions of the likely effects of term limits I drew on arguments made by people supporting and opposing the reform as found in Gerald Benjamin and Michael J. Malbin's book, *Limiting Legislative Terms* (Washington, DC: CQ Press, 1992), Appendix A.

3. This part of the law was voided by the 1995 U.S. Supreme Court decision, *U.S. Term Limits v. Thornton*, 514 U.S. 779.

4. Quoted in "Session Wrap-Up," *Arizona Capitol Times* (May 21, 1999), p. 17.

5. Ibid.

6. "Term limited representative may challenge own party's senator," *Associated Press State and Local Wire* (April 10, 2000).

7. "GOP bloc may swing budget vote," *The Arizona Republic* (June 9, 2003), A1, A2.

8. See General Accounting Office, *Campaign Finance Reform: Early Experience of Two States That Offer Full Public Funding for Political Candidates,* (Washington, D.C., Government Printing Office, May 9, 2003). Senator Pete Rios has suggested that open seats draw more candidates into the race, and while public funding evens spending, incumbents are still difficult to defeat because they have an advantage in name identification. Quoted in Mary Jo Pitzl, Chip Scutari, and Ashley Bach, "Candidate fillings hit state record," *The Arizona Republic* (June 13, 2002), 1, 16.

9. One former legislator we interviewed remarked that he did not think about term limits when deciding whether to run for the legislature, but after being elected, the recognition that he was only going to be there a maximum of eight years prompted him to behave differently than he otherwise would have within the legislature.

10. For example, see *Women in State Policy Leadership, 1998–2005: An Analysis of Slow and Uneven Progress* (Albany, NY: State University of New York: Center for Women in Government & Civil Society, 2006).

11. In something of a rebellion against the influence of the partisan staff, the incoming Senate Majority Leader Republican Tim Bee in 2006 terminated the employment of four senior advisors, declaring that they simply had served too long and had assumed too much authority. Said Bee: "The staff that we have has served us very well, but they've been here for a very long time, and I felt it was time for some new blood. . . . When you have staff that's been here longer than members, there sometimes can be a blurring of the lines in the roles." Quoted in Phil Riske, "Bee Fires 4 Top Senate Aides, Says Their Longevity Was a Detriment," *Arizona Capitol Times* (November 17, 2006): 1, 6.

6

Colorado Legislative Term Limits: The Worst of Both Worlds[1]

John A. Straayer

Proponents of state legislative term limits argued that the reform would eliminate what they saw as pernicious political ambition and careerism in these institutions and produce more politically responsive and demographically diverse "citizen-legislatures." Critics of the reform feared that term limits would leave the states with amateur legislative bodies subject to the influence of staffers, lobbyists, and governors[2] (Carey, Niemi, and Powell 2000, ch. 1, 2, 6). In Colorado, term limits appear to have produced the worst of both worlds. While few of the reformers' hopes have yet been realized, many of the negative consequences feared by critics have indeed materialized.

This chapter documents the first half-decade of Colorado's experience with legislative term limits. This experience has not been a happy one for the state's semi-professional lawmaking body. My conclusions are based on over one hundred formal interviews and informal conversations with legislators, lobbyists, legislative staffers, and journalists, the review of a vast assortment of legislative and other documentary materials, a mail survey of long-time observers of the Colorado General Assembly, and my own many years of direct observation of that august body.[3]

A BRIEF HISTORY

In 1990, Colorado became one of the first three states to adopt legislative term limits, along with Oklahoma and California. Adopted as initiative measure Amendment Number Five, with a statewide voter approval of 71 percent and majorities in every county, the reform applied to state legislators and all elective executive branch officials, all of whom were limited to eight consecutive years in office. State legislators are allowed immediately to run for a seat in the other chamber or, after being termed-out, they may run for a seat in the same chamber again after sitting out for four years. Thus, Colorado's are not lifetime term limits (like those found in six states), and its eight-year limit is slightly less severe than the nation's shortest limits (the six-year limits found in three states). In 1994, voters extended these limits to all elective local government officials.

As in so many states, Colorado's term limits were adopted in the political context of the anti-government and anti-incumbency mood of the late 1980s and early 1990s. Political circumstances, largely at the national level, had soured the public, but it was the states with direct democracy provisions in their constitutions that caught the fury of the public's impatience for institutional change. During this same period, Coloradans also passed some of the nation's most onerous tax and revenue limitations and other government restrictions through the ballot box.[4]

The Colorado General Assembly is a semi-professional state legislature[5] (Kurtz 2004). Its levels of compensation and staffing, and the time demands of legislative duty, are neither as high as in the professionalized bodies of California, New York, and Pennsylvania nor as low as in the citizen-legislatures of Wyoming, North Dakota, and New Hampshire. The General Assembly is composed of one hundred members, sixty-five in the House, and thirty-five in the Senate. For the past three decades, Republicans have held a majority in both chambers, except for four years when one of the chambers fell into Democratic hands.[6] The legislature meets annually for a constitutionally limited period of 120 calendar days. An initiative passed in 1988 established procedural rules banning the use of votes in party caucuses binding the votes of all caucus members and requiring some sort of committee action on all bills. Other rules limit members to the introduction of only five bills per session (with some exceptions) and establish a series of deadlines for bill introduction and completion of both committee and floor work on bills. Historically, Colorado has been a weak governor state, with the legislature's power firmly anchored in its control of the state budget process. But in recent decades, Coloradans have limited the power of their legislature by taking full advantage of the state's direct democracy provisions. Colorado is one of the top three states in the use of the initiative, referendum, and recall, using them not only to craft government institutions (like term limits), but also to pass scores of policy initiatives (Rosenthal et al. 2003, 206).

Through my copious interviews, documentary analysis, and an auxiliary survey, I have found that both advocates and critics of term limits believe that the Colorado experience has largely fulfilled the worst fears of the latter while failing to bring about the results desired by the former. Proponents' goals of curbing political careerism, diversifying legislative membership, boosting electoral competition, and sensitizing legislators to their constituents' needs have not been met. On the other hand, the lobby is stronger, the legislature has lost some power to the governor, its leadership is weaker, experience and institutional and policy memory of senior members have been lost, partisanship has increased, and civility and procedural orderliness have decreased. Many legislators, including some who voted for term limits, would now like to alter them, and several efforts to do so have been introduced and discussed, albeit not yet placed before the voters. However, the voting public is either unaware or unconcerned with this state of affairs since, in 2003, it rejected a very minor rollback of the reform, a ballot measure that would have suspended term limits for district attorneys. What follows is a more detailed report of term limits' impacts on legislative elections and representation, the institutions of the legislature, and the legislative process in the early years of the reform in Colorado.

COMPOSITION AND REPRESENTATION

Two of term-limit reformers' central goals were to boost competition and to reduce political careerism in the legislature (Carey et al. 2000; Colorado General Assembly Legislative Council 1990). They viewed the unlimited legislature as a bastion of entrenched, electorally-invincible incumbents who were closely tied to the political action committee coffers of interest groups and members of the lobby corps. The removal of these incumbents was supposed to usher in a new crop of demographically more diverse and constituent-sensitive "citizen-legislators" who would serve for a short period, bring some common sense to government, and then return to their homes and businesses around the state. In this way, the people would have their state government back. Or, at least, so went the argument.

Unfortunately for these reformers, in the first half-decade after term limit implementation in Colorado, almost none of this happened. The rate of legislative turnover changed little (see Figure 6.1). The number of open seats rose somewhat in the House, but not the Senate. Both before and after term limits, roughly one-quarter to one-third of all seats went uncontested by one of the two major parties. In 1994, the year of the national Republican sweep, eight incumbents lost out of sixty-six representatives and senators seeking reelection. Just two incumbents lost in the more normal year of 1996. But in three of the first post-term-limit elections, a total of just seven incumbents were ousted—the same or even less incumbent loss than before term limits. No changes were seen either in the pattern of party control or in changes in the individual legislative districts. In other words, term limits had no noticeable effects on electoral competition in the first three election cycles after their implementation.

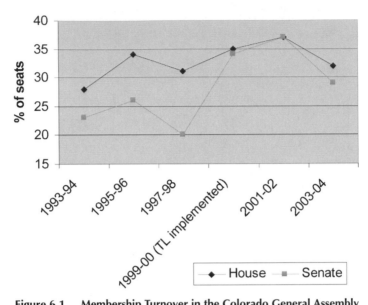

Figure 6.1.   Membership Turnover in the Colorado General Assembly
Source: Gary Moncrief, Richard Niemi, and Lynda Powell. 2004. "Time, Term Limits,
and Turnover: Trends in Membership Stability in U.S. State Legislatures," *Legislative
Studies Quarterly* 29: 357-81.

Neither did term limits have any obvious impact on the diversity of the
legislative body. With respect to race, ethnicity, gender, age, and party control, the General Assembly was the same before and after term limits (see
Table 6.1). Colorado has long been one of the leaders in female membership in state legislatures, ranking among the top three states for years. Since
term limits, nothing has changed. For years before term limits, 30–35 percent of Colorado legislators were women, and since the reform's implementation, the percentage has not changed. The number of Latino and
African-American members has increased slightly since term limits took effect, but this may be a reflection of the increasing diversity of the Colorado

Table 6.1.   Demographic Composition of the Colorado Legislature

Year	% Democratic	% Non-White	% Women	Ave. Age
1993–94	47.0	10.0	34.0	50.6
1995–96	40.0	10.0	31.0	50.3
1997–98	40.0	9.0	35.0	51.9
1999–00	35.0	12.0	34.0	52.6
2001–02	45.0	12.0	34.0	51.3
2003–04	45.0	13.0	33.0	52.4

Source: Colorado Legislative Directories, 1993-94 through 2003-04.

population. The percentage of Democrats in the legislature fluctuated with no apparent pattern after term limits, but Republicans continued to achieve solid majorities in each chamber. Again, this is nothing new.

The average age of legislators has not changed in any major way, although the combined House-Senate data shown in Table 6.1 masks some slight, but interesting, shifts. From 1993 through 2003, the average age of House members was virtually static, but in the Senate, the average age increased marginally and irregularly, rising from 51.26 in 1993 to 55.46 in 1999, following the exodus of the first group of term-limited members. Then it settled back to 52.97 in 2001, but it went up again in 2003 to 55.69. This post-term-limit pattern appears to be the product of an increased, but uneven, flow of House members to the Senate, who tend to be older than the average freshman not coming from the other chamber. Term limits also appears to have affected legislators' age spread. The last three pre-term-limit election cycles produced an average of ten lawmakers forty years old or younger and thirteen lawmakers over sixty. The average for the first three post-limit elections was fourteen lawmakers forty or younger and sixteen lawmakers over sixty. What consequence this change in age variance may have is not yet clear, although it may bode well for better representation because it signifies increased diversity in the legislative corpus.

Thus, the changes that term limit advocates desired—increased electoral competition, turnover, and membership diversity—did not materialize in Colorado, at least in the first three election cycles after the reform was implemented. On the other hand, term limits did cause one clear change in the demographics of the Colorado General Assembly—the reduction in the average length of service of legislators and especially the elimination of the small cadre of very senior members who had inordinate influence in lawmaking and the legislature. After the last pre-term limit election in 1996, eighteen of the sixty-five House members began the session with six or more year's experience, and eighteen of the thirty-five senators had ten years or more (combined House and Senate service). But after the third post-term-limit election in 2002, the number of such senior members in the House was down to eight, and in the Senate, the number was down to nine. Thus, in each chamber, the number of highly experienced members was halved by term limits. Term limits also reduced members' overall average years of legislative experience. After the 1992 election, House members started their term with an average of 4.20 years of legislative experience, and senators had an average combined House-Senate average experience of 8.03 years. After the last pre-term-limit election, in 1996, the numbers were 4.18 years for the House and 8.46 years for the Senate—very little change. But three election cycles into the term limits era, in 2002, these numbers fell to 2.48 for the House and 6.86 for the Senate. Thus, the decline in legislative experience has been quite dramatic in the House and less so for the

Senate, both in terms of average experience and the number of very senior members.

Advocates and opponents of term limits interpreted this expected change in legislative experience very differently prior to the implementation of the reform. Advocates looked forward to the change as the eradication of entrenched incumbents who were unrepresentative of the state and unresponsive to even their own constituents. These reformers heralded the increasing rotation in office as the hallmark of their hoped-for citizen-legislature. On the other hand, opponents worried that stripping the legislature of its most experienced members would also strip that body of institutional memory and expertise about both policy and procedure, leaving the legislative branch at the mercy of the information of lobbyists and executive agency personnel.

Whose interpretation of this change has been borne out by Colorado's early experience with term limits? In the eyes of virtually all our interviewees, the elimination of the small cadre of long-term legislative veterans has had mostly negative consequences. Issues such as taxation, transportation, education, insurance regulation, business-labor relations, and water resources are both technical and persistent year after year, and even decade after decade. One veteran lawmaker with many years of pre-term-limit experience put it succinctly, noting that: "Years ago, the big issues were schools, roads, and taxes. Now the big ones are education, transportation, and revenues. These new members think it's all new stuff."

In the pre-term limit era, these veterans were relied on by junior lawmakers to remember the politics and policy of issues that persisted over the years. They knew what was in existing law, they were familiar with the interests on the various sides of the issues, and they had a good sense of the consequences of current policy. More junior lawmakers, by and large, did not. Without these senior legislators' extensive knowledge, observers of the Colorado Legislature believe that post-term-limit lawmakers are more susceptible to distortions of issue history, past agreements, and policy consequences that are biased by lobbyists, legislative staff, and the governor, whether intentionally or not. This reduces the influence of the legislature in the policymaking process, and in the eyes of many of my interviewees, it reduces the quality of public policy. A former legislator commented: "The new [term-limited legislators] are in a hurry, and they don't always know what they're doing." A legislative staffer reported that there was "a loss of expertise in such areas as water, transportation, and capital development." Those close to the budget process noted that term-limited legislators tend to look at the budget in the short run, characterized by an "I-won't-be-here-in-ten-years" syndrome.

But perhaps the greatest source of disappointment for term-limits advocates should lie in the apparent expansion, not contraction, of the pool of ambitious political careerists. Dennis Pohill, the co-director of the Colorado Term Limits Coalition (CTLC), the group that placed Amendment Number Five on the 1990 ballot, stated that CTLC's primary goal was to return the legislature to being a citizen-legislature. That is, CTLC wanted to transform the General Assembly from what it believed was an aggregation of politicians concerned first and foremost with their political careers to a body of average Coloradans serving only a short period of time in the legislature. The CTLC believed that these legislators would be more in tune with, and more responsive to, their constituencies.

Unfortunately for the CTLC and like-minded reformers, the Colorado data make it clear that rather than purging the legislature of political careerists and supplanting them with average citizens serving only a brief stint of public service, term limits may have done just the reverse. One hundred ninety-one members left the General Assembly from 1990 to 2002 (see Table 6.2). Of the ninety-seven of these who left from 1990 through 1996, the immediate pre-term-limit era, 29 percent sought another elective office, while 43 percent retired from politics. From 1998 through 2002, the first three post-term-limit elections, fifty-eight members were term-limited from office. Of these, 53 percent immediately sought another public office, and just 25 percent left politics. During the same 1998–2002 period, thirty-six left the legislature voluntarily before being term-limited. Of these, 64 percent immediately ran for another elective office, and just 14 percent retired from politics. Thus, after term limits, the pool of ambitious officeholders in the legislature expanded. Many more legislators sought another office immediately after leaving the legislature under term limits than before them, whether they were term-limited from office or not. An insightful quip by a long-time statehouse lobbyist captured this seeming addiction to elective public life this way: "Once these guys get down here under the gold dome, they never want to go home." This pattern hardly suggests that term limits has established a citizen-legislature.

Finally, turning directly to the question of representation, term limits advocates may be heartened that there is some evidence to suggest that post-term-limit legislators are more interested in serving their constituents, re-

Table 6.2. Legislators' Immediate Post-Legislative Career Moves

	Sought Another Elective Office	Retired from Politics	Other	Total Departures
1990-96— Pre-TL	29% (28)	43% (42)	28% (27)	100% (97)
1998-2002—Post-TL:				
Term-limited departure	53% (31)	17% (10)	29% (17)	100% (58)
Voluntary departure (post-1998)	64% (23)	14% (5)	22% (8)	100% (36)

Source: Data gathered and assembled by the author.

gardless of their political ambitions. The General Assembly's Legislative Council, one of the main staffing units for the legislature, reports that since the implementation of term limits, there has been a steady rise in the number of member requests for staff assistance in responding to constituent requests for information and help[7] (Straayer and Bowser 2004). This may suggest that post-term-limit legislators have become more sensitive to their constituents' needs. However, even these data are subject to more than one explanation. More requests for help may simply reflect legislators' increased need for help, born of their limited experience.

INSTITUTIONS

Legislative leaders and committees make state legislatures work. Bodies of twenty to four hundred equal members simply cannot operate effectively without some structure and direction. Typically, the leader of the majority party in each chamber, sometimes in consultation with the leader of the respective minority party caucus, determines committee membership and chairmanships, schedules and controls floor activities, represents the institution to the press and the public, and plays a major role in deciding upon and advocating his or her party's policy agenda[8] (Rosenthal 2004, ch. 10). Standing committees in most state legislatures are closely connected to caucus leaders through the committee appointment and bill referral processes. Since, in most legislatures, bills receive their most careful scrutiny in these committees, their efficient and effective functioning is crucial for an efficient and effective legislature.

Legislative Leaders

Legislative leaders in the Colorado General Assembly have long enjoyed substantial formal authority in their chambers (Straayer 2000, ch. 4). The speaker of the House assigns majority party members to committees and selects the committee chairs and vice-chairs. Bill referral is also the sole responsibility of the speaker. Therefore, with the power to structure committee membership and decide where bills are heard, the speaker has a good deal of control over the fate of proposed legislation. The majority leader is the speaker's deputy and functions as the floor leader, having substantial control of the calendar and floor proceedings. The minority party leader plays a vital role as a watchdog of the process, serving as spokesperson and policy leader of the minority and assigning minority party members to committees, but otherwise, he or she has little formal power. In the Senate, majority party committee membership and chairmanships are formally controlled by the majority leader, but practically, these decisions are made jointly by members of a majority party leadership team. The Senate president alone has bill referral authority. The powers of the minority leader, like those of his or her counterpart in the House, are largely informal, except for assigning minority party members to committees.

Before term limits, the formal powers of legislative leaders were significantly augmented by informal powers in both chambers. For the eighteen years preceding the 1998 implementation of the limits, just two persons had served as speaker of the House, one for ten years and the other for eight. This continuity of leadership meant that rank-and-file legislators knew that cooperation with the speaker could help their cause and that conflict could lead to retribution. For example, Carl "Bev" Bledsoe, a retired eastern plains rancher entered the House in 1972 and was speaker from 1980 to 1990. He was soft-spoken, stern, serious about good public policy, and conservative in his attire, expression, and policy preferences.[9] With experience, Bledsoe learned to be strategic in his committee assignments and bill referrals, and as a result, he was able to have significant impact on the legislative process and its output. Members knew where Bev stood, and they knew that it was in their interest to support him. When problems of policy or behavior emerged, they were handled quietly, often in the speaker's office. The situation was similar in the Senate, where leaders were by no means unbounded in their influence, but they could and did succeed themselves year after year, developing considerable skill and experience and providing rank-and-file members with considerable incentive to be followers.

Term limits changed the power of legislative leaders and their relationship to the rank-and-file, especially for the House speaker and Senate president. While these top majority party leaders retained their formal authority and influence over committee membership and bill referral, a two-year rotation of these positions was set in soon after the implementation of term limits, making these leaders lame ducks the instant they win their positions. Furthermore, members are fully aware of the post-term-limit fluidity in leadership positions, and thus there has developed a constant quest for them. As one post-term-limit speaker stated: "The minute I was selected, the race began to succeed me."

Table 6.3 shows clearly this decline in leadership continuity, particularly in the senate. But the most significant development is not shown in the table—the establishment of a two-year-and-out pattern for the House speaker and Senate president, as of this writing. That is, from the onset of term limits in 1998, through four election cycles, every House speaker and Senate president was term limited after serving in the position for a single biennium. Roughly one-half of these leaders came to the position after having served previously in a second-tier leadership slot. While this system provides some training for leaders before they gain real power, the lame-duck nature of the top leaders weakens them considerably, especially compared to pre-term limit leaders. A

Table 6.3.   Leadership Turnover of the Colorado General Assembly

Year	House	Senate
1993–94	6 of 9	2 of 8
1995–96	5 of 9	3 of 8
1997–98	6 of 10	1 of 8
1999–00	8 of 9	4 of 8
2001–02	5 of 9	7 of 8
2003–04	5 of 9	7 of 9

Note: This table compares the number of members in leadership who were not in leadership the previous year to the total number of leaders. Leadership includes the entire formal list of majority and minority leadership.
Source: Colorado Legislative Directories, 1993-94 through 2003-04.

veteran lobbyist summed up the view of most close observers as to the results of this new rapid-rotation pattern: "They just blow off the speaker. They know she'll be gone soon."

The clout of the House speaker and Senate president has also been diminished by machinations of lower-level leaders in their efforts to position themselves for their rise up the leadership ladder in subsequent sessions. The eight-year limit in Colorado means that no one can ascend to a position of leadership with more than six years of experience. But many leaders below the top level now attain their first positions in their first or second term. All legislators know that they have only a few years to make their mark, but they also know that leadership positions will come open every session. Thus, the quest to climb the leadership ladder begins early, and it is constant. For example, going into the 2002 election, three House members, each with no more than four years of experience, fought for the majority leader position. In the process, each constructed his own political action committee to solicit money from lobbyists, and each distributed this money to fellow party members in an effort to earn their votes for the leadership contest. Each of these majority leader candidates even visited their party colleagues' districts and helped with door-to-door campaign work. This absence of clear and singular leadership has diffused power. Among my interviewees, there was a clear consensus that Colorado legislative leaders after term limits are less experienced and weaker, leading to less procedural orderliness and diminished party discipline.

Standing Committees

Just as term limits have triggered more rapid turnover in leadership, so too have they led to more change in committee membership and chairs, with destructive results for the role of these institutions in the Colorado General Assembly. While changes in committee chairs were common even before term limits, with one-third to one-half of chairs turning over following each election, since the reform was implemented in 1998, this turnover has increased, albeit not dramatically. Following both the 1992 and 1994 elections, the chairmanship of five of the ten standing committees in the House changed hands; in the Senate, it was five of ten after the 1992 election and three of ten after that of 1994. Following the 1998 election, nine of the ten House committees and seven of the ten Senate committees had new chairs. In the House, chair turnover dropped to four of eleven after the 2000 election. Since party control changed in the Senate following the 1998 and 2000 elections, all the committees had new chairs, but not directly due to term limits. In short, term limits changed committee chair turnover from a 50–50 proposition to almost a sure thing.

But what may be a more important consequence of term limits is the fact that new committee chairs are assuming their positions with less prior legislative experience and in a more partisan environment. The aggregate number of years of legislative service for House committee chairs dropped from seventy-four in 1993 to forty-one in 2001, rising somewhat to forty-eight in 2003. In the Senate, the decline was from eighty-eight in 1993 to sixty-five in 2001, rising to seventy-three in 2003.

Beyond these changes in the raw numbers, to what extent and in what ways does this decline in experience matter? In particular, do legislative committees in Colorado do their task of examining, screening, and crafting bills any worse? Judging from the opinions of my interviewees and my direct observation, several changes are apparent that may have a direct bearing on these committees' ability to do their duties. First, these committees are less orderly, and the interactions among their chairmen, members, and even witnesses are less civil. Also, committee members appear to be less knowledgeable about statewide issues and problems, and so bills are less well crafted when they reach the chamber floor. Confirming these observations, in the JPTL Knowledgeable Observers survey, 70 percent said that since term limits, committee members know less about issues and 84 percent said members are less courteous and collegial in committee.

Lobbyists

Critics of term limits predicted that the power of the lobby corps would grow as the less-experienced legislators, especially freshmen, would fall prey to the biased information and pressures of lobbyists (Carey et al. 2000; Colorado General Assembly Legislative Council 1990; Thompson and Moncrief 2003). At least in the first three sessions since term limits, it appears that legislators have relied increasingly on the lobby corps for information and cues, but probably not to the extent feared by critics. New members are cautioned by their leaders to be wary of making early commitments; "keep your powder dry" is the advice. Indeed, lobbyists often complain that the post-term-limit members are reluctant to make vote commitments, and when they do, their commitments are not always solid. At the same time, there has been a greater reliance on lobbyists, with 72 percent of the knowledgeable observers in the JPTL survey believing that lobbyists have gained influence in the Colorado General Assembly as a result of term limits. One lobbyist, a veteran of the legislature, observed: "I'm as effective now as I was when I was in the legislature. I know how the process works better than the members do." Another commented that he would no longer want to be a member, asking cynically: "Why would I want to have just one vote?"

Two perhaps less-anticipated consequences of term limits are about how influence within the lobby corps has changed and how the lobby itself has become more susceptible to the influence of legislators. First, before term limits, the influence of many veteran lobbyists was drawn from their close personal ties to long-term leaders—House speakers, Senate presidents, committee chairs, and budget committee members. But as these long-serving, powerful legislators have been term-limited out, these lobbyists have lost their clout. As a result, newer and often younger lobbyists compete more evenly with these veterans for influence. Just as important, for all of them, the job of lobbying is tougher. Each election brings in a large batch of new members, and the task of establishing relationships with them begins anew. And none of these freshmen can be ignored since no one knows which of them will rise to influential positions in just a few years. In short, lobbyists of the Colorado General Assembly must work harder since term limits.

In addition, many of my interviewees suggested that post-term limit legislators tend to be more aggressive in asking lobbyists to fulfill their needs. While this can include requests for information and endorsements, most frequently, this means campaign funds. In the JPTL survey, 82 percent of these observers, including many who were themselves lobbyists, reported that post-term-limits legislators are more aggressive in fundraising, and this means that they more frequently ask lobbyists and their clients for campaign contributions, not always in subtle ways.

There is some belief and concern that term limits have produced a decline in ethical interactions among lobbyists and legislators. As noted, lobbyists complain that lawmakers are less likely to keep their word on voting commitments and that they lean too heavily on them for campaign money. On the other side of the relationship, some legislators suggest that they have been threatened by lobbyists regarding their positions and votes. Some of my interviewees claimed that post-term-limit lobbyists are more likely to manufacture new and misleading stories about policy history and agreements. There were even reports of lobbyists being overtly disrespectful of legislators who were about to be term limited. While no major scandals emerged in the first three post-term-limit sessions, concerns of lobbyist-related problems were so high that, in 2003, the House and Senate leadership jointly established a lobbyist-populated task force to review ethics rules and make recommendations.

Legislative Staff

As is the case with the lobby, the influence of the staff of the Colorado General Assembly on the legislative process has increased, but not in the manner or to the extent predicted by critics. Most of Colorado's legislative staff is nonpartisan, in name and in fact. Two major staff units provide research and legal support. Legislative Council employs just over fifty full-time professionals who do both spot and long-term research, revenue forecasting, and fiscal analysis of bills, and who provide staff support for standing committees. Legislative Legal Services, a unit of similar size, drafts bills and amendments, revises statutes after each session and provides legal advice to the legislature. In addition, a staff of roughly fifteen professional analysts works for the Joint Budget Committee (JBC). Beyond these major staff units, one or two partisan staffers work for each top leader, the House and Senate have front desk clerks and a secretarial pool composed of partisan appointees, and a few partisan staffers work in the communications office of each caucus. But the bulk of legislative staff is made up of nonpartisan, full-time professionals.[10]

The influence of these professional staffers has grown somewhat with term limits, but this has occurred mainly through the provision of procedural advice, policy history, and revenue and budgetary analysis. By their own account, the professional staffers have very self-consciously tried to avoid the political thicket, especially since the advent of term limits. The exception here may be the staff of the JBC, but their increase in substantive influence has not been purposive. State budgets are always complex, and Colorado's is made all the more so by several recent constitutional provisions that both restrict revenues and determine expenditures. The term-limit-induced decline in the experience and budget knowledge of JBC members, along with the increase in budgetary complexity, has made these members more reliant on their staff for analyses and recommendations.

Term limits have also triggered (or at least coincided with) some important changes in staffing in the Colorado General Assembly. First, the directors of Legislative Council, Legislative Legal Services, and the Joint Budget Committee all retired since the adoption of the reform, stimulated to do so, at least in part, by changes in the institutional culture caused by term limits. But in all three cases, these directors were replaced by professionals from within the agencies themselves, easing the impact of the change in these important positions. Term limits have also led to an expansion in the number of partisan staffers in each chamber and a more-than-modest increase in their influence. For example, in the House, a legislator who was termed-out in 1998 was hired as a staffer to serve as an assistant and advisor to her party's caucus leadership, remaining in that post through the tenure of two speakers and majority leaders. Her role in party policy and strategy was significant. In the Senate, both parties increased the size of their media and partisan policy staffs after term limits.

LEGISLATIVE PROCESS

Term limits advocates predicted little about the effect of the reform on the legislative process itself. Critics suggested that there would be some impact on the balance of power. But observers of how term limits have actually played out in Colorado described a variety of impacts on the process, many of which may have important impacts on the output of that process.

Civility, Partisanship, and Norms

In the years leading up to term limits, the Colorado General Assembly always included many long-term veterans who functioned as role models for new members. Many of these veterans had long institutional and policy memories and a dedication to the legislature as an institution. Directly and by example, these members trained their newer colleagues in the informal rules, norms, and behavior patterns that facilitated a generally smooth and civil process. Partisan and ideological conflict existed, to be sure, but so did mutual respect and common courtesy, both within and across party lines. Furthermore, many of the seasoned veterans occupied formal positions in leadership or as committee chairs, giving them direct control over many aspects of the legislative process.

With the old-timers gone and legislative leadership somewhat enfeebled, and with a membership less knowledgeable about behavioral norms and less familiar with each other, term limits have led to more disorder, incivility, and increased partisanship in the Colorado General Assembly. Members are more inclined to commit "sneak attacks" on the chamber floors by proposing amendments to colleagues' bills without the courtesy of prior notice. Committee chairs and presiding officers on the floor have graveled down colleagues, refusing to recognize them or to allow continuing discussion. Members more frequently storm out of committees and off the floor out of anger. Minority party bills are much more likely to be killed in committee. The use of the "supermotion" has emerged, whereby a member will interrupt normal committee procedures, move to advance a bill immediately to the floor, and then defeat that motion, thus giving the bill a sudden and surprise death. Legislating is rougher and tougher, less congenial, less consultative, and more cutthroat than before term limits.

A particularly noteworthy episode of conflict and animosity occurred in the final three days of the 2003 legislative session when Republicans, holding the majority, surprised Democrats by bringing up a bill to redraw the 2002 court-ordered congressional district map.[11] Tempers flared, rules were jettisoned, and Democratic senators walked out of the chambers. The Democrats then tried a procedural ploy by asking to have the bill fully read on the floors, and Republican leaders complied by having sections of the bill read aloud simultaneously by a group of staffers at the front of each chamber. This episode epitomizes the lack of decorum, civility, and cooperation that has often characterized the legislature after term limits.

Both the responses to the JPTL survey and comments made in personal interviews confirm these changes in legislative behavior and norms after term limits. Fully 84 percent of the knowledgeable observers in the JPTL survey felt that post-term limit legislators in Colorado were less courteous in committee, and 78 percent saw this on the floor. Virtually every observer who was interviewed personally agreed. One commented: "There's been a decline in discipline. It was the informal, unwritten rules that made things work. They've been eroded." Another said: "They forget that legislating is a team sport." One legislative leader told his caucus: "Trying to work with you guys is like coaching little league football—everyone wants to be quarterback." Another leader put it more bluntly: "The newer people are different. They're more partisan, less collegial. There's more conflict. They chase trendy issues and don't know the rules. They don't respect the institution." Beyond simple civility, 84 percent of the JPTL observers believed that partisanship is up, 82 percent saw more aggressive fundraising, and 91 percent said that leaders were more focused on campaigns.

Ideological and Intra-Party Conflict

Another change in the Colorado General Assembly since term limits have been implemented has been an increase in intra-party ideological conflict, primarily in the Republican Party. It is not clear whether this was caused by term limits or simply happened to occur at the same time that the reform was implemented. Regardless of the initial causal mechanism of this trend, term limits seem to have accelerated it.

In the 1980s, long before term limits were even adopted, a group of very self-consciously conservative Republicans was elected to the House. Calling themselves the "House Crazies," they challenged and partially replaced the House Republican leadership, moving that chamber in a more fiscally conservative direction. In the 1990s, another influx of what many called the "New House Crazies" pushed a new, more extreme, fiscal conservative agenda overlaid with the social agenda of the Christian Right.[12] Term limits pushed out several influential moderate Republicans in 1998 and 2000, shifting the party's ideological balance farther to the right. The remaining moderate Republicans reported strong pressure to toe the hard-right policy line, including threats of retaliation or primary challenges if they did not. For example, moderate Republican Representative Gayle Berry was subjected to a brutal negative primary assault from the Christian Right in 2002, even though she was due to be term limited in 2004 (Straayer 2000).[13]

Other evidence of intra-party conflict and the ideological shift among legislative Republicans after term limits includes an increase in bills involving gun owners' rights, sexual preference, and reproductive choice, and even an attempt to impeach a judge over his ruling in a same-sex couple child custody case. This increase in intra-party ideological conflict may have been exacerbated by the drawing of more solidly one-party legislative districts, low participation in the legislative nominating process, and national trends. But at the very least, term limits made the legislature more responsive to these forces by pushing out moderates and reducing the time legislators have to get to know one another on a personal basis, thus dulling their sharp ideological edges.

Balance of Power

The influence of Colorado's governor has grown at the expense of its legislature since the implementation of term limits. In the JPTL survey, 73 percent of the knowledgeable observers felt this to be true, as did the vast majority of those I interviewed. But the reform is only one potential explanation for this trend. The identification of the causal effect of term limits on this relationship is made especially difficult because in 1998, the year term limits were implemented, Colorado elected its first Republican governor in twenty-four years, Bill Owens. Then, in two of the first three sessions after term limits were implemented, the GOP held a majority in each legislative chamber and the governor's office, the first instances of unified-party government in the state in over two decades.

Owens was aggressive in asserting his power and preferences, especially on budgetary matters. He and his budget director controlled the state's financial information tightly when they dealt with the Joint Budget Committee. He threatened to use the veto pen many times, and on many occasions, he did so. For example, in the 2002, 2003, and 2004 budgets, Owens vetoed certain pages of the budget bill in a way that greatly increased his budgetary flexibility.[14] Thus, it is difficult to determine whether, and to what extent, the Colorado governor's increased influence since term limits was due to unified government, Owens's personality, his skillful use of his formal powers, other factors, or to the reform itself.

Where term limits most clearly appear to have influenced the legislature's relationship with the governor is in the legislature's early reluctance to respond when challenged. One prime example was in the initial refusal by Republicans who, in 2001–2002, held the majority in the House but not the Senate, to support Democrats' desire to sue the governor for his veto of the budget bill definitions section. In 2003, following Republican recapture of majorities in both chambers, they did file a "friendly" suit to sort out legislative vs. executive budgetary authority. A defense of the legislative institution had to await the emergence of comfortable intra-party relations. Many of my interviewees suggested that the legislature's susceptibility to gubernatorial bullying stemmed from the Republican majority's felt need to support the governor of their own party. A lack of experience, knowledge, and institutional pride—all potentially a result of term limits—were also suggested to be significant factors in the legislature's reluctance to rise immediately to the challenge to legislative budgetary authority. Indeed, 70 percent of the JPTL survey respondents felt that legislators themselves were less supportive of their own institution after term limits.

Many of my interviewees also suggested another factor rooted in term limits that kept legislators from facing up to the governor—the governor's potential influence over their post-legislative futures. Most obviously, termed-out lawmakers might run for another elective office, and the financial and campaign help of the popular governor could be very helpful in such an endeavor. But the governor could solve a termed-out legislator's employment problems much more directly by giving him or her a state job. This possibility was very much in post-term-limit legislators' minds because following the 1998 election, a parade of term-limited Republican legislators secured cabinet-level or secondary-level jobs in the new administration. The hope for such a job of one's own might have much to do with a sitting legislator's acquiescence to a governor's entreaties.

Policy Outputs

Given all the institutional, political, social, and behavioral changes that have occurred in and around the Colorado General Assembly with the advent of term limits, is the public policy created by that body any different? While it seems likely that some such changes may have occurred, the question defies a definitive answer due to the lack of a common, precise assessment instrument. Many of my interviewees argued that bills are less well screened by committees that are weakened by a lack of experience. Some also argue that more poorly crafted legislation is passed by the full chambers. There is some sense that the agenda has shifted to the political right, but whether this can be attributed to term limits is unclear. There is broad consensus that major state problems are not addressed as they should be, but the question remains whether this is different, better, or worse than before term limits.

At least one change that has a clear impact on the legislature's policy output can undeniably be linked to the implementation of term limits, and that is the loss of what some of my interviewees called "policy champions" in the legislature. These were lawmakers who would spend a decade or more working on a particular policy problem, learning its ins and outs, introducing and advocating bills on the subject year after year, slowly perfecting policy instruments and programs, and building collegial support around the state and across the aisle. The loss of these policy champions may not soon be noticed. But in the long run, the consequences of replacing such members with short-timers may become evident as public problems fester and go unnoticed, or as major unanticipated policy consequences emerge from sloppy legislation.

ADAPTING TO TERM LIMITS

By the mid-1990s, it was clear both to the leaders of the legislature and to its staff units that when term limits began to jettison senior members, something would have to be done to replace them as sources of knowledge on process and policy. The informal mentoring and apprenticeships by which lawmakers were taught and indoctrinated into the legislative culture would be gone. To help replace them, the Colorado General Assembly greatly expanded its formal new-member orientation programs.

Before term limits, new-member orientation took the form of a Sunday evening dinner soon after the general election followed by two days of briefings by staff members, legislative leaders, and members of the press. In 1996, this program was expanded to four days, including a half-day in November, two in December, and one and a half days just before the opening of the legislative session in January. But with the implementation of term limits in 1998, the new member orientation was almost doubled to eight days. Also in 1998, the leadership had the staff prepare new member briefing books containing calendar deadlines, procedural rules, sketches of common floor situations, problems, and reactions, and other information that could be useful to freshmen. The director of the Joint Budget Committee staff put together a more specialized briefing book for the six JBC members.

In 2002, the new members program was again expanded and reorganized. The program was broadened to include such subjects as budgets and finance, policy areas like school funding, corrections and transportation, legislative-executive relations, media relations, and ethics. Mock committee and floor sessions were run and members were familiarized with staff information sources and computer systems. There is even a three-day orientation for legislators' spouses. The volume, complexity, and breadth of information presented in the new member orientation are far greater than the program before term limits. Indeed, legislators and staffers report that the amount of information in the post-term limit program can be overwhelming for freshmen. But the Colorado General Assembly clearly made a much greater effort to train its new members after the implementation of term limits, an effort that was undoubtedly needed given the large cadres of freshmen and the dearth of legislative experience that the reform produced in the body.

CONCLUSION

In an analysis of the impact of Colorado's legislative term limits just a year and a half after their initial impact, I concluded that the reform caused "lots of commotion, limited consequences" (Straayer 2003, 61–74). With time, the picture has changed. It is now fair to characterize its results in terms of its proponents' claims and critics' fears: term limits have wrought "the worst of both worlds."

Elections are just as costly since term limits were implemented in 1998, and incumbents win them just as often. Legislative turnover and electoral competition are largely unchanged. Political ambition and careerism have increased, not decreased, and there are no greater numbers of women or minorities in the legislature. Legislative leaders are weaker, and the lobby and governor are stronger. The Senate and House are more partisan, less orderly, and less civil than before the reform.

Of course, we must resist the temptation for overstatement. The Colorado General Assembly still functions, and it is likely that as many of its members care about the state and good policy as before term limits. Most legislators do their best, and the institution continues to have skilled and dedicated staff members. No major scandals erupted in the first three sessions under term limits.

The Colorado General Assembly is clearly not what it once was. But while the promises of reformers have not been fulfilled and the fears of critics have materialized, ultimately the test of a lawmaking body is the quality of the policy that is made there. But we may have to wait longer to determine if the institution's decline produces bad policy or fails to attend to the state's collective needs. The quality of the policy output of the legislature will likely take longer to manifest itself, and its assessment will be much more complex than simply assessing the characteristics of the legislature itself.[15]

NOTES

1. This chapter was originally presented at the Life with Term Limits Conference, Ray C. Bliss Institute, University of Akron, April 29–30, 2004.

2. The 1990 "An Analysis of 1990 Ballot Proposals" published by the Legislative Council of the Colorado General Assembly in advance of Colorado's term limits election contained these pro and con arguments. Pro: "Limiting terms of office will allow more individuals . . . to serve the public (and) will invigorate the political system by making room for new policy-makers with new perspectives on addressing public policy issues" (p.21). Con: term limits will "strengthen the hand of permanent bureaucrats, congressional staff and lobbyists, none of whom are elected by, or accountable to, the public" (p.22).

3. All interviewees were assured of anonymity. All unattributed quotations in this chapter are from these interviews, conducted primarily in 2003 and 2004.

4. Failed initiated tax or revenue limiting measures were on the ballot in 1986, 1988, and 1990, all prior to the successful 1992 passage of the Taxpayers Bill of Rights (TABOR). A general fund appropriations increase limit of 6 percent annually was adopted by statute in 1991 and made constitutional by the 1992 TABOR language. Furthermore, a successful initiated measure in 1992 funneled most state gambling revenues to parks, trails, and other "outdoors" programs, local elected officers were term-limited in 1994, a 1996 ballot measure attempted to tag congressional candidates who would not take a term-limits pledge with a ballot "scarlet letter," and a successful initiated measure in 2000 locked guaranteed appropriation increased for K–12 schools into the state constitution. Collectively, these measures have substantially gutted the legislature's fiscal powers.

5. Colorado ranked fifteenth among the states in legislative professionalism on a 2004 legislative professionalism index developed by Karl Kurtz of the National Conference of State Legislatures, Denver, Colorado. Karl Kurtz's numbers fit with other such rankings.

6. The years of Democratic control were 1975–1976 for the House and 2001–2002 for the Senate. Between the time of this study and the publication of this book, Democrats took control of both chambers in 2004, and in 2006, they both increased their House and Senate margins and captured the governorship.

7. Reported to author by Legislative Council staff members.

8. Clearly, the nature of leadership varies depending on both the formal authority and personal abilities and style of the incumbents. But most commonly, house speakers, and to a lesser degree, senate presidents, control committee membership and chair selection and, along with majority leaders, exercise considerable procedural control. They are also the most public legislative faces and voices.

9. This characterization of Speaker Bledsoe comes from the author's personal observations and acquaintance with him.

10. The state auditor is an officer of the legislature who also employs many nonpartisan professional staff members, but their activities have very little direct impact on the legislative process other than to produce reports which may trigger the introduction of bills.

11. See T.R. Reid, July 2, 2003, "GOP Redistricting: New Boundaries of Politics?," *Washington Post*; Jon Sarche, March 6, 2007, "State Republicans' redistricting chal-

lenge dealt final blow," *Ft. Collins Coloradoan;* and Bob Ewegen, July 29, 2006, "Republicans reopen gerrymander wound," *Denver Post.*

12. See Straayer, 2000, 165–70; Lynn Bartels, August 2, 2006, "Lies, dang lies . . . ," *Rocky Mountain News;* Fred Brown, May 21, 2006, "A diminished delegation," *Denver Post;* Kate Martin, April, 2006, "A party divided," *Loveland Herald-Reporter;* Julia Martinez, March 17, 2005, "State conservatives redefine roles," *Denver Post.*

13. Additionally the consequences of this development in Colorado's Republican Party were witnessed in the divisive 2004 U.S. Senate nomination contest between Pete Coors and Bob Schaffer, in the 2006 gubernatorial loss by Republican candidate Bob Beauprez, in the 2005 ballot measure, Referendum "C" and in a host of Republican primaries. The events have been heavily reported by the Colorado media and are chronicled in an unpublished manuscript by John A. Straayer, tentatively entitled "Colorado's Great Downhill Run."

14. The pages that were vetoed were the "definitions" section of the budget bill. The absence of many definitions provided the governor with additional latitude in moving funds within major allocation categories.

15. Since the completion of this study, there have been additional changes in the legislature which may be partially attributable to the delayed impact of term limits. In 2004 the Democrats gained control of both chambers for the first time in over 40 years, and in 2006 they increased their margins and won the governorship as well. In 1998, sixty-one of the one hundred members were Republicans; by 2007 their numbers had shrunk to forty-one. Further, in 1998, twenty of the Republicans were women; in 2007 the GOP female count stood at six.

While it would be an enormous stretch to suggest that term limits caused this change in party and gender numbers, the limits may have structured conditions so as to accelerate the impact of broader changes which were occurring in the state and, especially, within the Republican party. Colorado faced a fiscal crisis beginning with the 2001 recession, with which the then-dominant Republican Party failed to cope. This failure boosted the fortunes of the Democrats. Concurrently, the more hardcore social-agenda right wing element in the Republican Party increasingly influenced the nominating process and when seats were vacated by incumbent Republicans, by voluntary or term-limited causes, the party looked less and less appealing to female candidates. Entering the 2006 primaries, for example, there were forty-five Democratic women seeking the party nomination for legislative seats, but only sixteen female Republican primary election candidates.

Republicans who I have questioned on the matter offer two possible explanations. One is that the party agenda has changed and appeals less and less to women. Issues such as families, health care and children have given way to concerns with abortion, immigrants, gays and guns, and these later issues resonate less well with women than does the former set. A second theory is that some in the more right-leaning crowd see the proper role of women as mothers, subservient to the man of the household, who should stay home and raise children.

All in all, Colorado's legislature a decade or so after the initial impact of term limits is very unlike the pre-term-limit institution. But the post-2004 changes, as significant as they are, most likely bear just a modest and delayed relationship to term limits.

7

Out with the Old Heads and in with the Young Turks: The Effects of Term Limits in Semi-Professional State Legislatures[1]

Christopher Z. Mooney, Jason Wood and Gerald C. Wright

In recent decades, "semi-professional" state legislatures have had, as John Straayer characterized the effect of term limits on Colorado in a previous chapter, the "worst of both worlds." States with semi-pro legislatures tend to be middle-sized states with middle-sized public problems. But in the late twentieth and early twenty-first centuries, "middle-sized public problems" are in any absolute sense very large problems, indeed. These states typically have at least one major metropolitan area and all the troubles and advantages that modern American mega-cities provide. They have large and diverse economies and millions of residents. Today, they deal with the significant challenges of either shifting from a manufacturing to a service economy (like Connecticut and Maryland) or dealing with an influx of immigrants from within and outside the U.S., as well as new industries (like North Carolina and Nevada).

To deal with these challenges, these states have legislatures that are neither full-time, fully staffed, nor fully paid. Most legislators do not devote their full attention to lawmaking because they simply cannot afford to do so. For example, no one can even support himself or herself on the $28,000 per year paid to a Connecticut lawmaker, let alone support a family. Fortunately, these bodies only meet for relatively brief periods, allowing their members to make a living with their "real" jobs outside the legislature. Furthermore, these semi-professional legislatures have many fewer staff than do their more professionalized counterparts; thus, their staff cannot compensate for these lawmakers' lack of attention to their jobs. In short, these states have copious public problems but meager help from their legislatures to deal with them.

122 Christopher Z. Mooney, Jason Wood, and Gerald C. Wright

Colorado, Arizona, and Indiana are prime examples of states with semi-professional state legislatures. Each has a major city—Denver, Phoenix, and Indianapolis, respectively—and mixed and changing economies and populations. They are challenged to solve major public problems and provide quality services to their residents, but their legislatures are clearly part-time enterprises, more like the city councils of mid-sized cities than their counterparts in California, Ohio, and Illinois. These legislatures' sessions run for three or four months each year, their professional staffing is modest, and their members' salaries range from $30,000 per year (Colorado) to as little as $11,600 (Indiana). Clearly, these are state legislatures with their hands full.

How do semi-professional state legislatures cope under these conditions? As we saw in the previous two chapters, and as we will see in this one, an important coping mechanism is the tradition of "old heads" controlling these legislatures. That is, semi-professional legislatures rely on a small cadre of long-serving members for their policy knowledge, their memory of previous legislative debates and battles, their understanding of the complex institutions of state government (including the legislature itself), and their gravitas in dealing with those outside the legislature, including the governor, lobbyists, and the media. These old heads fill important leadership and committee positions, controlling much of the legislative process. They are also important in training and acculturating new members, both formally and informally. These old heads devote much more of their time to legislating than do their colleagues, and they are often, but not always, compensated for their efforts through extra leadership stipends. In short, a semi-professional legislature's old heads hold down the fort for their colleagues, allowing the legislature to function smoothly and sustain a balance of power with the other actors in the state's political system.

Given this scenario of the functioning of semi-professional state legislatures, how should we expect term limits to affect them? As we have seen in the previous two chapters, while term limits do not much affect the overall level of turnover in these bodies, a strikingly important effect is to decapitate them of their old heads. This leaves these semi-professional legislatures with no members who have long service and institutional knowledge and who are respected by external political actors. As we shall see, most of the significant effects of term limits on semi-professional legislatures are either the direct or indirect effects of the purging of their old heads.

In this chapter, we compare the composition, institutions, and power relationships of the Arizona Legislature and the Colorado General Assembly with those of the Indiana General Assembly, our control case for the assessment of term limits on semi-professional legislatures. Indiana's legislators are not limited in the number of terms they can serve, but the Hoosier legislature parallels the term-limited bodies in Arizona and Colorado in most other important respects. By comparing these three bodies, we will demonstrate that the main impact of term limits on semi-professional state legislatures has been to deprive them of their vital senior legislators. This loss of their old heads has, either directly or indirectly, led to the loss of power relative to other actors in the process, reduced effectiveness of legislative committees, decreased comity within these bodies, weaker leaders, and less-informed legislators, in general. While the normative implications of these impacts can be argued, there is no denying that term limits have dramatically altered semi-professional legislatures, and not necessarily in ways predicted by term limits advocates in the 1990s.

THE INDIANA GENERAL ASSEMBLY IN BRIEF—1993–2004

Before making comparisons with Arizona and Colorado, consider a little background about the nature and context of the legislative process in Indiana. The politics and policymaking of the Hoosier state during the study period (1993–2004) were nicely summarized by former House Speaker Mike Philips when he stated "not all that much has changed." After analyzing a wide range of information, including many interviews with close observers of, and participants in, the legislative process in Indianapolis, statistical data about various aspects of the process, and data from the JPTL's knowledgeable observers survey and the national survey of state legislators, we find that Philips was, not surprisingly, right on the mark. During the twelve-year study period, there was only very modest change in Indiana's legislative politics. This makes the state a good control case in our efforts to assess the effects of term limits.

Our interviewees generally spoke approvingly of the functioning of the Indiana General Assembly. Although they routinely described the institution as being strongly partisan, our respondents conveyed great respect toward the legislative process in Indiana and those who participated in it—even those who might have been in opposition to the respondent himself or herself. The legislative process was said to be characterized by mutual respect and comity, on the one hand, and by partisanship, on the other—characteristics that are not necessarily compatible. Furthermore, the Indiana Senate and House of Representatives were said to operate with different environments. The Senate serves to "cool" the House, paralleling Washington's comment to Jefferson about the chambers of Congress. While the House is more innovative, competitive, and anxious to deal with the state's problems, the Senate is more deliberate, orderly, and careful in the legislation it allows to pass through the process.

While its partisanship is largely a reflection of the close competition between the two parties on the state's political stage, the General Assembly's other broad characteristics—stability, comity, and mutual respect—are the result of its group of long-serving, senior members who control the chambers through strong party caucuses and effective leadership. Caucus leaders were especially strong during the study period due to the development of leadership campaign committees that raised and funneled resources into targeted races throughout the state. In the House in particular, the close party balance of seats contributed to intense electoral competition and greater partisanship, both of which helped shore up leadership power. Some respondents felt that this electoral competition led to less compromise and cooperation than in earlier times. But counterbalancing this, Indiana's legislature had less membership turnover than many semi-professional state legislatures during the study period. This contributed both to strong institutional memory about the legislative process and policy and the development of many working relationships, and even friendships, among rank-and-file members, sometimes even across party lines.

COMPOSITION, REPRESENTATION, AND ELECTORAL COMPETITION

Given this general characterization of the Indiana General Assembly during the study period, let us turn to a more detailed comparison of the three semi-professional legislatures, beginning with some traits of their members and elections.

Composition and Representation

Term limits proponents argued that one of the principal benefits of the reform would be to alter the composition of legislatures, purging the bodies of professional politicians in favor of average citizens and increasing the representation of a variety of underrepresented groups (Will 1993). But in general, we find that term limits had virtually no effect on the composition of semi-professional state legislatures in the outward characteristics of gender, race, and ethnicity, but that the reform may have had a minor impact on legislators' average age. More important, term limits appear to increase the level of state legislators' political ambition, exactly the opposite of the effect for which reformers had hoped.

First, the previous two chapters describe how the composition of neither the Arizona nor the Colorado legislature changed much after the implementation of term limits in those states. Female representation remained flat or even declined. Historically, Colorado has had among the nation's highest proportions of women in its legislature, with typically 30 to 35 percent female in the decades prior to term limits. After the implementation of the reform, female legislative membership in Colorado remained stable. The Ari-

Table 7.1. Demographic Composition of the Indiana General Assembly

Year	% Democratic	% Non-White	% Women	Ave. Age
1993–1994	51.33%	8.00%	19.33%	52.52
1995–1996	43.33%	9.33%	20.67%	53.11
1997–1998	46.00%	8.67%	18.67%	53.93
1999–2000	48.00%	8.67%	18.00%	54.47
2001–2002	47.33%	8.00%	17.33%	56.39
2003–2004	46.00%	7.33%	18.00%	58.40

Source: *Indiana General Assembly Legislative Directory*, Indiana Chamber of Commerce: Indianapolis, IN (various years).

zona Legislature, another long-time national leader in female representation, actually had slightly fewer women in its ranks under term limits. Similarly, term limits had little impact on the ethnic and racial composition of the Arizona and Colorado legislatures. While Arizona elected more Latino lawmakers, these gains were offset by losses of Native-American and African-American members. Likewise, the Colorado General Assembly, which consistently had less than 10 percent Latino and African-American members before term limits, saw no change in minority representation.

The data from our control state, Indiana, confirm term limits' lack of impact on these racial, ethnic, and gender traits of state legislatures. The Indiana General Assembly changed little on these traits between 1993 and 2004 (see Table 7.1), with the percentage of women hovering around 19 percent and its non-white representation holding steady at around 8 percent. Thus, the term-limited state legislatures' stability on these traits after the implementation of the reform is paralleled in the non-term-limited legislature, demonstrating clearly their lack of effect.

On the other hand, the patterns of legislators' ages in these states offers an interesting comparison that may give a small insight into term limits' effects on the composition of state legislatures. The average age of Arizona and Colorado house members held steady after term limits were implemented, while their senate members aged slightly. In Indiana, both chambers saw a slow, steady increase throughout the study period. Perhaps the modest effect in the term-limited senates is the result of more termed-out house members moving to the upper chamber. The term-limited houses stay more stable in age as new representatives rotate through on an eight-year cycle. The Indiana General Assembly increases in average age as its stable membership (see the discussion of turnover below) ages.

Careerism

In the 1990s, reformers argued that term limits would reduce legislators' careerist ambitions (Will 1993; Fund 1992; Petracca 1991a). That is, lawmakers would think of their work in the legislature less as a long-term vocation and more as a short-term avocation. These "citizen-legislators" were supposed to bring the common touch and sensibilities to the state capitol and be more independent of interest groups and the "capital culture." On the other hand, critics of term limits argued that such lawmakers would merely be dilettantes, whose lack of policy and procedural knowledge would leave them unable to assess the veracity of the information and advice of lobbyists, bureaucrats, and staffers (Cohen and Spitzer 1996; Polsby 1991). These arguments lead to some hypotheses that we assess later in this chapter, but here we assess the impact of term limits on legislators' careerism and legislatively relevant knowledge.

While it is more difficult to measure validly a legislator's attitude toward his or her job as a legislator than it is to measure a legislator's gender or race, we find good reason to believe that term limits have not eliminated legislators' ambitions for political careers, as reformers had hoped. In survey data discussed in the previous chapters, most term-limited Arizona lawmakers reported that they would seek another political office after they left the legislature, no fewer than before term limits. Indeed, while less than 40 percent of departing pre-term-limits legislators in Colorado sought another elective office, 50 percent of term-limited lawmakers did so. Why is political ambition sustained or increased in these term-limited, semi-professional legislatures? Perhaps instead of attracting citizen-legislators who wish only to dabble in lawmaking, a term-limited legislature attracts those who intend to use it as a political springboard to higher office. They know they will have a limited legislative career, so they invest less time and effort in the position and work toward enhancing their prospects for a post-legislative career. Alternatively, and perhaps more likely, the type of person attracted to a term-limited legislature is the same as that attracted to a non-term-limited legislature, but these limits force them from office before their political ambition is fully sated. Indeed, perhaps both these processes are at work.

This seeming inability of term limits to reduce political careerism in Colorado and Arizona is in direct contrast to the situation in the non-term-limited Indiana legislature, where dramatic changes in its members' occupational make-up strongly suggest a decrease in political ambition. While precisely identifying state legislators' actual occupations is notoriously difficult, virtually all of those interviewed about the Indiana Legislature agreed that the pattern of non-legislative employment there had changed in recent years, both during and before the study period. Indiana legislators once were mainly lawyers, farmers, and small business owners, but by the early 2000s, they were much more likely to be public employees (some of whom were compensated for their time working in the legislature), retirees, and those who did not need to hold a full-time job because their spouses did so.

The near-universal explanation for this change was that the demands of leg-islative life have turned the position into a full-time job, one for which the meager part-time salary no longer is adequate compensation. The result has been that legislators are now first elected later in life (perhaps contributing to the increasing average age) and burning out sooner. Our respondents be-lieved that because of this, new members during our study period were less politically ambitious than those who served in the 1970s and 1980s, whether in terms of running for higher office or even simply staying in the state legis-lature very long. One of our interviewees estimated that only about 25 per-cent of each new freshman class would be long-serving legislators, while the rest would serve a few sessions and return home. This sets up the dynamic that is common in non- and pre-term limited semi-professional state legisla-tures: many minimally committed, overworked rank-and-file members and a small cadre of senior old heads dominating the institution. In such an envi-ronment, term limits are unlikely to decrease political careerism.

Policy and Procedural Knowledge

Another argument of term limits' opponents was that the reform would re-sult in lawmakers who were merely dilettantes, whose lack of policy and pro-cedural knowledge would leave them unable to assess the veracity of the in-formation and advice of lobbyists, bureaucrats, and staffers (Cohen and Spitzer 1996; Polsby 1991). Later in this chapter, we will assess the cumula-tive effects of this and other potential effects on the relative power relation-ships among the various institutions. But a couple of questions from the JPTL knowledgeable observer survey allow us to test the effect of term limits on legislators' knowledge directly, and the results confirm the reform's oppo-nents' concerns. In a very clear and consistent pattern, these term-limited semi-professional legislators are believed to be less knowledgeable about is-sues in their committees, statewide issues, and how the legislature operates after term limits, while in our control state, Indiana, the observers saw no change in these characteristics over the study period. Just as tellingly, the same pattern of observations was seen in response to a question about legis-lators' inclination to defend the legislative institution—in term limits states, this inclination decreased, while in the non-term-limits states, it stayed the same. Thus, according to these knowledgeable observers, term limits have led members of semi-professional legislatures to know less and care less about legislation and the legislature, respectively.

Electoral Competition

Another argument made by the proponents of term limits was that the re-form would increase competition for seats in the legislature (Citizens for

Term Limits 2002; U.S. Term Limits, Inc. 2003; Steen 2006). Incumbents were said to have an unfair advantage over their challengers, so opening up more seats by force would level the playing field and increase competition, both in primaries and in general elections. The chapters on Colorado and Arizona show that term limits' impact on electoral competition is not obvious in single-state analyses. In these states, the only evidence of greater electoral competition was the slight increase in the number of legislative candidates in the primaries and the increase in campaign spending. Of course, the latter change both parallels national trends and is also decried by term limits' advocates. On the other hand, the partisan composition of neither the Arizona nor the Colorado Legislature underwent dramatic transformation after term limits were imposed, as it might have done if electoral competition increased greatly. More important, these states experienced no decrease in uncontested legislative races, which would have been another indictor of more competition. Other scholars have suggested that term limits actually decrease attempts at unseating incumbents, with potential challengers simply waiting for an open seat and then battling it out with other challengers in the primary (Lazarus 2006; Cain, Hanley, and Kousser 2006). While the evidence from these semi-professional state legislatures does not test this hypothesis directly, it does fit with that scenario.

Political·competition in our control state, Indiana, during the study period looked much the same as it did in our term-limits states. First, the cost of campaigns increased and the process of fundraising, recruitment, and even campaign strategy became more centralized. Legislators used to be completely responsible for their own campaigns and their costs were low, often only $10,000–$30,000 for a senate seat, in the experience of some of our interviewees. But throughout the study period, intense fighting over a few targeted races pushed up average spending steadily. For example, the 2002 race in the 86th House district saw a Republican incumbent defeated by thirty-seven votes in a campaign where combined spending topped $825,000—for an Indiana House seat that paid $11,600 annually!

But extremely expensive fights were a rarity in Indiana during the study period, and while average campaign costs increased steadily, average electoral competition did not, at least at the micro-level. The usual election saw low turnover of individual members and of party seats. Figure 7.1 shows that Indiana typically had between 10 and 20 percent turnover in any given election, somewhat lower than what we saw in Colorado and Arizona, both before and after those states implemented term limits. Table 7.2 shows that, with the exception of the Republican Revolution of 1994 (which was quickly reversed in 1996), even less partisan change happened in legislative seats. This suggests a stable system and little electoral competition throughout the study period, at least in individual districts, paralleling the experience of Colorado and Arizona at this time.

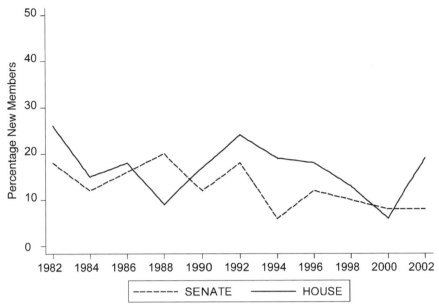

Figure 7.1. Membership Turnover in the Indiana General Assembly
Source: Correspondence with Gary Moncrief from data examined in: Moncrief, Gary, Richard Niemi, and Lynda Powell. 2004. "Time, Term Limits, and Turnover." *Legislative Studies Quarterly* 29:357-82.

At the macro-level, electoral competition in the Indiana General Assembly, especially in the House of Representatives, was much more intense than the micro-level numbers suggest. The Democrats continued to be competitive in the House, and even held control of the chamber toward the end of the period. In what is generally regarded as a solidly Republican state, this is surprising. Part of the explanation for this appears to be clever targeting

Table 7.2. Seats Changing Parties in the Indiana General Assembly

Election Year	House		Senate	
	D to R	R to D	D to R	R to D
1994	12	0	3	0
1996	2	8	1	1
1998	0	3	1	1
2000	0	0	2	1
2002	4	2	0	0
2004	5	2	1	0

Source: Calculated by the authors from the *State Legislative Election Returns, 1967–2003* database, Thomas M. Carsey et al., Release Version I. (http://www.unc.edu/~carsey/research/datasets/data.htm), and the Indiana Secretary of State (http://www.in.gov/sos/elections/elections/index.html).

of races by Democratic house leaders. In the 1998 election, only five of the one hundred house winners got 55 percent or less of the two-party vote, and all of these were Democrats. In 2000, there were eleven such competitive races, of which Democrats won seven. The Democratic majority worked to craft a favorable partisan gerrymander for the House after the 2000 census, and the effort appears to have been remarkably successful. In 2002, the Democrats kept their house majority of 51–49, and they did so with only 40.4 percent of the statewide vote. At the same time, the Indiana Senate had only modest electoral competition, at both the micro- and macro-levels, with its Republican majority better reflecting the statewide vote.

What Indiana's experience demonstrates is that electoral competition can rise, fall, or hold steady, regardless of term limits, sometimes depending on idiosyncratic events and personalities. But for the most part, the experience of Indiana on state legislative electoral competition in this period parallels those of Colorado and Arizona. Therefore, the comparison of these semi-professional legislatures on this dimension provides no evidence to support reformers' predictions that term limits would increase electoral competition in state legislatures.[2]

INSTITUTIONS

Next we consider the impacts of term limits on the three principal institutions of state legislatures: legislative leaders, committees, and parties. In general, we find that term limits have yielded less effective leadership, weakened committees, and increased the intensity of partisan conflict.

Legislative Leaders

In Arizona and Colorado, term limits appeared to have produced major changes in the role and power of legislative leadership. The direct effect has been to cause these leaders to come and go much more quickly than before term limits. As a result of their lack of experience and their lame-duck status, these term-limited leaders were seen as having far less power and control than did those leaders prior to term limits. In Arizona, where formal power is still concentrated in the hands of legislative leaders, more frequent challenges (notably the "Mushroom" and "Cellar Dweller" Rebellions) have made leaders' jobs more difficult. Likewise, in Colorado, term limits have fundamentally altered how legislative leaders function. As in Arizona, these leaders still retain certain formal powers, such as assigning members to committees and referring bills, but their traditionally strong informal influence has been weakened dramatically.

Two sets of factors appear to be at work in this weakening of term-limited legislative leaders; one set of factors has to do with the leaders themselves, and the other set pertains to the rank-and-file members. First, compared to leaders before term limits, term-limited leaders come into power with much less experience and a clearly defined and very short time to serve. Term limits force the most experienced legislators to retire, so leaders have, at most, only a few terms of legislative experience. Furthermore, both the Arizona and Colorado legislatures have fallen into an informal two-year rotation cycle for their leaders, with leaders moving up from one leadership post to another after each election. By the time a person rises to the top majority or minority party position, he or she is in his or her last term. Thus, as soon as they take their positions, top legislative leaders are lame ducks, with the concomitant short time horizon both for pushing an agenda and for wreaking retribution on those who would oppose them. In addition, as soon as leaders are elected, the competition for their successors begins, causing further distraction and limiting the leaders' power.

The second set of factors limiting leaders' power in term-limited legislatures is the willingness of rank-and-file members to challenge them, especially on policy. In a term-limited legislature, new members have a clearly delimited timeframe in which to accomplish their agenda. Therefore, they are less willing to defer to the wishes of leadership and more anxious to advocate their individual concerns sooner. These rank-and-file legislators fear their leaders' retribution less due to the latter's high turnover. The removal of this fear of retribution has had a crippling effect on the ability of leaders to control members in Arizona and Colorado. Combine this with the steady or increased political ambition of members of term-limited legislatures that we have already discussed and you have legislatures that are far harder to handle being run by leaders with fewer informal tools and less experience. This is not a good recipe for strong leadership control of a state legislature.

The contrast between the leadership of our term-limited, semi-professional state legislatures and our control legislature in Indiana could not be starker, further supporting our conclusion that term limits decrease legislative leadership power. Throughout the study period, Indiana had a relatively stable and strong set of legislative leaders (see Table 7.3). The leaders of the Indiana General Assembly are chosen by secret ballot within the party caucuses. Each chamber's majority party caucus elects its top leader—speaker of the House and president pro tempore of the Senate—and, as in many legislatures, these decisions are ratified by a party-line vote on the floor of the respective chamber. The Indiana Senate had remarkable consistency in its top leadership throughout and before the study period, with president tempore Senator Robert Garton being the longest serving legislative leader in the country by 2004.[3] While the speaker of the house is generally regarded as the

Table 7.3.   Leadership Turnover in the Indiana General Assembly

Year	House	Senate
1993–94	4 of 14	4 of 15
1995–96	2 of 14	8 of 17
1997–98	2 of 14	5 of 18
1999–00	1 of 16	6 of 20
2001–02	0 of 16	0 of 19
2003–04	3 of 16	11 of 21

Note: This table compares the number of members in leadership who were not in leadership the previous year to the total number of leaders. Leadership includes the entire formal list of majority and minority leadership.
Source: *Indiana General Assembly Legislative Directory*, Indiana Chamber of Commerce: Indianapolis, IN (various years).

most powerful position in the General Assembly, Garton's long tenure and pervasive control of the flow of business in the senate was felt by many of our interviewees to balance the stronger formal power enjoyed by the speaker. Currently, the speaker is Representative Patrick Bauer, who, in contrast to Senator Garton's long service, had completed just one session as speaker when we conducted our interviews at the end of our study period. Due to the changes in party control, speakers in the Indiana General Assembly have not had long tenures in recent decades. However, they have consistently had long service within their chambers and party caucuses.

In our study period, these top Indiana leaders also helped develop strong campaign support for their members. While most senators and representatives had safe seats and were expected to raise money to fund their own campaigns, the leadership targeted members in tight races and supplied them with extra resources. Prior to the study period, speakers typically did polling and recruiting, and they had established campaign committees, but the level of leadership involvement by both the senate and the house caucus leadership was much greater by the end of the study period, including such activities as raising and distributing considerable campaign money, direct mail, media campaigns, and telephone banks.

Thus, through long and unlimited tenure, formal powers, and campaign support, legislative leaders in Indiana were stronger and getting stronger throughout the study period. Contrast this with the clear decrease in power of legislative leaders in Arizona and Colorado after term limits and the conclusion is clear. For good or ill, term limits unmistakably have reduced the power of legislative leaders in these semi-professional state legislatures.

Committees

Legislative committees in Arizona and Colorado also suffered from term limits. In both states, the turnover of committee members increased modestly, decreasing the committees' ability to examine and craft legislation with care and knowledge. There was a consensus among observers that committee members were less informed on issues and more poorly crafted bills were getting to the chamber floor due to this lack of knowledge. The most important effect of term limits may have been on the greater turnover of committee chairs, who are now taking up their gavels with less experience, procedural knowledge and skills, and policy information than before the reform. According to observers, this has led to committee systems in these states characterized by far more chaos and incivility than before term limits.

In our control state, Indiana, the senate and house committee systems were taken quite seriously throughout the study period. No significant changes were reported in either the formal or informal operations or power of the committees. Few amendments to bills reported out of committee were made on the floor in a given session, and while each chamber has a provision for bill discharge, they are almost never used. Indeed, in 1988, the house passed a rule to make it harder for the speaker to pull bills from committee for floor action, and that rule was in effect throughout the study period. In both chambers, the number of committees was relatively stable, and there was little turnover of chairs. Thus, the stability and importance of Indiana's standing committees and the change in those of Arizona and Colorado suggest that term limits do indeed yield a significant degradation of the power and role of these bodies. If standing committees are central to the effective and efficient operation of a state legislature (Francis 1989), then term limits may also be said to degrade policymaking in the states.

Political Parties, Partisanship, and Comity

The impact of term limits on the role of party, partisanship, and comity in our semi-professional legislatures is less obvious than the impact on leadership or committees. First, there is no clear effect of the reform on the partisan balance in a chamber. None of the states—term limited or control—saw a major change in the balance in either of its chambers. Republicans held handy majorities in both chambers of the Colorado and Arizona bodies and the Indiana Senate throughout the study period. The Indiana House switched party control in 1998, 2004, and 2006 and had a close balance throughout the study period.

But trends in the partisanship attitudes and comity in these bodies is less easy to pinpoint with our data. On one hand, the studies of the term-limited Arizona and Colorado legislatures found that participants in, and observers of, these bodies believed that there was an increase in partisanship and a decrease in comity after term limits were implemented. This was attributed to long-serving moderates being termed-out and replaced by more ideologically extreme legislators, the lack of time for members to make friendships and respectful relationships across the aisle, and the loss of old heads who indoctrinated new members into a legislative process that was less confrontational, partisan, and ideological. These changes in the working atmosphere of these term-limited legislatures was further attributed to some of the other effects of term limits, such as weakened leadership and committees, more members looking to make an immediate impact on policy, and the general lack of issue understanding associated with new legislators.

While those in the term-limited legislatures themselves attribute these changes to term limits, a look at the working relationships in our control state raises some doubts here. Historically, Indiana has long had strong, competitive legislative parties, but with some differences emerging between the house and the senate in the last decade. In partisan balance, the house has been very competitive while the Republicans have maintained solid control of the senate. For example, at the end of the study period, the Democrats held a bare one-vote edge (51–49) in the house compared to the Republican dominance in the senate (32–18). While the senate has been under Republican control for all but two years since 1970, the house has been closely split since 1992, including suffering through a contentious power sharing arrangement that arose out of a 50–50 tie following the 1996 election. These close margins have led to vigorous partisan conflict and high levels of party cohesion in the house.[4] In the senate, the Republicans' longstanding, comfortable majority and non-confrontational leaders have led to a substantially less partisan atmosphere than in the house. Thus, the factor that appears to be determining the level of partisanship in the chambers in this study is not term limits, but the competitiveness of the parties themselves, and the fact that partisanship seems to be increasing everywhere over the course of the study period.

On the other hand, a striking feature of our interviews with observers of the Indiana General Assembly is that even during discussions of the high, and increasing, levels of partisanship that characterize that body, our interviewees seemed to have consistently positive opinions about their opponents, the level of comity in the process, and the quality of policymaking in general in the state. One legislator said that she frequently had informal conversations with members of the other party at receptions and dinners, and through these functions got to know them as individuals. This is confirmed by the JPTL's Knowledgeable Observers survey, where Indiana scored the highest of the nine study states on the item about participants being "collegial and courteous to other members." When asked about this directly, a legislator answered that, yes, almost everyone behaved quite respectfully because "we all know one another."

At least part of this comity among participants in the Indiana legislative process can be attributed to the development of long-term relationships among these actors, as was mentioned directly or indirectly by many of our interviewees. Furthermore, interviewees described the socialization and mentoring processes that long-serving members—old heads—spearheaded formally and informally both to introduce new members to other members and to demonstrate the importance of cooperation and mutual respect among legislators in making the process run smoothly and well. Thus, if term limits appear to have had little effect on the partisanship or party balance of these semi-professional legislatures, it seems to have affected the comity of the institutions indirectly. Without the old heads to mentor the new members and without their ability to establish long-term relationships among one another, the comity of these bodies has deteriorated.

BALANCE OF POWER

To this point, we have focused on term limits' effects on the behavior of state legislators. Of course, as legislative behavior changes, so may the behavior of those who regularly interact with lawmakers, as those non-legislators adapt to changing circumstances. In this section, we explore the question of whether term-limited legislatures have their power reduced relative to other actors in the policymaking process: the governor, lobbyists, and legislative staff.

Governor

The governor seems a likely beneficiary of the changing political environment surrounding term-limited state legislatures since those features of a legislature that have historically been important in supporting its role in policymaking—especially leadership and committees—have been degraded by the reform. But mapping out the cause-and-effect relationships between gubernatorial power and term limits is difficult due to the small number of cases available and the fact that any changes are confounded by differences in governors' personalities and political and administrative skills.

Colorado has historically had a weak governor, but this seems to be changing in the term-limited system. The governor has become increasingly aggressive in asserting his power, particularly with regards to budgetary matters. He has used the veto more than usual, and he has taken steps to reduce the ability of the legislature to use the line-item budget in its favor. While this change is not wholly attributable to term limits, term limits probably were responsible for the legislature's reluctance, or inability, to fight back against the increasingly aggressive actions of the governor. One effective tactic of the governor that was directly related to term limits was his moving into his cabinet or sub-cabinet many termed-out legislators. This not only gave him a team with strong links and leverage with the legislature, it also suggested that soon-to-be-departing legislators might want to acquiesce to his wishes if they wanted good post-legislative employment with the state. Likewise, Arizona went from governors who were weak or damaged by ethical concerns just before and early in the study period to having governors who appeared to be stronger after term limits were implemented.

Thus, in the single-state studies, it appears that term limits may increase a governor's influence in semi-professional states. However, an examination of our control state demonstrates that this conclusion may be premature. Institutionally, Indiana's governor is relatively weak (Beyle 2004). And indeed, during our interviews with those in and around the legislative process, the governor was rarely mentioned spontaneously. When asked directly about the role of the governor in legislative policymaking, respondents indicated the strongest governor had been Robert Orr (Republican, 1980–1988) and that more recent governors (including all those in our study period) had left a "vacuum" in terms of agenda-setting and policy leadership. While this lack of involvement with the legislature may have been due to all three of these governors being Democrats facing one or two chambers controlled by Republicans, our interviewees seem to believe that it was more a matter of their personal styles than anything inherent in the political culture of the state or the constitutional limitations of the governor's office. In short, while there was some mixed evidence in the JPTL's knowledgeable observer survey that governors in states with semi-professional legislatures gained power after term limits, the more detailed evidence from interviews suggests that any such changes in gubernatorial power is not necessarily attributable to term limits.

Lobbyists

A comparison of these three semi-professional state legislatures suggests that not only have term limits changed the influence of lobbyists, but they have also transformed the way lobbying is conducted. In Arizona, perceptions about the influence of lobbyists depend on who was asked. Veteran legislators typically reported that new legislators were increasingly dependent on lobbyists for information, while newer legislators said that they were very suspicious of lobbyists and their information. Legislators in Colorado appeared to increase their reliance on lobbyists, but legislators also expressed a good deal of leeriness about lobbyists and their information.

These perceptions in the term-limited states were in stark contrast to those we found in the control state. Our observers of the Indiana Legislature characterized the relationship between lobbyists and the legislature in quite positive terms. Veteran legislators reported relying regularly on lobbyists both for political information about constituency preferences and effects and for policy guidance on ways to craft legislation to achieve a particular objective. Committee chairs among our interviewees said they tried to talk with lobbyists on both sides of an issue to get a complete picture. Overall, the relationship between lobbyists and legislators in Indiana was seen as well developed, well understood, and well valued by legislators and staff. Thus, the change in the term limits states and the lack thereof in the control state suggests that term limits did indeed decrease the respect legislators have for lobbyists and, thus, it is likely that their influence and the extent to which their information is used in the legislative process have been reduced.

But while these descriptions of lobbying, lobbyists, and their relationship to legislators in the term limits and control states are quite different, the JPTL's knowledgeable observer survey shows no discernible difference in the perceptions of lobbyists' overall influence over lawmaking. On average, the survey respondents in each of these three states believed there to be a moderate rise in lobbyist influence over the study period. What explains this apparent contradiction? A closer look at the interview data shows that while things indeed did change for lobbyists after term limits—and in fact, they changed dramatically—Lobbyists have adapted very well to their new environment, allowing them to sustain their influence.

The single-state analyses of Arizona and Colorado made clear the change in how lobbyists operated after term limits. In both Arizona and Colorado, term limits removed the importance of long-term relationships between veteran members and lobbyists. This served to level the playing field for younger lobbyists and those who rely on information rather than personal connections in their work. Lobbyists were also thought to be putting more effort into educating and cultivating relationships with new members. And with all these new members, the job of the lobbyist was made more difficult by term limits.

But our respondents in Indiana also suggested that the lobbyist-legislator relationship had changed, both during the study period and before. First, this relationship had become more formal than in years past, with less wining and dining and more provision of lawmaking support. There was also some feeling that the lobbyists in Indiana were "less powerful but more necessary" than in the past. There were more lobbyists, so members had multiple sources of information on important issues, and since the issues were more complex, lobbyists' policy expertise was more important.

So in this respect, the changing role of lobbyists is similar in the term-limited and non-term-limited state legislatures. Lobbyists of each of these semi-professional legislatures became more important and busier during the study period. This may be the result of similar pressures and constraints that override term limits. Increased constituent demands, growing policy complexity, and more intense interest group activity may simply be overwhelming these part-time lawmakers, forcing them to rely more on lobbyists and forcing these lobbyists, increasingly in competition with more of their colleagues, to work harder. The difference may only be in the attitude that lawmakers in the term limits and non-term-limits states have toward these lobbyists and their own need for them. While non-term-limited legislators, many of whom have either been in office for several years or have been socialized by their senior colleagues, appreciate the job that lobbyists do, less-experienced, term-limited legislators use their help, but resent having to do so.

Staff

While state legislative staff usually work quietly and unobtrusively in state capitols, they loom large in analysts' thinking about the effects of term limits. Like governors, lobbyists, and other non-legislators who work in and around the state lawmaking process, these staffers were predicted—for good or ill—to gain influence after term limits, primarily due to their time and expertise (Cohen and Spitzer 1996; Polsby 1991). But semi-professional legislatures notoriously lack the large and stable staff corps of fully professionalized legislatures, like in California and Ohio. Indeed, Kousser (2006) found that while staff in some respects take up the slack for less-experienced term-limited legislators in California, they could not do so in less professionalized legislatures. Supporting this line of thought, the JPTL knowledgeable observer survey yields little evidence of staff overall influence changing more in term limits states than in non-term-limits states during the study period.

However, interviewees in both term-limited semi-professional legislatures in this study did report an increase in the importance of legislative staff, but the change was somewhat different in each state. In Arizona, these observers reported that the nonpartisan staff became more important in providing basic information on how the legislative process worked and that the partisan staff became more important in providing policy direction. Some observers even felt that the partisan staff had gained too much influence. In Colorado, on the other hand, only the nonpartisan staff was seen to have grown in influence, through the provision of both procedural advice and policy analysis. Little change in the role or importance of legislative staff during the study period was reported in Indiana. Thus, while term limits may well lead the legislature's staff to play a more prominent role in the legislative process, the specific changes that occur in a given semi-professional body depend on the ways in which those staff were arranged prior to term limits being implemented.

CONCLUSION

Semi-professional state legislatures have perhaps the hardest job of any of the fifty-one state and national lawmaking bodies in the United States. Professionalized legislatures—such as those in California, Ohio, and Illinois—govern larger and more complex states, to be sure, but they have far more time, money, and staff at their disposal to analyze public problems, weigh arguments, and make decisions. At the other end of the spectrum, citizen-legislatures—such as those in Arkansas, Maine, and Kansas—have somewhat less money, staff, and time than do the semi-professionals, but they typically lack the diversity of population and economy and the major urban centers that states with semi-professional legislatures have. Semi-professional state legislatures—like those in Arizona, Colorado, and Indiana—typically have resources that resemble those of citizen-legislatures more than those of professional legislatures, but they govern states that have more in common with those that have professional legislatures than those that have citizen-legislatures. Historically, semi-professional legislatures have dealt with this dilemma by developing a cadre of old heads, senior legislators who devote extra effort to their legislative responsibilities, allowing the legislative process to work well and indoctrinating new members into the legislative culture, for good or ill. Given this coping mechanism of these semi-professional legislatures, there was good reason to suspect that they would be especially affected by term limits.

That said, perhaps the most surprising finding of this study is the muted nature of term limits' impacts on semi-professional legislatures. These have not become Jeffersonian-Platonic ideal legislatures, as term limits advocates had hoped, but neither have they become completely dysfunctional, as the reform's opponents had feared. Term limits do not appear to have changed the demographic composition of these bodies in any significant way. Electoral competition has not increased, and the influence of governors, legislative staff, and lobbyists has not changed greatly.

But term limits have wrought some changes in these legislatures, even if they have been less dramatic and more complex than either the reformers or their opponents had predicted. Some of the change we found in these semi-professional legislatures is attributable to the loss of old heads in the chambers. By definition, term limits create a body in which there are none of the long-serving members upon which semi-professional legislatures have long relied. As a result, legislative leaders are less powerful under term limits, due to their high turnover and reduced experience. Committees and committee chairs are less influential for the same reasons. These are very significant changes, since legislative leaders and committees are probably the two most important institutions in state legislatures. Strong leadership and hard-working committees with knowledgeable members are needed for our legislatures to play an effective policymaking role in the states. Thus, term limits' weakening of leaders and committees in semi-professional legislatures is not a positive development for the effectiveness of our state legislatures.

Most of term limits' other effects that we have identified may be attributed to changes in the legislators themselves. These changes may simply be caused by the lack of members' experience that term limits necessitate. Legislators are less knowledgeable of the issues because they simply have not had time to learn more. They know and care less about the legislature itself because they have less professional and emotional investment in it. These attributes of inexperience are exacerbated by the lack of old heads being there to help socialize and acculturate new members.

Another set of changes in legislators that term limits seem to have caused is perhaps less benign, especially from the perspective of term limits reformers. These reformers had hoped that term limits would purge state legislatures of professional politicians, those who thought of politics as a career and, therefore, acted while in office in ways that benefited themselves, rather than in ways that benefited their constituents or the state as a whole (Will 1993; Fund 1992; Petracca 1991a). Their ideal was a body made up of citizen-legislators, serving briefly, bringing their personal experiences, expertise, and ideas to state lawmaking. But as we have seen, term limits have not eliminated thoughts of a long-term political career; these thoughts have just been modified. Rather than planning a long career in the state legislature, term-limited legislators look to other offices to satisfy their goals.

Ironically, term limits in semi-professional legislatures may even encourage political careerism. Under term limits, a lawmaker with any amount of political ambition knows that he or she must look beyond the legislature, and so begins thinking of his or her next office early on. Such an incentive structure may even attract more people who see the legislature primarily as a launching pad for their career. And regardless of any such differences in recruitment, term limits—especially short ones—leave many legislators' political appetites far from satisfied, encouraging them to run for higher office. Without term limits, members will be more prone to stay in their safe legislative seats as long as their political ambition burns, since moving on risks the loss of their current political position (Lazarus 2006). In a semi-professional state legislature, this can mean frustration, overwork, and burnout, decreasing a legislator's interest in another office. While we do not have the sort of evidence needed to test this hypothesis rigorously, the patterns of behavior in the three semi-professional state legislatures in our analysis fit this scenario well.

Thus, term limits have had a significant impact on semi-professional state legislatures, even just a few years after their implementation. These effects were not as dramatic as predicted by those in the battle over the reform's adoption in the 1990s. Some of these effects have been subtle and some have been unexpected. Furthermore, it is important to remember that some years may pass before the various political actors in these states understand term limits fully and adapt to them completely. Indeed, some of the early effects may cause reactions that lead to other changes down the line. For example, lobbyists may develop more effective means of alleviating new legislators' trepidations about dealing with them and, thereby, gain more influence. Or legislators may hire more legislative staff to compensate for some of the shortcomings in their policy and procedural knowledge. As with any political reform of this magnitude, term limits merit long-term monitoring, especially in those legislatures that are the most susceptible to problems that the reform could cause—the semi-professional state legislatures.

NOTES

1. We would like to thank Brian Bartoz, Nathan Bennett, and Ricardo Herdandez for their research assistance on this chapter, and Tom Carsey and Gary Moncrief for some of the data used in our analyses.

2. Term limits may affect electoral competition for other offices by terming out politically experienced legislators before their ambition is spent. These termed-out legislators may go on to seek seats in Congress, local offices, or other positions (Tothero 2003; Powell 2000; Lazarus 2006). The JPTL did not collect data to test this potential effect of term limits.

3. Senator Garton served as president tempore from 1980 until he was defeated in his 2006 Republican state senate primary.

4. This is evident in roll call voting data from the 1999–2000 sessions, where the R^2 between party membership and NOMINATE scores (which measure roll call vote liberalism-conservatism) calculated for the competitive votes for the house is .951. Interestingly, in the senate, the relationship is just as strong (R^2=.957), demonstrating that partisanship is important in both chambers of the Indiana General Assembly.

III

CITIZEN LEGISLATURES

8

Term Limits in the Arkansas General Assembly: A Citizen Legislature Responds

Art English and Brian Weberg

In 1992, 59.9 percent of the voting citizens of Arkansas approved Amendment 73, a constitutional limitation on the terms of office of their state legislators. It was a banner year for the term limits movement, with a total of twelve legislatures joining the club that fall. In Arkansas the margin of victory was relatively low compared to the overwhelming voter approval of term limits in other states. But, whatever Arkansas citizens may have lacked in enthusiasm for Amendment 73, they made up for by the rigor of its provisions.

Compounded by a biennial session schedule, Arkansas' term-limit law may have a more restrictive effect on lawmakers than in any other legislature. Turnover among members has increased dramatically but there has been little change in demographic makeup, with the exception of women whose numbers have increased with term limits. Republicans also appear to have benefited from term limits, giving them a toehold in one of the nation's most dominant Democratic assemblies. New leadership and new power vested into leadership positions, especially in the House, have not countered a concurrent shift of power to the executive branch. Lobbyist influence may be declining as term limits cut off established relationships and force lobbyists to deal with a more freewheeling and less tradition-laden membership.

A BRIEF HISTORY

The effect of term limits on the Arkansas General Assembly must be viewed within the context of the legislature, the state's political culture, and the political environment surrounding the term-limits initiative. It should be first noted that Arkansas has a citizen legislature. The Assembly meets only in odd years for sixty days unless extended by a two-thirds vote. Legislators currently earn a constitutionally specified salary of $12,500 annually with periodic cost of living raises and modest salary bumps for the Speaker of the House and Senate President Pro Tem. Actual annual salaries as of July 1, 2007 were $15,060. The supporting staff is relatively small, growing only when the Assembly is in session. Legislators themselves have vocations outside the Assembly, especially in areas such as business, insurance and real estate; others are educators, administrators and attorneys. Most have deep roots in their communities, with those who reside within fifty miles of the Capitol commuting daily when the legislature is in regular biennial session and leaving the capital city for home on weekends. The state's political culture is an intimate one. Politicos in the state know each other and run into each other on a regular basis. The weekly newspapers in the counties and towns and the state's only major daily—the *Democrat-Gazette*—cover politics comprehensively. Seldom is a political development secret in Arkansas for very long and legislators, members of Congress, constitutional officers, and even a former president are seen in the general stores, movie theaters, and restaurants of the state on a frequent basis. Where else but in Arkansas can you call a United States Circuit Court of Appeals Judge and be put right through without a secretary asking who's calling, or see your United States Senator hitting balls next to you at the driving range, or be in a local restaurant and have the former President of the United States take a table only a few feet away?

It is surprising within such a context that term limits would gain so much favor with the state's electorate. That is not to say that the legislature and the state's other political institutions are viewed in such a positive light. Indeed, the high level of media scrutiny on the state's political institutions and their inhabitants often illuminates their misdeeds in greater proportion than perhaps in other states. Nonetheless, the adoption of term limits in Arkansas had more than one cause. First was the initiative of U.S. Term Limits, a national advocacy group which fervently believed that elected officials who had been in office for a long time, especially members of the United States Congress, were far more interested in their own career than the interests of the citizens who had elected them. For example, the preamble of Amendment 73 states very cogently the aims of U.S. Term Limits and its supporters:

> Preamble: The people of Arkansas find and declare that elected officials who remain in office too long become preoccupied with reelection and ignore their duties as representatives of the people. Entrenched incumbency has reduced voter participation and has led to an electoral system that is less free, less competitive, and less representative than the system established by the Founding Fathers. Therefore, the people of Arkansas, exercising their reserved powers, herein limit the terms of elected officials (Constitution of the State of Arkansas of 1874, 1996).

U.S. Term Limits and its allies had a point. During the time they were sponsoring term limit proposals in states with voter initiatives, Congress was embroiled in a banking scandal in which some members had written checks that were cleared by the House bank even when there were insufficient funds in their accounts. Even though members' salary deposits covered these "hot checks" at the end of the month, this preferential treatment did not set well with ordinary citizens. Many citizens may, in fact, have thought the members were drawing sums in addition to their taxpayer supported salaries. In Arkansas the scandal was highly visible with two of the four members of the state's congressional delegation having written hundreds of these types of checks. Both congressmen were to see their elected political careers end because of the scandal. The effect of the scandal on the congressional institution, the strength and passion of U.S. Term Limits, and an Arkansas General Assembly with few legislators willing to speak out against term limits, provided a very favorable environment for the adoption of term limits in Arkansas.

Amendment 73 limits lifetime service in the Arkansas Legislature to three two-year terms in the House and two four-year terms in the Senate. Citizens of the state who are eligible for elective office can anticipate a legislative career that will last no longer than fourteen years, assuming they win all of their elections and pursue the maximum opportunity to serve at the State Capitol, although it is possible, but rare, that a member of the Senate could serve a total of twelve years in that chamber if they draw a two year term during reapportionment. These are among the most restrictive state legislative term limits in the nation.

Two key features of the Arkansas Legislature compound the effects of Amendment 73. First, up until the advent of term limits, the influence of seniority and lengthy legislative service were hallmarks of the institution. Membership turnover averaged about 18 percent between 1988 and 1996 although several long-serving members enjoyed legislative careers measured in decades rather than years. Second, Arkansas is one of the only states that retains a biennial legislative session calendar. House members limited to three two-year terms attend only three regular floor sessions during their tenure. Term limits severely collapse the time legislators have to learn the nuances of state policy, the legislative process, the crafts of deliberation, compromise and leadership—or to accomplish their personal and political goals. Theoretically, a member of the House might serve only 180 days in his or her entire House career.

Amendment 73 took effect first in the Arkansas House in 1998 when forty-nine of the one hundred House members were termed out, resulting in an overall turnover that year of over 56 percent. Term limits hit the Senate in 2000 when thirteen of thirty-five Senators were forced to leave. Today, few members in the legislature who were first elected prior to the term limits era remain and the 2004 election marks at least the beginning of the end of their legislative careers.

COMPOSITION AND REPRESENTATION

One of the expected effects of term limits was that legislatures would experience dramatic turnover leading to new members and new ideas. In the Arkansas General Assembly turnover has historically been less than in most states. The reasons for this are several. For one, scholars have found that Arkansas legislators, with their deep roots in the community and their part-time status, were very happy running for term after term in the legislature (Rosenthal 1981). The part-time nature of the Assembly provided members with ample opportunity to earn a living in their primary vocation while also serving their constituencies as lawmakers. Reinforcing the lack of turnover was the one-party Democratic make-up of the state legislature and the lack of competitive elections. Many legislators stayed in the Assembly to make business connections and foster their private careers. In consequence, it was common for the legislatures of the 1970s and 1980s and earlier to have numerous members with ten years or more service. In the 78th General Assembly, which we use as baseline here because it was the last one prior to term limits, 81 out of 135 members had served ten years or more. Of course these long-serving legislators provided an ample target for those favoring term limits to argue there were too many legislators serving too long.

Once term limits were adopted higher turnover became a given. As Figure 8.1 dramatically shows, House turnover jumped to 56 percent in the first year term limits took effect. In the Senate the first effects were in 2001 and 2003 where turnover was almost 50 percent. Large numbers of new members are now a reality every two years, but as Table 8.1 indicates, many new Senate members are from the House and many of the new House members are from local government—primarily the county legislatures also known as the quorum courts. Several Senate members have even migrated back to the House. If term-limits supporters posited an Assembly of yeoman citizens coming directly from their communities without political or elected experience, that ideal has not been achieved. Still, term limits have changed the Arkansas General Assembly forever. With term limits in force there will never be another legislator like John Miller, who entered the House in 1959 and served almost forty years. When he left the House in 1997 after term limits kicked in, he took that institutional experience and knowledge with him. Nor will there ever be another legislator like Max Howell who began his legislative career in the House in 1947 and entered the Senate in 1951 serving in that body until 1993. Howell and several other senior legislators dominated that Senate for many years, perhaps underscoring the argument made

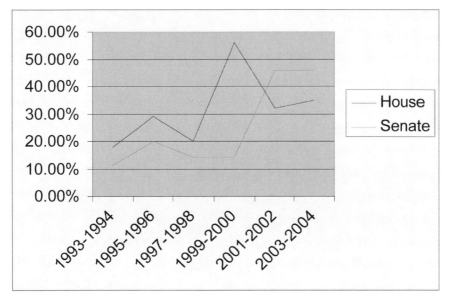

Figure 8.1. Membership Turnover in the Arkansas Legislature, 1993–2004

by term-limits proponents about long-serving legislators. Howell's power was illustrated by his traditional "duck dinner" just before the start of the Assembly's biennial session where he awarded the best committee leadership positions to his Senate supporters and cronies and, along with Knox Nelson, dominated the legislative life of the Senate. Howell's hold over the Senate was noted by fledging Governor Bill Clinton in 1978 when he quoted Howell as giving him the following advice about his nascent governorship: "Son, I've been in politics since you were born; I'll probably be here when you die; I'll sure enough be here when you're governor and then you'll wish you were dead" (Blair 1988, 167).

Demographic Change

Supporters argued that term limits would bring greater diversity to the Arkansas General Assembly. New members would be younger and the divesting of incumbent seats would allow more females and minorities to enter the Assembly. So far this has not occurred to any great degree. The average age of legislators, for example, has remained remarkably stable in both chambers. Where legislators seemed to grow old in the chamber prior to term limits, the ages of those taking their places has remained in the high forties and low fifties. As has been noted, legislators are deeply immersed in their communities. The kinds of people who seem to be running and

Table 8.1. County Legislative Experience in the Assembly and Prior House Experience in the Senate, 1985–2007

Year	1985	1987	1989	1991	1993	1995	1997	1999	2001	2003	2005	2007
County Legislative Experience	8	10	11	12	15	17	17	18	21	17	13	14
Senators with House Experience	9	8	8	6	7	9	8	8	21	29	29	28

Table 8.2.   Demographic Composition—Arkansas House

Year	% Democrat	% Non-White	% Women	Ave. Age
1991-1992	91.00	9.00	8.00	52
1993-1994	90.00	10.00	12.00	53
1995-1996	88.00	9.00	16.00	52
1997-1998	87.00	10.00	22.00	51
1999-2000	76.00	12.00	20.00	47
2001-2002	70.00	12.00	14.00	50
2003-2004	70.00	12.00	15.00	50

winning legislative seats reflect the maturity of their occupations, with an increasing number of retired people running for legislative office. Perhaps young aspirants to a political career have been dissuaded by the more limited opportunity to make a part-time career in the Assembly for their law practice or business brought about by term limits. It was this type of legislator, the "advertiser," that according to Barber (1962) used legislative service to promote his or her vocation. These legislators were not, however, the active "lawmaker" legislators who spoke forcefully on the floor, introduced legislation, and embraced the legislative process at every turn. Nonetheless, term limits has forced legislators to become more like Barber's "lawmakers" with a much more limited legislative career in front of them. And, if there are now fewer "advertisers" in the Assembly, this would seem to be a strong argument for term limits. Additional evidence and study are needed to flesh out these propositions.

As shown in Tables 8.2 and 8.3, term limits have not had a significant effect on the number of African Americans and females in the Arkansas Legislature either. African-American membership has been extremely stable over the last decade. Although female representation in the legislature has increased, term limits is likely only a partial cause given the greater representation of women in elective bodies throughout the nation since the late 1980s and early 1990s.

Table 8.3.   Demographic Composition—Arkansas Senate

Year	% Democrat	% Non-White	% Women	Ave. Age
1991-1992	88.57	8.57	2.85	50
1993-1994	85.71	8.57	2.85	49
1995-1996	80.00	8.57	2.85	48
1997-1998	80.00	8.57	2.85	48
1999-2000	82.86	8.57	0	50
2001-2002	77.14	8.57	11.43	49
2003-2004	77.14	8.57	20.00	52

What has changed dramatically is the number of females in the Arkansas Senate. In 1991 the Senate continued its long time pattern of female under-representation with only one female member. However, with the first impact of term limits taking place in the Senate in 2001, followed by a second wave in 2003, the percentage of women rose to 11 and then 20 percent. Was term limits responsible for this large increase in female senators? We believe that it was for a reason related to term limits. Table 8.1 shows the large number of current Senators with House experience. Five of them are women who have served in the House, indicating that incumbency and House experience provide a strong jumping-off point for women interested in the Senate, a chamber that before term limits seldom had female representation.

Elections

Supporters of term limits believed that Arkansas elections, particularly leg-islative elections, would become dramatically more competitive with the on-set of term limits. If true, more competitive elections would certainly be a change in the state's electoral culture. Arkansas is not a heavily partisan state although it elects mainly Democrats. Most Democratic candidates tend to be center-right or conservative in their political philosophy. Republican candi-dates tend to be more to the right of the political spectrum than Democrats are to the left. Democratic and Republican activists, however, following a national trend tend to be more polarized (Barth 2003). Of the two parties, the Repub-licans are the more cohesive and ideological. Arkansas voters, like most of the candidates who run for Arkansas state and local office, tend to be more gener-ally conservative and not strongly party driven. Several of the state's leading po-litical scientists have pointed out that the state's largest political party may in fact be its independents (Blair 1988; Schreckhise, Parry, and Shields 2001).

In Arkansas incumbents frequently win elections at both the constitutional and state legislative level. Blair (1988), for example, found that no incum-bent in the Senate and only four in the House lost in primary challenges, with just one Senate incumbent tasting defeat in the general election—an electoral turnover rate of only four percent. It was expected that term limits would change that dynamic by encouraging primary challenges, creating open seats, and removing entrenched incumbents. Looking at the candidate filings for 2004 primary and general elections can give us some additional in-sight in assessing this proposition.

As shown in Table 8.4, the data do not support the notion of increased legislative competitiveness under term limits. In fact, only three incumbents were defeated in the general or primary elections. In the Senate, which oddly had no term-limited seats up in 2004, only four incumbents were chal-lenged, two by term-limited House members, one of whom was encouraged and financially supported by the Governor because of the incumbent's

Table 8.4. Legislative Elections, 2004 General Primary

	Seats Up for Election in November 2004	Contested Seats in May Primary	Incumbents Defeated in May Primary	Contested Seats in November General Election	Incumbents without Opposition in November General Election
Senate Total Seats = 35	18	4	1	3	11
House Total Seats = 100	100	27 (term-limited = 23) (not term-limited= 4)	2	27 (term-limited=16) (not term-limited = 11)	70

opposition to the Governor's school consolidation plan. The data also indicate that House term-limited seats were characterized by more primary challenges than untermed seats. That termed seats would generate more primary challenges is no surprise even though several termed seats had no primary or general election challengers. What is notable from the candidate filing data is that so few House incumbents drew general election opponents. Even though conventional political wisdom posits that the best time to beat an incumbent is in their first reelection, it appears that with seventy House members unopposed, would-be challengers may be waiting to run until an incumbent's final term. Coupled with a possible disincentive to run because of an abbreviated legislative career due to term limits and an increasing number of safe seats because of one-party dominance in certain regions of the state, this evidence raises very serious questions about candidates' choices under term limits.

A final unintended impact of term limits is evident when the names of the candidates filing for legislative office are closely examined. In several instances where the member is term limited, we found that a spouse or child of the term-limited incumbent had filed for the seat. Keeping the seat in the family as an incumbent's term ends is certainly not the norm, but it is also not surprising that this kind of "incumbency" occurs because of the strict term limits in Arkansas and the desire of some public officials to continue in office.

Representation

Arkansas legislators, as noted above, are part-time. Their occupations are those that would be found in any small and medium size town in a relatively rural state. Legislators are country lawyers, public school teachers, insurance and real estate agents, college professors, and general store merchants. Regular sessions, although longer since term limits, do not usually last over ninety days. During the session the pace is fast and furious. A 1991 study of work styles in the Arkansas General Assembly found that 75 percent of the legislators interviewed (N=36) worked at least fifty hours and 50 percent said they worked seventy hours or more a week during the regular biennial session. About two-thirds of these legislators also reported that they devoted about 70 percent of their time during the session to lawmaking activities (English 1991). About one-third of the sample, however, said they devoted at least half their time to constituent matters during the session and it was not unusual for legislators to spend fifteen to twenty hours a week when not in session handling constituent problems in the district and attending interim committee meetings in Little Rock. The evidence we have regarding Arkansas legislators is that they are hardworking people who take the job of representation seriously.

**Table 8.5. Legislative Roles in the
Arkansas General Assembly**

	1983	*1991*
Trustee	23%	8%
Delegate	25%	34%
Politico	52%	58%
	N=85	N=38

Arkansas legislators are very accessible to their constituents. During the session citizens call the Capitol switchboard, frequently leaving messages asking their legislators to support a particular bill. The home numbers of the legislators and their e-mails are readily accessible to constituents and, when back in the district, members often make a beeline for the general store, restaurant, gas station or other common meeting place to find out what his or her constituents are thinking. Given this array of "home style" activity it would seem that legislators would be expected to pick up on the instructions of their constituents and act as "delegates" in their representational behavior. Poised against this hypothesis is the expected effect from term limits that legislators would tend to act more as "trustees" in their role orientation because of a shortened legislative career and diminished accountability, especially in a legislator's final term.

As shown in Table 8.5, data from 1983 and 1991 data present an interesting insight into the representational attitudes of legislators prior to term limits. This evidence suggests that most Arkansas legislators—back in the days of low turnover and senior leadership—either looked to their constituents for guidance or exercised judgment depending upon the situational context of the issue they were confronting. The trustee role was taken by the smallest portion of legislators during both studies, especially in 1991, our baseline year. This finding suggests that Arkansas legislators did not perceive themselves as Burkean trustees in their representational style. Despite the fact that most legislative issues are neither highly visible nor directly relevant to a representative's district, the delegate and politico roles seemed to fit Arkansas legislators the best—a fit that made sense when considering the small and intimate world of Arkansas government and politics.

However, the data we collected from our 2002–2004 interviews and the knowledgeable observer study paint a somewhat different picture. A few legislative respondents thought that term limits weakened the legislator/constituent connection because many citizens no longer have a strong attachment to their representative. Studies and polls over the years have shown that many constituents do not even know the name of their representative or the office they hold. As several legislators mentioned in the 1991 study and our 2002–2003 interviews, they will sometimes meet constituents who ask, "Well Senator, how are things back in Washington?" The knowledgeable observers survey supports the view that Arkansas legislators are dealing with constituents in approximately the same ways as they did ten years ago in terms of communication styles: person to person meetings and mail. What is different, according to these observers, is that legislators are spending less time solving constituent problems, while placing more emphasis on generating pork for their district (Knowledgeable Observer Survey).

This latter finding can be interpreted in a couple of different lights. Getting pork for the district is a form of constituent service that usually points to a legislator's effectiveness in assisting constituents in the district. On the other hand, it might also be seen as a way for the legislator to claim credit as a means of using his or her term-limited office as a springboard to another elective or appointive office. Or, it could even indicate a move to a broader approach for the legislator in solving district problems—something that term-limit supporters would likely advocate—as opposed to individual problem solving for constituents that do not contribute to the greater good of the district. At this point insufficient evidence is available to decipher which representational strategy is most likely to be followed by term-limited legislators. Interviews and survey data suggest that representational relationships are likely to suffer more under term limits simply because the amount of time that a legislator has to develop relationships with constituents is so much less before a legislator is replaced than prior to term limits.

INSTITUTION

Leadership and Lobbyists

Two areas in which the impact of term limits is apparent are legislative leadership and the legislature's relationship with the fourth branch of government, lobbyists. Leadership in particular has undergone significant change under term limits, especially due to increased turnover (see table 8.6).

Table 8.6.   Committee Evolution in the Arkansas General Assembly

Year	Number of Committees	Number of Committees Chaired by Same Chairperson	Mean Seniority of Standing Committee Chairs
1977	30	4	19.7
1987	35	7	25.2
1997	36	0	16.3
2007	68	0	7.6

In the past, leadership, through formal position, seniority and legislative expertise, dominated the rank and file of the Arkansas legislature. Nowhere was this more evident than in the Senate of the 1970s and 1980s where Max Howell and Knox Nelson controlled the membership by assuming most of the key formal and informal positions of power themselves. For example, in Howell's last year in the Senate, he chaired the Senate's Judiciary and Efficiency Committee, sat on the powerful Joint Budget Committee, and was vice chair of the Rules, Resolutions, and Memorials Committee.

While leadership centralization characterized the Senate, a strong seniority system was dominant in the House (English and Goss 1986). Senior leaders dominated the legislative process, and it often took five or six terms in the House and several in the Senate before a legislator became a committee chair or vice chair. Those who offended the leadership in some way never achieved formal Assembly power despite numerous reelections. Two and three term legislators, never mind first-termers, had little power. They were expected to learn the ropes and not make waves. Senior committee chairs and members of the Joint Budget Committee ran the show, made the important decisions, and bargained for the Assembly on key issues with the governor.

Term limits brought change to both chambers in the following ways. First, with senior legislators removed from both the Senate and House, a leadership vacuum was created. In the Senate, power equalized and fragmented. Of the Senate's nineteen standing, joint, and select committees in 2003–2004, only one person—a newly elected but former long-serving member of the House—chaired more than one committee, which was a far cry from the days of Nelson and Howell when power was concentrated in just a few leaders. In the House a similar division of legislative power existed. Furthermore, in both the House and the Senate, Republicans, because of their increased numbers and seniority in a term-limited, more equalized legislature, found themselves chairing important committees on which they would not have even had the opportunity to serve in past legislative sessions. Second, under term limits the predictability of who becomes the Speaker of the House or Pro Tem of the Senate no longer runs along the formerly well-established track of seniority. In fact those positions now attract significant competition. For example, in a post-term-limits race for Senate Pro Tem, the most senior member of the Senate, a Republican, was defeated in an intense factional contest in which several of his own party's members actually supported his victorious Democratic opponent. Third, the Speaker of the House and the Pro Tem of the Senate, both somewhat ceremonial positions in the past (in part, because they were only one-session offices), have become more powerful relative to other legislators because their formal power now stands out relative to the junior status of other legislators. For example, as term limits approached and a Republican governor assumed office, House Democrats broke with tradition to elect the same person as speaker for two consecutive sessions in order to combat a Republican governor whom they opposed.

In the 84th Assembly, which confronted the highly charged issue of school consolidation, the Speaker of the House and Pro Tem assumed very visible positions in the media war with the governor over his plan. While they were not the only legislators involved, their central position as spokespersons for the Assembly thrust them into the fray much more than legislative leaders in the past, who often operated well under the media radar screen.

A fourth and very important impact of term limits on legislative leadership has been the change in leadership structure, particularly in the House. Since the invocation of term limits the House has gone simply from a Speaker, Speaker Pro Tem model to four assistant speakers Pro Tem, one for each Congressional district, widening the Speaker's leadership circle and assigning greater status to these legislators. The other related development is a new and striking one. In both the House and the Senate there are now formal floor leader positions—majority and minority leaders and whips—who by law also become members of the powerful Legislative Council, the body which essentially serves as the legislature when that full body is not in session. Also, in the House before term limits, committee placement was largely a function of seniority. Under term limits the Speaker of the House considers seniority, caucus recommendations, and individual member preferences. Under the new practices in the 2003 session House Republican members were able to stack the House Judiciary Committee so that they could successfully influence tort reform legislation. In the Senate, a less formal, clubby body even with term limits, committee selection is most influenced by seniority and majority party leadership.

Fifth, one of the most interesting, and in some ways, most attention-getting effects of term limits, has been on the experience levels of the leaders in the House and Senate. In the past, a legislator had to have upwards of fifteen to twenty years of legislative service before becoming Senate Pro Tem or Speaker of the House (English 2003). Under term limits Speaker designates are now selected in their second two-year term. House rules do specify, though, Speaker designates be selected in January of even-numbered years so as not to detract from the power from the current Speaker during the legislative session. Under this system the transition to a new Speaker can be made without overt conflict with the existing Speaker. In the Senate a member may be selected as Pro Tem just after reelection to a second four-year term. In consequence, recent Assemblies have seen incredibly youthful leadership, particularly in the House. For example, Speaker Bob Johnson was only thirty-three when he assumed the reins of the 82nd Assembly (1999), the first Assembly after term limits took effect. Similarly, Shane Broadway, first elected at twenty-four, became Speaker designate at twenty-six and Speaker at twenty-eight. It is fair to say that prior to term limits both of these legislators would have had to serve six or seven terms and been into their forties before they would have attained the legislative stature to run for Speaker or Pro Tem. Former Speaker Capps noted in an interview that "it took twenty years before I became Speaker. You had to wait your turn." Term limits in this sense have provided leadership opportunities based more on competitive merit than seniority. In past Assemblies seniority and merit were often considered together in the selection of leadership.

Finally, and perhaps most importantly, is the emergence of the Speaker as the most powerful legislator in the House. This is due primarily to the Speaker's power to appoint committee and subcommittee chairs and vice chairs, as well as the leadership team of assistant speakers and members of the House Management Committee. Since committee chairpersons and vice chairpersons are respectively paid an additional $200 and $100 per month in addition to the added prestige and power they have as chairpersons, there is a certain environment of goodwill that is created toward the Speaker. The rising importance of the Speakership under term limits was illustrated by the race for the Speaker designate position for the 2009 session. As the 86th session drew to a close the four candidates for Speaker were throwing elaborate receptions supported by lobbyist contributions in substantial part to line up commitments for the January 2008 election. Candidates for Speaker have formed leadership PACS to funnel contributions to potential supporters within the legislature (Brummett 2007). It is ironic that one of the impacts of term limits appears to be the creation of a more Congress-like campaign system for the selection of Speaker.

Although lobbyists appear to have increasing influence in the selection of House Speaker, there is little evidence of an overall increase in the influence of lobbyists on legislators. In general, lobbyists are disconcerted by the changes wrought by term limits. Long-term, cultivated relationships are no longer present. Lobbyists have always been influential in the Assembly and they frequently entertain legislators at group-sponsored breakfasts and evening receptions. Established groups that can hire contract lobbyists or have in-house lobbyists, such as utilities, the farm bureau, business interests, and teachers, are by far the most powerful groups in Arkansas (English and Carroll 1992). Term limits have not slowed the level of contacts made by lobbyists, but they have forced them to work harder. For example, at a 2004 meeting between legislative leaders and several powerful lobbyists, most of the agenda was taken up with a discussion of how term limits adversely effect the legislature-lobbyist relationship and made the legislative process that much more difficult. Another lobbyist complained about the amount of work it took to educate new legislators about key issues. Still, lobbyists are adapting to the new dynamics created by term limits. Our interviews found that lobbyists now try to identify potential legislative leaders very quickly, cultivating those relationships as soon as possible. Another strategy that groups are utilizing, and that appears to be on the rise, is the employment of termed-out legislators as lobbyists. Prior to term limits, although the top-rated lobbyist in an informal 1999 poll rated former Speaker Cecil Alexander the most powerful Arkansas lobbyist, most influential lobbyists tended to be in-house and contract lobbyists who had cultivated close relations with legislators over the years (*Arkansas Democrat Gazette*, 1999). In fact, out of the top thirty lobbyists, Alexander was the only former legislator. A similar newspaper poll, just four years later, found that four of the top ten most powerful lobbyists were former legislators, including two former Speakers of the House (*Arkansas Democrat Gazette*, 2003). Interest groups have realized they must work harder and longer to continue to maintain their level of influence prior to term limits. One way they are doing so is by hiring former influential legislators who have been termed out.

Committees

Committees have also been impacted by term limits. In the House, in particular, a major development starting with the 83rd General Assembly has been the institutionalization of a subcommittee structure. The subcommittee structure was expressly created to provide members with the opportunity to learn committee norms and operations and to provide members with the opportunity to prepare for holding leadership positions on the full standing committees in their second and third terms. Each of the ten standing committees now has three permanent subcommittees, each with a chair and vice chair.

While the vice chair of the standing committee usually winds up chairing one of the subcommittees, the result of this innovation has been to give many term-limited legislators the opportunity for additional committee responsibility and experience. In the 83rd Arkansas House, for example, twenty legislators were either chairs or vice chairs and twenty additional legislators chaired subcommittees. Of the one hundred members of the House, forty were either committee chairs or vice chairs. As the old joke goes even if you didn't know a House member, you would not be too far off by greeting him or her with "How are you today, Mr. (or Madam) Chairman."

One other aspect of the committee process that needs to be addressed is whether committees are functioning more effectively under term limits. Again while data are limited here to interviews and the results of the knowledgeable observers' survey, a couple of generalizations may be offered. First, several legislators thought that it was now much easier to get a bill out of committee because committee chairs were less skilled at killing bills, both good and bad. Second, as equality of power has been substituted for the committee chair's power, a larger number of bills are being introduced and adopted in the Assembly. While supporters of term limits point to these results as encouraging fresh ideas, opponents argue that term limits lead to the passing of more "bad" bills. According to the knowledgeable observer survey, over the past ten years, committee chairs have become much less knowledgeable about the issues before their committees, less courteous, less likely to seek public comment, less likely to amend bills in committee, less willing to compromise, and less polite to their committee peers. These data certainly support the idea that the committee process has been undermined by term limits. Nevertheless, our measurement of how well the committee structure is functioning under term limits could be improved with prospective rather than retrospective measures.

Staff

In the Assembly, staff assumes a central role because of the part-time institutional setting. Members have no personal staff unless they use their monthly $800 administrative stipend to hire a part-time person who can help with constituency work, especially during the regular session when long and harried workweeks are typical. Sometimes an intern from a local university or college is found, but the Assembly has always faced space constraints; House members, in particular, have few places for an intern to work because only the leadership has office space. The formal staff of the institution resides in the Bureau of Legislative Research supervised by the Legislative Council. The fifty-plus employees of the Bureau, along with a handful of staffers who work with each chamber directly (administrative support, information officers, legal counsel, personnel/fiscal officers and constituent relations specialists), constitute the staff of the Assembly. In addition, the legislature employs over two-hundred people in its Division of Legislative Audit, but these workers are generally not engaged in the day-to-day activity of the legislative process. The Bureau, in particular, is a key institution for new incoming legislators elected under term limits. Each committee has a Bureau staff member who provides support to one or more standing committees. The legislative bill drafting service of the Bureau is the key unit in drafting bills for legislators, who depend greatly on the office's ability to draft bills expertly and quickly.

Within this context it is clear that the Assembly's staff is very important to the operation of the legislature. With far fewer attorneys in the Assembly— and lobbyists uncertain about which legislator to approach to introduce their legislation—the four or five members of the Bureau's bill drafting services assume a critical role in the movement of legislation. With senior legislators now having just four years of experience in the House and, at most, ten years of experience in the Senate, it is arguable that staff members could increasingly supplant their expertise for that of legislators. This proposition would seem to be an even more likely one under term limits considering that many staffers in the Assembly have been there for a decade or more. Of the ten key staff listed in the 1991 Southwestern Bell legislative directory under the "officers of the House and Senate," six of them were still there at the beginning of the 2003 session. The parliamentarian of the House, for example, has been in that position since the 1973, and the Director of the Bureau of Legislative Research recently retired after the 2005 session after celebrating his fiftieth year of legislative service.

Given this small, but rapidly graying, "band of brothers" assisting the Assembly, staff influence would seem certain to increase, a concern because of the inherently undemocratic nature of unelected staff. Interestingly, data from our interviews and the knowledgeable observers survey do suggest increased staff influence but not in a pernicious manner (Knowledgeable Observer Survey). The survey data show that legislators now rely on staff to a higher degree than a decade ago, in a statistically significant way. Our personal interview data paint a picture of hardworking staff who, while asked to do more, stay well within the bounds of what legislative staff are expected to do: provide research and support, but not policy advice. For example, the Bureau's legal staff, after providing appropriate counsel, will defer to legislators' preferences, even in cases where those preferences duplicate existing laws or where they might cause constitutional defects in the draft legislation. Committee staffers are happy to respond to questions even though many questions may be ones that veteran legislators would have automatically known in preceding sessions. Several of our staff respondents pointed out that while term-limited legislators know less and depend upon them more, they also treat them with more respect and deference than legislators did prior to term limits.

While all of this is very logical, perhaps it might also be explained by the "role reversal" of legislators and staff. Before term limits many Arkansas legislators had as much or more seniority in the Assembly as staff. With term limits, legislators are now perennially the new kids on the block compared to most legislative staff. The greater dependence on staff has made them more important in a term-limited legislature, but so far it appears that staffers have not injected themselves inappropriately into the policymaking process. Finally, the Assembly responded to term limits by shoring up its staff expertise. For example, the lack of senior legislators has meant a concomitant decrease in budget expertise among legislators, especially in the House with the departure of two former legislators who had served both in the House and the Senate and then returned to the House. In response, in the 86th Assembly the Speaker's office added the Speaker of the 85th Assembly to its staff as an administrative assistant/budget analyst and a legislative/policy analyst. This former Speaker, whose first session was in 1971, is the legislature's acknowledged expert on education. In the Senate, constituent services were bolstered with the addition of the position of Coordinator of Constituency Services and the hiring of the Bureau of Legislative Research's leading budget analyst as Senate Chief of Staff.

LEGISLATIVE PROCESS

Party Change and Partisanship

Term limits have also had an impact on party representation in the Assembly. Long dominated by Democrats, term limits opened up long-time Democratic seats in areas of growing Republican strength and gave Republican representation a tremendous boost.

As Table 8.7 illustrates, in term-limited seats Republicans picked up eighteen seats in the House and three in the Senate whereas Democrats could only turn one seat their way in both the House and the Senate in 2000 and 2002. Of course, Democratic dominance in the Assembly continues, but Republicans now have enough seats to warrant minority leaders in the both chambers and the number of Republican chairpersons, given only token representation in the not too distant past, now has to be taken into consideration by the majority party. In addition, since most tax increases under the lengthy, highly detailed and frequently amended Arkansas Constitution require a three-fourths majority for passage, Republican legislators are now at veto strength in both chambers. The much higher number of Republicans in the House also allows the GOP the opportunity to be much more competitive for seats in the Senate and statewide constitutional and congressional office in the future. The increased number of Republicans in the House, aided by term limits, has provided a sort of farm system for a state party long in need of grassroots representation. In the 2004 election cycle, for example, the term limited Republican minority leader ran for the 2nd Congressional seat (Little Rock

Table 8.7. Seats Changing Parties in the Arkansas Legislature, 1992–2002

	House				Senate			
	Untermed		*Termed*		*Untermed*		*Termed*	
Year	*D to R*	*R to D*	*D to R*	*R to D*	*D to R*	*R to D*	*D to R*	*R to D*
1992	0	0	—	—	—	—	—	—
1994	0	0	—	—	1	0	—	—
1996	4	2	—	—	2	0	—	—
1998	3	1	—	—	1	1	—	—
2000	0	1	11	1	0	1	1	0
2002	0	0	6	0	1	0	3	0

and Central Arkansas), while a Republican Senate member from tradition-ally Republican Northwest Arkansas won the Republican nomination to oppose first term U.S. Senator Blanche Lincoln. Not to be outdone, a Dem-ocratic term-limited member of the House ran for the 3rd Congressional seat in Republican-dominated Northwest Arkansas, the state's fastest grow-ing region in population and economic development. This evidence lends credibility to the claim that term limits can stimulate an increase in two party competition.

Civility and the Rules of the Game

Legislatures, of course, are human institutions. In Arkansas, the Assembly brings together one hundred members in the House and thirty-five members in the Senate every two years to represent constituents, make law, and mon-itor the other institutions of state government. Like virtually all-legislative bodies, the Assembly operates with both formal and informal rules, the lat-ter deeply ensconced in the legislative culture and often more important than the formal rules of the legislative process. How term limits has im-pacted the informal workings of the Assembly is thus a very important ques-tion because it goes to the heart of the legislative process—the ability to work together in the stressful situations of who gets what, when, and how. One of the few studies that examined the Assembly's informal rules and folkways found that legislators mentioned fifteen unwritten rules, of which four were particularly important: apprenticeship, keeping one's word, respecting col-leagues, and specialization (English and Carroll 1983).

While our data are limited, it appears that term limits have created a very different working environment for legislators. First, and very simply, term limits have affected the norms of apprenticeship and specialization. Legis-lators now simply do not have time for an apprenticeship and, in conse-quence, their assertiveness in some situations may impact adversely upon institutional civility. Several of our respondents mentioned that legislators do not seem to care as much about their colleagues' feelings or keep their word with lobbyists about supporting their legislation.

Legislative specialization also seems to have suffered. For example, it ap-pears that term limits have made legislative service less attractive to attor-neys, in part, because limited terms minimize the vocational side-benefits traditionally associated with service. To illustrate, in the 1991–1992 session the Senate had sixteen members with law degrees. In the 2003–2004 Sen-ate, however, just two members had law degrees, underscoring a tremen-dous decrease in legal expertise. Those opposed to term limits point to the inimical effects they can have by terming out legislators with specialized ex-pertise in important areas of the legislative process.

Data from the knowledgeable observer survey support the proposition that new legislators are less likely to know and embrace the unwritten rules of the game. Legislators are less likely than ten years before to be defenders of the legislature when it is under attack, and they are less likely to be collegial and courteous in committee meetings or generally polite to other members. Our overall findings call into question the view that term limits contribute to a smoother functioning legislature. A state legislature that is less likely to "get along and go along" is probably less likely to be efficient, responsive, and accountable in dealing with the incredible diversity of demands that must be confronted and reconciled.

Balance of Power: Executive/Legislative Relations

Relationships with the executive branch are harder to analyze. The Arkansas governor has, in fact, many advantages the Assembly does not have. In Arkansas the executive has both the general and the item veto, although both can be overridden by a simple majority of the Assembly. The executive has broad appointment powers, including the power to appoint members to the politically powerful and constitutionally independent Highway and Fish and Game Commissions. In addition the governor appoints members to a myriad of commissions and boards that regulate the state's businesses and officiate over its educational institutions. And, the governor is the only elected official under the constitution that can call the legislature into special session, which gives him extraordinary power in terms of timing and setting the agenda for the legislature. Perhaps even more significantly, the governor is at the center of the state's political system at all times simply because the job is "full time" with a support staff of over fifty people.

The governor and his chief budget officers, the head of the Department of Finance and the Administration Director in particular, comprise the primary budgetary force in state government as the Assembly has become increasingly reactive in this most important of all executive/legislative relations, especially as senior leadership has moved out of the legislature. The governor also dominates the media stage of the state political system from his state-of-the-state address to his many opportunities for press conferences, and television and radio appearances. One regular radio program called "Ask the Governor" provided Governor Huckabee with a very effective bully pulpit to chide legislators during the 2004 session over their opposition to his school consolidation plan. And, as has been evidenced by our interviews and observations, under term limits experienced cabinet heads seem to have a greater advantage over legislators seeking information about their agency's budget. During one budget hearing we observed that only the veteran legislators—virtually all of them term limited and soon leaving the legislature—were asking the tough questions. Another established lobbyist told us that one agency director, after some enthusiastic questioning by a term-limited legislator during a budget hearing, said, "I don't worry much about those guys. He'll be gone next year and I'll still be here." This may, in fact, be the largest impact of term limits on executive/legislative relations: it appears to have institutionalized an inequality of power in the legislature's ability to oversee the executive branch bureaucracy. Finally, while Amendment 73 also term limited the constitutional officers of the state, it nonetheless provided them with a maximum of two four-year terms. Since the vast majority of Arkansas governors have been elected to two terms, an Arkansas governor will normally have an advantage over legislators in budgetary conflicts simply because he and his full-time cabinet and budget staff are likely to have experienced more budget cycles. In sum, the formal and informal powers of the executive, its dominance with the media, its experience and staff, give significant advantages to the executive that are increased under term limits.

Nevertheless, the Arkansas General Assembly, even under Democratic governors, has not been the completely malleable, especially when significant interests were at stake. While former Governors Dale Bumpers and Bill Clinton were able to obtain tax increases for educational reform it was not easy, and Governor David Pryor (D—1974–1978), typically acknowledged as the most popular politician of the last fifty years in Arkansas, saw his plan for enhancing the taxing power of local governments rejected by a recalcitrant legislature dominated almost entirely by his own party (Ledbetter, Moore, and Sparrow 1979). Much more recently the Assembly made sure that Republican Governor Mike Huckabee would not be able to use capital development project funds at his discretion—a customary power that other governors had exercised. The legislature also fought Huckabee tooth and nail over school consolidation, ultimately forcing him to abandon his own plan, resulting in a bill becoming law without his signature that only consolidated school districts of less than 350 students. Even more recently, newly elected Democratic Governor Mike Beebe, with a sizeable popular mandate from the electorate and large Democratic majorities in the Assembly, still had to work out some compromises with the Speaker of the House before a very popular three percent reduction in the sales tax on food was passed. Governor Beebe, who had served almost twenty years in the Arkansas Senate and who was the leader of that body during the 1990s, said in a speech at the 2007 annual meeting of the Arkansas Political Science Association that there was no doubt in his mind that term limits had strengthened the governor's office at the expense of the Assembly. If term limits have made the legislature weaker in relation to the governor, this pattern has yet to fully play out and it will be interesting to see how well future governors work with the legislature when their partisanship is inapposite and/or when their popularity is lower.

CONCLUSION

The Arkansas General Assembly is a far different institution since term limits. It is a legislature made up of new faces and increased local government experience. It is a legislature with increased Republican representation, a change in the political landscape that has gone hand in hand with incremental Republican realignment largely in the Northwest portion of the state and the growing suburbs in other regions in the state. Term limits have also produced a new opportunity structure in Arkansas. Members of the General Assembly are introducing more bills and more legislators appear to be looking for opportunities to continue their public service careers after their legislative service. A more open committee structure has emerged that provides leadership opportunities for legislators willing to work hard and take advantage of their leadership potential. At the same time it appears that the power of individual chairpersons particularly in the House has been reduced while the power of the Speaker has substantially increased.

Institutional change is a significant effect of term limits in the Arkansas General Assembly. Today's freshman Senator or House member is likely to be an important committee chair the very next session. Legislative staff members are being asked more questions, although sometimes not the most insightful ones, and orientation sessions for Arkansas legislators have now become a permanent part of a new legislator's routine. Leadership change has taken place too. Floor leadership positions have become permanent fixtures in both chambers, most likely with the goal of exercising leadership control over a much more individualized and fragmented legislature. Legislators are also leaving the legislature to take jobs as lobbyists, which may actually increase the power of already powerful interest groups. There is also some evidence that some term-limited legislators find members of their own nuclear family to keep their seat in the Assembly.

The loss of what is commonly called institutional memory has been one of the chief arguments against the continuation of term limits in Arkansas. The argument appears to be a strong one. What is lacking is not political experience in a legislative body—which is indeed helpful—it is chamber specific experience. Members of the House coming to the Senate are generally quite unfamiliar with the more informal norms and traditions of the Senate, and with few veterans left to pass them on there has been a concern among members of a loss of Senate identity and a lessening of Senate influence in the legislative process. On an individual level many of our Senate respondents expressed discontent about the lack of opportunity to continue in public service because of term limits. While a number of them run for Congress (and several have been successful), take jobs as lobbyists or in state government, or even return to the House, others wishing to continue in public service find themselves frustrated when no opportunities to do so emerge.

In response to this situation, the 84th General Assembly sent (as one of the three amendments it could constitutionally submit during a regular legislative session) an amendment to the state's voters that would have doubled the number of years a member of the House could currently serve from six to twelve, and extend the number of years that a state Senator could serve from eight to twelve. That adaptation demonstrated the Assembly believed that additional time was needed to conduct legislative business. Unfortunately for its supporters, the amendment had at least two significant problems. First, it did not extend term limits for constitutional officers, which suggested the Assembly was looking out strictly for its own needs. Second, and most grievously, the amendment was seen as self-serving since it emanated from the Assembly itself rather than from more disinterested groups in the electorate that wished to implement a constitutional initiative to extend the terms. The result was a forgone conclusion; the extension amendment was defeated by 70 percent of the voters—ten percent more than voted for term limits in the first place.

Term limits, as we have argued, have changed the Arkansas General Assembly. Whether it is for better or worse is still a matter of argument. One thing is clear. After the 2004 vote to extend term limits, they are certainly going to be part of the Arkansas political landscape for the foreseeable future. Indeed, if term limits are going to be extended or abolished in Arkansas, that initiative will have to come from some place other than the Arkansas General Assembly, which ironically, was only partially responsible for them in the first place.

9

Institutional Change and Legislative Term Limits in Maine

Richard J. Powell and Rich Jones

As the first state in which term limits forced legislators from office in both houses of its state legislature, Maine has served as a bellwether for other term-limited states, especially those with less professionalized legislatures.

Even though Maine's term limits law is among the most lenient in the nation, the effects of this reform on Maine's government have been dramatic. With increased turnover, the overall level of political experience in the Maine legislature has decreased significantly. The accompanying loss of institutional memory has led to a host of significant changes. Most notably, the influence of staff members and the executive branch has risen, while the power of leadership and committees has decreased. These changes have also contributed to changes in the bicameral relationship between the two legislative houses, with the Senate increasing its influence relative to the House under term limits.

A BRIEF HISTORY

Maine voters adopted term limits in a referendum held during the November 1993 special off-year election. In an election that attracted one-third of the electorate, almost 68 percent of those voting supported the term limits.[1] The term-limits law limits members of the Maine House and Senate to four consecutive two-year terms. It also limits the terms of the Secretary of State, Treasurer, Attorney General and State Auditor—all of whom are either elected or, in the auditor's case, selected by the Legislature. Notably, it included a unique provision that counted the years already served when the term limits provision took effect for the 1996 elections. As a result, in 1996, thirty Maine legislators (twenty-six Representatives and four Senators) were among the first in the nation to be forced from office by term limits.

Despite their initial retroactivity, Maine's term limits provisions are relatively weak compared to the other states because the law applies only to consecutive terms. Termed legislators can thus run for the same chamber after sitting out just one term and can immediately seek election to the other chamber. Similarly, the length of Maine's term limits, eight years for representatives and senators, falls in the middle of the range allowed for House members and is equal to most of those allowed for Senators in other states with term limits. In addition, Maine's term-limits law is a statutory provision—rather than a constitutional amendment as found in many states—making it easier for the Legislature to amend or repeal it. However, there is very little political support in the legislature for changing the term-limits law because of its popularity among Maine's citizens and the fact that it was enacted by voter referendum. Thus, there appears to be little likelihood that Maine will soon follow the path of Idaho and Utah, which repealed term-limit laws in 2002 and 2003 respectively.

Among state legislatures Maine is unique in several regards. First, Maine ranks near the bottom of all states in traditional measures of legislative professionalization. For example, Maine's legislature is a part-time, citizen legislature in which most members maintain active careers outsides the legislature. Lawmakers are paid just $11,384 a year for the first regular session and $7,725 a year for the second regular session, plus a housing allowance of $38 per day and $32 per day in reimbursement for meals. Moreover, Maine's legislators have neither personal staff nor personal office space. It meets in short sessions, typically lasting six months in odd numbered years and four months in even numbered years.

Second, Maine's legislature is very large relative to the size of the state. While Maine has only 1.2 million citizens, its legislature is one of the largest in the nation with 151 members of the House of Representatives and 35 members of the Senate. The fact that Maine legislators represent relatively few constituents is in keeping with a strong Yankee tradition of active citizen participation and a moderate consensus-seeking political tradition.

The term-limits movement was gaining support nationwide in the early 1990s with adoption of provisions in California, Colorado and Oklahoma. In 1992, two Maine political consultants circulated petitions to place legislative term limits on the ballot as a citizen petition. Once the required number of signatures was collected the petition was sent to the Legislature for its consideration. When the Legislature failed to approve it, it automatically became a ballot referendum as required by law.

The three years preceding the vote on term limits were tumultuous in Maine politics. In 1990, a particularly acrimonious election ensued in which Republican Governor John McKernan was reelected by a slim margin. Immediately following the election, Democrats accused McKernan of hiding a budget deficit. A protracted budget fight between the Governor and Legislature in early 1991 caused the state government to shut down for seventeen days. This was exacerbated by a heated battle over the state's worker's compensation law. As a moderate state with a history of consensus-oriented politics, citizens were highly dissatisfied with the bitter partisan battles being fought in Augusta.

Citizen dissatisfaction with state government continued to run high into 1992. A ballot-tampering scandal involving an aide to then-House Speaker John Martin (D-Fort Kent) following the 1992 elections added to the negative view of the legislature and the House Speaker. Martin, who had been serving as speaker for nearly two decades, had long been a controversial figure in Maine politics. Many observers of Maine politics believe that a desire to remove Martin from office was a primary motivation of those supporting term limits. Citizen support for term limits was not the result of a single factor, but during the campaign over the term limits referendum, Martin became the "poster child" for the term-limits movement in Maine.

THE EFFECTS OF TERM LIMITS ON
THE COMPOSITION OF THE MAINE LEGISLATURE

Maine's citizen legislature has always had relatively high turnover. As shown in Figure 9.1, turnover in the House of Representatives was typically in the range of about 25 percent. In the Senate, turnover was a bit lower at about 20 percent. Of course, one of the central goals of term-limits advocates was to increase turnover by removing long-term members and bringing new faces into state legislatures. The adoption of term limits in Maine clearly accomplished this goal.

In looking at changes in the rate of legislative turnover over time, we see that the effects of term limits actually became apparent before they even took effect. In anticipation of being termed from office, turnover rose dramatically for the legislature elected two years before term limits was to begin removing legislators from office. In 1995, turnover jumped to 47 percent in the House and 31 percent in the Senate. This was caused by a number of long-term members leaving office to pursue other opportunities, including campaigns for Congress. Such moves became less risky since they were facing removal from office within two years anyway.

Under term limits, turnover has remained at levels higher than before, ranging from 30–46 percent in the House and 8–43 percent in the Senate. The relatively low turnover in 1999 illustrates the cyclical nature of term limits turnover. Since large classes of new members entered the Legislature in 1995 and 1997 we would expect turnout to be lower in 1999 since those

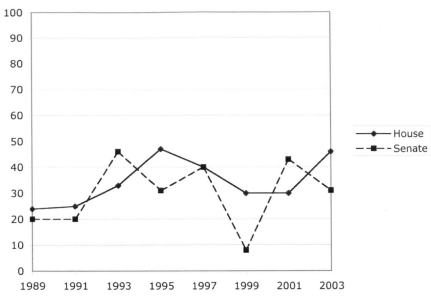

Figure 9.1. Membership Turnover in the Maine Legislature (%), 1989-2003

legislators had not yet reached their four-term maximum. And, in fact, turnout increased again in 2001 and 2003 as more legislators reached their maximum tenure in office.

Term-limit advocates and political observers also anticipated that term limits would lead to a change in the types of people elected to state legislatures. Notably, it was expected that term limits would increase the number of women legislators, because a number of long-time male legislators would be removed from office. Although underrepresented, prior to term limits women were represented in the Maine Legislature in much higher percentages than in most other states. As shown in Table 9.1, women typically held about 30–35 percent of the seats in the House and about 10–12 percent of Senate seats. Under term limits, the gender composition of the

Table 9.1. Demographic Composition of the Maine Legislature

Year	% Democratic	% Women	Ave. Age
1993–1994	59.68%	31.70%	49.8
1995–1996	48.92%	27.30%	50.6
1997–1998	53.76%	25.80%	50.5
1999–2000	53.23%	27.40%	50.6
2001–2002	56.99%	30.10%	53.0
2003–2004	57.53%	26.88%	53.6

Maine Legislature has changed but not necessarily as expected. Overall, the total number of women serving in the Legislature has remained fairly stable in the range of about sixty members. However, the representation of women in the House has actually dropped to about 23–25 percent. In the Senate, on the other hand, women have increased their representation. In large part, this has been accounted for by a migration of experienced female members from the House to the Senate.

Overall, the Maine Legislature has experienced a significant increase in turnover under term limits. However, the gender composition of the Legislature has changed very little. The remainder of this discussion focuses on the impact of increased turnover resulting from term limits on the Legislature and its place in Maine politics.[2]

THE INSTITUTIONAL IMPACT OF TERM LIMITS ON THE MAINE LEGISLATURE

Legislative Leaders

Without a doubt, one of the most significant effects of term limits on the Maine Legislature has been on the role played by party leaders. This was an almost universal sentiment expressed among those interviewed. Because term limits removed long-tenured members from the Legislature, leaders now come to their positions with limited experience in the legislature and even less experience as legislative leaders. As shown in Tables 9.2 and 9.3, term limits have had a dramatic impact on the level of experience possessed by leaders, but not always in expected ways. Notably, term limits have had a different impact on the House and Senate. Under term limits, the House has seen heavy turnover in its leadership every session. Turnover in the Senate has also been high, but not at the same levels as in the House.

The differential experience of the leadership in the House and Senate is even more apparent when we look at the average total years of legislative experience held by leaders, a measure that includes prior service in either

Table 9.2.   **Leadership Turnover**

Year	House	Senate
1993–1994	2 of 5	3 of 5
1995–1996	3 of 5	4 of 5
1997–1998	4 o 5	2 of 5
1999–2000	3 of 5	1 of 5
2001–2002	4 of 5	5 of 6
2003–2004	3 of 5	2 of 5

Table 9.3.   Experience of Party Leadership in the Maine Legislature (Mean Years)

Chamber	1991	1993	1995	1997	1999	2001
House	13.5	16.0	14.0	8.0	8.9	5.6
Senate	11.8	9.7	6.2	5.8	6.8	6.3

chamber. In 1993, House leaders had served an average of 14 years in the Legislature and Senate leaders served 9.7 years. By 2001, the average experience of leaders in the House dropped to just 4 years, but increased to 13.3 years in the Senate. This shift is accounted for by the fact that a significant number of termed House members have migrated to the Senate, while almost no Senators have moved to the House. Thus, Senate leaders have become much more experienced than their counterparts in the House. As discussed below, this has contributed to a general feeling among those connected to the Legislature that the Senate has become more powerful relative to the House since the advent of term limits. This might also contribute to legislators' notions that the House is more chaotic than the Senate and has more splinter caucuses and mavericks that can challenge a leader. The Senate has tended to have more cohesive caucuses.

Particularly in the House, the lack of experience and the fact that leaders will be termed out of their leadership position at a specific date have combined to alter the power of leaders and the roles they perform. Under term limits, legislators now have a much better chance to serve in their party's leadership since legislative leaders are generally limited to one term in a leadership position, thus creating much greater turnover. In the House, a clear leadership ladder has emerged in which legislators move from whip, to floor leader to Speaker of the House, generally over three successive terms. Therefore, the three most recent House Speakers had all served just three terms in the House upon taking power. As noted above, Senate leaders have had somewhat more legislative experience with most of them having served in the House previously.

In some ways, this marked a return to the traditional path followed by Maine's legislative leaders prior to the 1970s. For most of Maine's history, there had been frequent turnover among presiding officers, although in many cases they had more than six years of legislative experience prior to their selection for leadership. In the 1970s and 1980s, as the Maine Legislature took on a more professionalized, careerist look, leaders such as John Martin in the House and Charlie Pray in the Senate began to serve numerous terms in office, accumulating a great deal of power in the process.

The inability of current leaders to succeed themselves limits their ability to impose sanctions on and influence the members, thus reducing their power as legislative leaders. Speakers and Senate Presidents are lame ducks the instant they are sworn in. Members know they can outwait the leaders and many do. As a result, members are reported to be more critical of the leaders and more willing to challenge them than in the past. Members also tend to show less allegiance to the leaders and are less reliant on them. Since the leaders readily acknowledge their lack of power to sanction members and impose penalties for not supporting their positions, they must now gain and maintain power through persuasion and coalition building rather than by using institutional power. As one leader explained, "Going to the members and saying 'I need your vote' doesn't work anymore. Now there is a need for massaging and educating the members, showing them how policy intersects with politics."

Additionally, term limits have evened the playing field by ensuring that all leaders (and rank and file legislators for that matter) have roughly the same amount of legislative experience. Several interviewees asserted that John Martin was powerful, in part, because of his mastery of the legislative process gained from many years of experience. Under term limits most leaders have roughly the same level of experience.

Leaders' roles have changed somewhat under term limits. They are required to educate the members about basic procedures, processes and policies to a greater extent than they did in the past. They must also explain the role of the legislature and pass on the norms of behavior in their chambers. This becomes more difficult as the legislative leaders, particularly those in the House, take their leadership positions with limited legislative experience themselves.

Leaders continue to play an important role in elections. Specifically, they are expected to recruit candidates, help raise campaign funds and get their party's candidates elected. Although leaders were expected to play an electoral role prior to term limits, this role has become more important because the increased legislative turnover caused by term limits has increased the need to recruit candidates and organize campaigns.

Another complicating factor for leaders has been Maine's adoption of a "clean elections" law that took effect with the 2002 campaign. In the 2002 election a sizeable number of legislators accepted public funding under this law. In fact, as one leader told us, accepting money from the leaders' campaign fund is considered by many candidates to be politically disadvantageous because it causes the appearance of being beholden to leadership. As a result, members now have less need for campaign contributions from the leaders and the leaders have one less source of leverage over the members. However, active campaigning for legislative candidates is still an expected role for legislative leaders. In fact, observers cited the willingness of one legislator to travel the state in support of legislative candidates as a significant factor is his election as whip, floor leader and, eventually Speaker of the House. This was often cited by interviewees as the approach legislators are likely to take under term limits to move into leadership positions.

Under term limits, House Speakers and Senate Presidents now have a single term to make their mark and leave a legacy. Thus, they come to office with a sense of urgency in accomplishing their policy goals. This is reflected in the fact that major policy initiatives are more likely than in the past to originate with party leaders rather than committee chairs. As a result some leaders have been less concerned about institutional issues and processes. They want to act quickly and are less concerned about the long-term institutional rules, procedures, and norms that typically govern the legislative process. This short tenure has the effect of leaders being less interested in the management of the legislative institution. Increasingly, under term limits this role is being assumed by legislative staff particularly those on the Legislative Council staff and in the offices of the House Clerk and Senate Secretary.

Under term limits the path to leadership has changed, with potentially significant effects on the legislative process. Traditionally, leaders were chosen from the ranks of committee chairs. However, the two most recent House Speakers, Michael Saxl (D-Portland) and Patrick Colwell (D-Gardiner), and the person likely to be the next House Speaker have followed the same career path from whip to floor leader to Speaker of the House. Recent Senate leaders have followed similar paths. As a result, observers note that leaders now have a limited understanding of how committees develop consensus on legislation and the time needed to do so. They point out that, in some cases, leaders have imposed unrealistically short deadlines for action and emphasized moving legislation over building consensus and agreement. Bills have been pulled out of committees before committee members have had an opportunity to work through the issues and gain consensus. This tends to disrupt the work of the committees and affects the ability to get legislation passed on the floor. Likewise, leaders have less ability to train new committee chairs on how to run their committees because they have not had the experience of doing so.

Committees

The Maine Legislature uses Joint Committees with Senate and House co-chairs. There are three senators and eleven representatives on each committee and a total of seventeen Joint Committees. There has been no substantive change in the number of committees or the committee jurisdictions since the passage of term limits. However, committees were restructured in the mid 1990s when Republicans controlled the Senate. These changes were intended to reduce the number of committees and to streamline the committee system.

Most interviewees assert that the committees are weaker under term limits. According to a number of observers, committee reports are more likely to be challenged on the floor now than in the past. This includes committee reports

Table 9.4.   Experience of Committee Chairs in the Maine Legislature

Chamber	1993	1995	1997	1999	2001
House	8.8	7.9	4.1	6.4	4.7
Senate	8.3	4.0	7.5	10.1	7.4

adopted unanimously or with large majorities. As one observer commented, "In the past these reports were not debated on the floor they were just voted upon." Because experienced members have been termed out, the amount of substantive expertise on the part of committee chairs and members is reduced. As shown in Table 9.4, in 1993 House committee chairs had an average of 8.8 years of legislative experience and Senate chairs had an average of 8.3 years. By 2001, the experience of committee chairs declined to 4.7 years in the House and 7.4 years in the Senate. In recent sessions nearly all freshman members of the Senate served as a co-chair of a committee. As a result, numerous interviewees told us that members give less deference to the work of committees than they did before the imposition of term limits. One legislator told us about a unanimous committee report that was overturned on the floor because a group of legislators knew more about the particular issue than the committee members. Another former member put it more bluntly, stating, "Committee reports do not mean anything any more."

The passage of the appropriations bill in 2001 departed significantly from the traditional process for adopting this legislation and provides a vivid example of some of the changes that have occurred under term limits. The Appropriations Committee developed a bill that included a number of compromises that were not satisfactory to a number of members. However, it was passed out of the committee unanimously. Several attempts to amend it on the floor of the House were defeated with the support and involvement of leadership. The Senate leaders however, worked to rewrite the bill and amend it on the floor. The amended bill was sent to the House for concurrence with limited warning to the House leaders. In the past, the bill would have been sent back to the Appropriations Committee for the issues to be resolved rather than amending it on the floor. A number of observers pointed out that the more experienced Senate leaders took advantage of the more inexperienced House leaders. They also led the newly elected senators to believe that this is the way things were done traditionally. This process created hard feelings between the chambers and, in particular, among the House leaders and Senate leaders. This example illustrates both the decreased influence of the committees in the legislative process and the increased power of the Senate relative to the House under term limits.

The decrease in experience among committee chairs and members has meant that committee staff now plays a more active role in scheduling committee meetings and organizing the bills that will be heard during the meetings. One aspect of the scheduling function is that legislative leaders turn to staff more often now to ensure that committees are meeting their deadlines for considering legislation. In the past the chairs performed these functions and directed more of the committees' actions. Staff has also been increasingly called upon to provide historical information on how the Legislature dealt with the issues in the past and to explain basic principles about issues to bring new people up to speed. As one former legislator observed, "The nonpartisan staff know more than the committee members."

A particular problem that observers report, because members have limited experience, is an increase in the number of previously disposed issues being revisited. New legislators are not sure who to talk to about proposed legislation and are not aware of what was previously tried. Moreover, these less experienced members are said to be more likely to propose overly simple solutions for complex problems. Because legislators are now limited to four terms in the Legislature, they feel the need to move very quickly upon taking office to file their bills. These combined trends lead to a dramatic increase in the number of bills that have been introduced since term limits took effect. In 1995, the legislative session prior to term limits taking effect, 1,586 bills were introduced. By 1999, this rose to 2,276. Bill introductions settled back to 1,852 in 2001 after leaders made a concerted effort to reduce workload (see a more detailed discussion of this in the final section).

In addition, because term-limited members have a shorter time horizon, several observers pointed out that it is more difficult for committees to deal with complex, long-term issues. Most of the members and chairs have not had experience in dealing with some of the major issues. It also takes time to lay the groundwork to pass major legislation and most members are focused on the near term because they will be termed out after eight years. As one observer said, many members hold the view that, "My job is not to solve the budget problem long term; it is to focus on the next two years."

In the 2002 session some committees operated effectively while others foundered. According to interviewees there is variability in the skill and experience of committee chairs. Some new committee chairs adapt to their roles very quickly, perhaps drawing upon prior experience in government or in related non-governmental positions. However, many new chairs have had a difficult time running the committee meetings and effectively dealing with the issues before them. There is a generally acknowledged need for more training for committee chairs.

Legislative Staff

Staff can be divided into two main categories—partisan and non-partisan. The partisan staff work for the party leaders and caucuses and in the offices of the Clerk of the House and Secretary of the Senate. The offices of the House Clerk and Senate Secretary also perform a number of non-partisan parliamentary and bill processing services to their respective chambers. While the offices of the House Clerk and Senate Secretary are not regarded as solely partisan, they are appointed by the majority party and are perceived by members as playing semi-partisan roles.

The purely partisan staff are found in the offices of the party leadership. These staff provide policy analysis, media relations and constituent services help to the members of their caucus. There has been a slight increase in the number of partisan, caucus staff during the past 10 years. According to data collected by the National Conference of State Legislatures, the Maine Legislature had 190 total staff members in 2003, with 156 of them serving in full-time positions. Maine ranked 41st among all states in number of legislative staff. Of the staff working for the Maine Legislature, 24.7 percent of them can be classified as political staff.[3]

Non-partisan staff are generally found within a central staffing agency called the Legislative Council. They provide bill drafting, committee staffing, general research and fiscal analysis services to all members of the Legislature. The number of non-partisan staff has remained fairly constant since the imposition of term limits. The staff structure has also remained essentially the same.

Legislative staff perform more of an educational role with respect to the legislators since the imposition of term limits. Most staff have years of experience in their jobs. The less experienced legislators elected under term limits increasingly turn to them for background information on issues, help in understanding legislative rules and processes and historical information on actions taken by past Legislatures. While legislators always used staff for this type of help, staff report an increase in demand for these services since the imposition of term limits. For example, staff in offices of the House Clerk and Senate Secretary report an increase in the number of members who request help in scripting the phrases used to make motions and move legislative actions. The fiscal staff provides more briefing materials on the budget and fiscal issues under term limits. Some movement in this direction occurred before term limits as the budget process was changed to include more legislators, however, the demand for these materials increased under term limits. As described previously, committee staff provide more historical information on issues and more frequently help the chairs schedule bills under term limits. Legislators also turn to their partisan staff more frequently for political and policy advice than they did before term limits. For example, members appear to be going to the Clerk of the House and the Secretary of the Senate for procedural as well as political advice. The nonpartisan staff feels they have lost power because the members have less of an institutional focus and favor those staff that can help them politically.

In the initial debate over the enactment of term limits, critics asserted that term limits would shift power in state legislatures from the lawmakers to the legislative staff. Although some observers assert that the legislative "bureaucracy" has gained power under term limits, many others see no shift in power among legislators and staff. In fact, many of the nonpartisan staff asserted that their roles have been diminished under term limits as more members have taken on of short term political orientations, showing less interest in issues related to the legislative institution. Many observers say that legislators now turn more frequently to the partisan staff for assistance because they are more likely to know them through their election campaigns and are initially less aware of the services available from the nonpartisan offices. To compensate for this, nonpartisan staff are spending more time reaching out to the new legislators at the beginning of their terms to help explain the role and services provided by the nonpartisan staff.

Although our interviewees expressed some disagreement over the extent to which staff may have become more influential under term limits, there was a near unanimous recognition that staff now represent the key repository of institutional memory in the Legislature. Since there are fewer and fewer members with lengthy careers in the Legislature, members must now rely on the staff for historical perspective and institutional continuity. Relatively few legislators are able to speak with authority on what was done in previous legislatures.

Lobbyists

Without a doubt, one of the central concerns of term-limits opponents was that lobbyists would be greatly strengthened by term limits. The fear was that an experienced corps of lobbyists would find it easy to influence inexperienced legislators. Our interviews suggest that the role of lobbyists has changed under term limits, but there is disagreement about whether lobbyists are more or less powerful.

Much like legislative staff, lobbyists perform more of an educational role under term limits than they did previously. Traditionally, lobbyists have helped legislators understand how proposed legislation would affect their clients and why their clients want certain policies adopted. However, under term limits lobbyists are increasingly asked to provide information on how past legislatures dealt with issues. Observers report that lawmakers also turn to lobbyists for help in understanding legislative rules and procedures.

On the other hand, term limits has created some difficulties for lobbyists as well. The influence of lobbyists is largely a function of their ability to form relationships. However, the turnover caused by term limits means there are more new legislators that lobbyists must meet and get to know. In addition, many of the legislators that lobbyists know and have relationships with are termed out of the legislature. Both factors combine to make it more difficult for lobbyists to do their jobs. In addition, the adoption of the "clean elections" law (after the imposition of term limits) has reduced legislators' reliance on campaign contributions from groups represented by lobbyists. In fact, lobbyists reported an increase in the number of new legislators who go to great lengths to avoid talking to them, seemingly holding the view that lobbyists are an inherently corrupting group.

BALANCE OF POWER

Interestingly, most of the people we interviewed felt that other actors and institutions in the process have gained power and they have either lost power or their power has remained constant. In other words, there is widespread agreement that term limits have altered the internal and external power relationships for the Maine legislature, but little consensus on the specific nature of these shifts. One member of the executive branch argued that power has not shifted; it has simply disappeared. According to this perspective, the legislature and state government overall are weaker as a result of term limits.

While there was considerable disagreement about the specific nature of power shifts, the most frequent position, particularly among legislators, was that the governor and/or the executive branch in general have gained power. This is thought to be true mostly because the governor and the executive branch have greater expertise on issues, they maintain institutional knowledge of issues, and they can wait out the legislature as needed. Repeatedly, our interviewees suggested that legislators lack the institutional memory on issues and the knowledge of issue areas to effectively counter the power of the executive branch.

When pressed, however, legislators were uncertain whether this perceived shift of power toward the governor was solely the result of term limits. During its first six years under term limits, Maine had a very popular Independent governor, Angus King. Numerous interviewees cited the political savvy and policy knowledge possessed by Governor King and his ability to utilize his independence to gain influence over state policy. Those observers we interviewed before 2003 were generally less certain about how term limits would influence the balance of power during periods of partisan control. However, in 2003 the governorship returned to partisan control with the Democratic administration of John Baldacci. The interviewees we talked with in 2003 and 2004 continued to express the view that the executive branch was being strengthened at the expense of the Legislature because of term limits.

Our interviews indicate that the increased influence of the executive branch extends to departmental heads and agency staff as well. Many observers told us that legislators lack the policy-specific experience to effectively question executive branch officials. In particular, legislators are increasingly deferential to departmental heads during committee hearings. One senator explained that term limits exposed the Legislature's weakness in exercising oversight of the executive branch, leading to the creation of a new oversight agency within the Legislature itself, the Office of Program Evaluation and Governmental Accountability (OPEGA). The creation of OPEGA is just one of several adaptations the Legislature has undertaken in an effort to adjust to the realities of term limits.

ADAPTATIONS

Maine legislators and legislative staff recognize that term limits have significantly altered the legislative process and the norms of legislative behavior by removing longer tenured members and leaving a legislature with less collective experience. Although our interviewees identified a mix of positive and negative effects, there was widespread consensus about most of the effects of term limits on the Legislature and its place in the broader environment of Maine politics. Often times, different members had different interpretations of the same phenomena. For example, the positive effect most often mentioned to us was that term limits have created opportunities for more members to serve as legislative leaders and committee chairs. This is a corollary to the most frequently cited observation that term limits have had the greatest impact on legislative leaders. The current leaders point out that they owe their position in part to the fact that term limits forced out their predecessors. On the other hand, it is the relative inexperience of leaders that is most frustrating to many members.

The second most frequently cited positive aspect of term limits is that they bring new people into the legislature. Although Maine has always experienced fairly high turnover among lawmakers, term limits guarantees that each seat will turnover after eight years, if not before. New people bring new ideas, visions and priorities to the legislature. According to several observers this turnover helps to promote evolution within the Legislature as the new members question assumptions and revisit important issues. The downside of this trend is that it has led to a substantial increase in workload in which legislators are constantly seeking to "reinvent the wheel" because they are increasingly unfamiliar with the actions of previous legislatures.

Observers also pointed out that the Maine term-limits law is relatively weak, allowing lawmakers to return after sitting out a term or moving from one chamber to the other. Not all new legislators are policy neophytes. Many of them have served in other government posts or held policy-relevant positions in the private sector. For example, in 2003, a former state budget director was elected to the Legislature and immediately became active on the Appropriations Committee. Similarly, some termed legislators returned to the Legislature, including John Martin who served multiple terms in the Senate after having served as House Speaker for over two decades. Other positive aspects identified by interviewees include: more qualified members are attracted to the legislature because term limits set a defined length of service; they turn out long tenured members which ensures that the Legislature remains a citizen-based, part-time body consistent with Maine's political traditions; individual legislators are empowered by term limits, which results in more internal competition among the members for power; and, committee chairs elected under term limits are not as beholden to the executive branch commissioners. That being said, far more observers felt that term limits had a net negative impact on the Legislature.

It is not the mission of this chapter to render a verdict on the ultimate success or failure of term limits. Instead this section seeks to explain the ways in which the Maine Legislature had adapted to the new political realities created, in part, by term limits.

TRAINING INITIATIVES

With an increase in the number of new legislators entering the Legislature under term limits, there emerged a clear need for enhanced training programs to educate legislators about legislative procedures and the policy issues they would face. As a result, the Legislature conducts an orientation program for new legislators, which has been expanded since the imposition of term limits. The House of Representatives conducts training that includes a mock session and training on legislative rules. In 2001 and 2003, the Legislature and the Margaret Chase Smith Center for Public Policy at the University of Maine cosponsored a forum for all legislators on policy issues to provide background information from several perspectives. Similarly, the Legislature has continued to develop a statewide bus tour for legislators at the start of each new session so that members can become familiar with the issues facing the various regions of the state.

Sensing a need for increased training, during the fall of 2002 the Legislative Council created a curriculum committee to develop training programs for the Legislature. The committee included both legislative leaders and rank and file members. The committee laid out ideas for training programs and recommended institutionalizing them. In addition to training, the leaders assigned veteran members as mentors for the new legislators. The goal of the mentoring program is to provide continuous on the job training by helping new members understand legislative procedures, conveying norms of legislative behavior and passing on historical information about past legislative actions.

Most interviewees stressed the need for additional training, both on policy issues and how to more effectively perform their roles as legislators, committee chairs and leaders. Many emphasized the importance of increasing the training of committee chairs.

LEGISLATIVE RULES AND PROCESSES

In 1999 the Legislative Council created a Special Committee on Legislative Rules. The committee considered a number of changes in the way the legislature operates in response to the effects of term limits. The ideas considered included limits on bill introductions, changing the number of votes to move bills out of committee and changing the session schedule. The Legislative Council considered the ideas but made no major rules changes. One interviewee stressed the need for the legislature to rethink how it conducts its business in response to term limits. In this legislator's view, the Legislature should change committee processes to increase public input, improve scheduling and emphasize more important issues during committee deliberations by reducing the amount of time spent on minor bills.

Although the Special Committee's suggestions for changes to the rules were not followed, the attention they brought to the institutional challenges brought about by term limits led to some informal changes. For example, while no formal limits were placed on the number of bill introductions, legislative leaders went to great lengths to convince members to be more selective in the bills they introduced. This led to a decrease in the number of bill introductions in 2001 and 2003, although not to pre-term-limits levels. These efforts have alleviated some of the strain on the Legislature's resources.

ROLE OF LEGISLATIVE STAFF

As we discussed previously, under term limits, legislative staff provide more summary and background information to help legislators better understand policy issues confronting the Legislature. For example, the fiscal staff report conducting an orientation program for Appropriations Committee members and producing more summary documents. Some documents address basic budgeting functions while others contain more in-depth information on policy issues. Increasingly, the staff is posting these documents on the web and using electronic means to communicate with the more technology savvy members.

The records maintained by committee staff could be particularly useful in helping to train new committee chairs. Staff maintain records on the bills considered by each committee, the testimony they receive and amendments offered during the committee meetings. This information is maintained in committee files for several sessions before they are transferred to the state archives. The legislative library also maintains similar files on issues. These files could be used to provide "institutional knowledge" on legislative actions to future lawmakers.

ENHANCING OVERSIGHT

Perhaps the most ambitious attempt to counteract the effects of term limits came in the form of the creation of a new oversight agency housed with the Legislature itself. In response to the increased difficulty of a term-limited legislature in exercising its executive oversight functions, legislators sought an institutional solution to the problem. The Republicans provided the primary impetus for this change with the stated intention of eliminating government "waste" and increasing governmental accountability. The proposal was also supported by some Democrats who were concerned about the loss of the Legislature's influence vis-à-vis the executive branch under term limits.

Ultimately, the Legislature created the Office of Program Evaluation and Governmental Accountability (OPEGA), which was modeled after similar agencies in other states, especially Florida. This office was to be staffed by professional, non-partisan staff and would be charged with assisting the Legislature in its oversight functions. As of now, OPEGA is still in somewhat of a limbo. Although it was created by statute, subsequent funding has been slow to develop. Further, it became part of a larger political controversy in 2003 and 2004 when the Democratic Senate President delayed making the appointments necessary to breathe life into the new agency. Nevertheless, this new agency represents an attempt by the Legislature to adapt to the realities of term limits.

NOTES

1. Matthew C. Moen and Kenneth T. Palmer, "Maine: The Cutting Edge of Term Limits," in *The Test of Time: Coping with Legislative Term Limits*, ed. Rick Farmer, John David Rausch, Jr., and John C. Green (Lanham, Maryland: Lexington Books, 2003), 48–50.

2. According to the 2000, U.S. Census, Maine is the "whitest" state in the nation with only 3 percent of its population classified as non-white. As a result, the Maine

Legislature has also had very few non-white members either before or after term limits. Due to the limited number of non-white legislators, it is not possible to reliably assess the impact of term limits on the racial composition of the Legislature.

3. We thank Brian Weberg of the National Conference of State Legislatures for providing us with these data on staff in the Maine Legislature.

10

It's All About the Turnover: Term Limits in Citizen Legislatures[1]

Michael Smith

The impact of term limits is not a one-size-fits all phenomenon. Proponents of term limits attacked the growing professionalism of U.S. legislatures: longer sessions, higher pay, full-time careers serving in office, longer incumbencies, and more staff. They sought to undo what they perceived as the negative effects resulting from this growing professionalism in Congress and the state legislatures.

These pro-term-limit arguments presuppose that legislatures have become more professionalized than in the past. This is true of Congress and of legislatures in such heavily-populated states as California, New York, Illinois, and Ohio. But one irony is that term limits have also been imposed in the state legislative bodies that had never varied from the "citizen legislatures" model of short sessions, low pay, minimal staff, dual careers, and small districts. Thus the study of term limits in certain states offers a new wrinkle in the debate: how have term limits played out in state legislatures that had never become highly professionalized in the first place?

A BRIEF HISTORY

Arkansas voters imposed term limits on the state legislature in 1992 with Maine voters doing the same in 1993. Kansas, lacking any constitutional provision for petition initiative, lacks term limits. Arkansas and Kansas feature very similar populations figures of around 2.7 million people each (U.S. Census, 2003 and 2002 estimates, respectively). Maine is smaller, with just under 1.3 million citizens (U.S. Census, 2002 estimate). None of these three states features legislative pay high enough for the job to be considered

a full-time one (in spite of the increasing workload), and personal legislative staff in these three states ranges from none at all (Arkansas and Maine)
to one secretary for every three rank-and-file house members or one senator (Kansas).

Districts in these states have few residents compared to those in larger
states. Door-to-door campaigning is still the expected norm for anyone serious about winning elections. Campaign fundraising is not the full-time-
plus job that an Ohio or California legislator would face, and when these
legislators go home, they can still expect to be recognized at the grocery
store by constituents who know them personally. These citizen-legislators
must work a second job, be independently wealthy, or rely on retirement
income in order to supplement minimal pay. All three states are more rural than the nation as a whole, but their characters are changing. Each state
overall is struggling with slow growth, but with some spots of population
growth that defy the states' lackluster trends. In the case of Kansas, this
would be Johnson County, near Kansas City. Often cited as a national ar-
chetype of suburban sprawl (Peirce and Hagstrom 1983; Frank 2004)
Johnson County features high incomes, high growth, and major employ-
ers such as Sprint telecommunications. Otherwise-poor Arkansas faces
boomtown growth in the northwest section of the state: home of the flag-
ship state university, many retirement communities, and the headquarters
for Wal-Mart, the world's largest publicly-traded corporation. Half of
Maine's population is concentrated in a tiny seaboard strip around Port-
land. The rest of the state—nearly its entire land area—forms a single congressional district featuring more land area than any other one east of the
Mississippi River.

Arkansas, Maine, and Kansas entered the 1990s without ever having varied from the citizen-legislature model. Yet Arkansas and Maine both provide for citizen-initiated ballot initiatives, and their voters still saw the need
to impose term limits. Still in effect today, these laws vary widely. Arkansas's
are the most harsh, allowing for three, two-year terms in the house and two,
four-year terms in the Senate. These are lifetime limits: once having served
up to one's limit, one can never serve again. However, Arkansas's law did
"grandfather in" terms served before the law took effect, thus delaying the
law's impact. Long-serving legislators were free to serve up to six more years
in the house, and eight in the senate, after the law took effect in 1992.
Maine's voters opted to limit both house and senate members to four consecutive two-year terms in each body. However, the limits are for consecutive terms only, not lifetime ones. Maine legislators may "sit out" one or
more terms and run again, starting the term-limits clock anew. Then again,
Maine's voters opted to make the impact of their law more immediate by
not "grandfathering in" terms served before the law took effect, meaning
that all of the state's most experienced legislators were forced from office as

State	Arkansas	Maine	Kansas
Year passed	1992	1993	No term limits
House	3 two-year terms	4 two-year terms	No term limits
Senate	2 four-year terms	4 two-year terms	No term limits
Consecutive or lifetime?	Lifetime	Consecutive	No term limits
"Grandfathered?"	Yes	No	No term limits

Figure 10.1. Term Limit Laws in Citizen Legislatures

of the next election following the law's passage in 1993. Kansas has neither the petition initiative for citizens to change laws, nor term limits.

COMPOSITION AND REPRESENTATION

Turnover

The small size of these states has always insured that each state legislator represents far fewer constituents than do their peers in larger states. This has given a primacy to door-to-door campaigning and other "retail, not whole-sale" political strategies that do not require as much fundraising as elections in large states. Low legislative pay has probably been a major cause of the fact that, even before term limits, turnover in all three state legislatures was substantial (and remains substantial even in Kansas, with no term limits). In Maine, turnover for the legislature as a whole was typically more than 20 percent before term limits. In Arkansas, turnover was lower pre-term limits: just under 20 percent for the house and just under 10 percent for the senate in 1993–1994. Despite "grandfathering" of earlier terms into the law, turnover in Arkansas rose after the 1993–1994 session. Anecdotal evidence suggests that this resulted from legislators' anticipating term limits' full effect. They responded by seeking other elected offices or different jobs. Kansas's turnover for the past ten years varied greatly in the house, with averages around 20 percent but a low of 12 percent and a high of over 40 percent. Turnover is astonishing in the Kansas Senate: all seats are on the ballot during presidential election years, and during those years the turnover rate exceeds 40 percent! Given that a major goal of term limits' proponents was to increase turnover, they can rest assured that this is not necessary in Kansas.

In the Arkansas General Assembly, term limits have correlated with more turnovers, fewer attorney-legislators, more Republicans, and the curious phenomenon of spouses, sons, and daughters of term-limited state legislators seeking the seats being vacated by their own relatives. Some of these phenomena—most notably the seat gains made by Republicans—may be coincidental or simply hastened by the imposition of term limits.

In Maine, term limits have pushed turnover rates from high to even higher. They have created a cycle in which many legislators are elected in certain election cycles (starting with the first election after the law took effect), and then there is a lull in competitive elections lasting for several cycles until these legislators reach their term limits. Lacking term limits, Kansas nevertheless features high turnover, particularly in the state senate. One legislator said, "we do have term limits in Kansas—it's called legislative pay!" The implication here was that the low pay forced legislators out of office after a few terms. Interestingly, Arkansas and Maine both feature lower legislative pay than Kansas, yet the last featured the highest legislative turnover pre-term limits. Thus, legislative pay alone does not explain the turnover numbers.

What may indeed explain the high turnover in Kansas is the state's "three party state" dynamic (Loomis 1994; Smith 2003) in which the dominant Republicans are deeply divided into moderate and conservative factions. These factions compete fiercely with each other and often act as separate party organizations, occasionally leaving the minority Democrats to act as tiebreakers or even leading them to surprising upset victories in this bastion of red-state America. The Kansas GOP also features many, highly-contested primaries in which conservatives and moderates square off against one another. This increases the defeat of incumbents and contributes to the high turnover. It may also make the work environment less attractive and lead to more retirements.

In sum, Kansas's turnover rates rival those of the other two states, in spite of the facts that Kansas features no term limits and offers higher legislator pay than do the other two states. At the other end of the spectrum, Arkansas began the period with low turnover, which necessarily became much higher after term limits took effect. But Maine featured high turnover before term limits, and these rates climbed even higher after term limits. Prior to term limits, there was a great deal of variation in turnover between the three states, which could not be explained by legislator pay. Term limits serve to mask these differences and drive turnover in Arkansas and Maine up to levels similar to those of non-term-limited Kansas.

Women and Racial Minorities

Some term-limits proponents hoped to open up more legislative seats for women and racial minorities, making the legislature more inclusive and more representative of society as a whole. Robert Kurfirst (1996) labeled these proponents "term-limits populists." Such advocates are bound to be disappointed with the results in citizen legislatures. While women have gained a few seats in the Arkansas Senate, there has not been any other significant change in the diversity of state legislators during the ten-year period studied. Overall, term limits may serve to open up representation only when a group has virtually no representation in the state legislature. Such was the case in the Arkansas Senate. In some sessions shortly before term limits, it had no female members at all. Today it features a few.

Arkansas is the only one of these three states that features a large, dispersed population of any non-white racial group. The state has a large African-American population and has been at the center of well-known civil rights struggles in the past. By contrast, Maine is one of America's "whitest" states, and Kansas features only a few counties with significant minority populations. African-Americans, by far the largest non-white racial group in Arkansas, were not represented in the state legislature in proportion to their share of the state population before term limits took effect. The imposition of term limits has done little to rectify this situation. Both before and after term limits, African-Americans in Arkansas are usually elected only from "majority-minority" districts. Because the state also features many districts where African-Americans are a substantial portion but not a majority of the population, the state's Black communities remain underrepresented. Maine's only significant minority communities are American Indian reservations, but there is little in the way of racial minority representation in the state legislature. Kansas, like Arkansas, features a few nonwhite legislators elected from majority-minority districts in Kansas City and Wichita. But overall the Sunflower state's racial minority population is a good deal smaller than that of Arkansas. Minority legislators are even more scarce in Topeka than they are in Little Rock.

There is an enormous gap between Arkansas and the other two states when it comes to women serving in the legislature. Kansas and Maine are relatively progressive, with approximately one-third of each state's legislature made up of women. In Maine, this holds both before and after term limits. Women lag far behind in Arkansas, but at least their numbers have grown from under 7 percent of the legislature to over 15 percent during the period studied. It is impossible to know whether term limits caused this change, hastened it, or merely happened coincidentally. However, the gains made by women, particularly in the Arkansas Senate, are the only substantial gains made by women or racial minorities in any of the three states studied during the ten-year period. The percentage of female legislators in Arkansas remains far below that of Maine or Kansas. It may be that term limits have an impact on composition only when one group is very drastically underrepresented in the state legislature.

Other Changes

Aside from gender and race, term limits have brought some major changes to who is represented in the statehouse. Most notable is the dramatic decrease of attorneys serving in the Arkansas General Assembly. This has had substantial institutional effects, reducing the number of freshmen legislators that can use their legal expertise to review legislation and increasing reliance on centralized staff to review legislation for constitutionality and general workability. Researchers found no major shifts in the Maine Legislature's composition. In Kansas, the most dominant shift has been from rural to suburban representation. This occurs with redistricting every ten years. It reflects the state's shifting population. Several Kansas legislators told researchers that the state's lack of term limits is putting the brakes on an inevitable power shift from rural legislators to suburban ones. Western Kansas residents choose to reelect legislators for many terms, while suburban residents are less likely to do so. This helps depopulating western Kansas retain legislative clout that would otherwise be lost due to population decline in their areas (and growth in the suburbs).

Experience

Neither Arkansas nor Kansas had substantial changes in the average age of legislators during the ten-year period studied. Maine's trend of legislators getting older was present before term limits took effect and has continued, flying in the face of some proponents' hopes that younger legislators with "new ideas" would be elected. Few will be surprised to learn that since term limits, Maine's legislators have had, on average, less lawmaking experience than their predecessors. Many term-limited house members are seeking senate seats in Maine, thus widening the "experience gap" between the house and senate in the Pine Tree State. The senate has the advantage in institutional knowledge. Given that the senate is considered the upper chamber, this may seem a given in any state. However, such is not the case in Kansas. In the Sunflower State, turnover is much higher in the senate than the house, mitigating any institutional advantage the upper chamber might otherwise have. Some Kansas House leaders told interviewers that they had negotiated the last year's budget directly with the governor and nearly bypassed the senate altogether. In Arkansas, there is now a pronounced tendency for newly-elected legislators to have experienced serving in another elective office prior to the statehouse. As in Maine, the most common career path is from house to senate. However, unlike their counterparts in Maine, Arkansas researchers also found substantial numbers of new legislators that had served in *local* offices before coming to Little Rock. This helps counteract the loss of institutional knowledge inherent in term limits. Term limits proponents may be gratified to see this "rotation in office"—that is, a phenomenon of professional politicians forced to run for different offices rather than getting comfortable and making a career of staying in the statehouse.

Representation

At the core of a representatives' job, of course, is representation. Term limits shorten time horizons and refocus a representative's time priorities. Proponents hoped this would bring a renewed focus on the interest of the state. They sought less use of seniority for home-district pork, which often sealed incumbency advantage in the next election. Have their hopes been met?

To study representation, researchers combined the aforementioned field studies with a survey of knowledgeable observers in the states. The results are telling. In Arkansas, the survey found representatives elected under term limits to be more, not less focused on bringing home "pork barrel" spending to the home district. But otherwise, districts got less attention—the same survey found Natural State legislators spending less time seeking public input on legislation. Furthermore, they were less likely to support and defend the institution of the legislature itself—moving closer to the behavior of congresspersons who Richard Fenno (1978) saw "run[ning] for Congress by running against Congress."

Maine's situation shows some similarities to that of Arkansas. Pine Tree State legislators in the term-limits era were also more likely than their predecessors to pursue "pork" for their home districts. Again mirroring their Arkansas colleagues, Maine legislators were less likely to support and defend the legislature as an institution. There is one notable difference: term-limited Maine legislators are also more likely than their predecessors to send newsletters and other communication home to constituents. Overall, both states' term-limited citizen legislatures suggest a mixed impact of term limits on attention to the constituents: more pork, more newsletters (in Maine), but less giving of a legislators' most precious resources: time. Are these changes truly due to term limits?

Kansas is the telling case. Lacking term limits, the Sunflower State's experiences serve as a control. Some of the changes observed in Arkansas and Maine may be coincidental with term limits, not caused by them. Indeed, in term-limit-free Kansas, legislators are also less likely than their predecessors to support and defend the legislature as an institution. This suggests that term limits may not be the cause of this change in the other states. Today's Kansas legislators are less likely than their forerunners to seek public input on legislation. This suggests that term limits may not be the cause of similar problems in the other states. And finally, Kansas legislators are now more likely to send newsletters and other communication to constituents—again suggesting that a similar pattern in Maine may not be caused by term limits. Thus, this study finds few strong relationships between these measures of representation and term limits. However, term limits may correlate with the Maine and Arkansas legislators' increased tendency to pursue pork barrel spending—no such trend was observed in Kansas. This pattern directly contradicts the hopes of term-limit advocates who hoped that term limits would lessen the focus on pork and bring a Burkean, "whole state" orientation to the capitol.

THE INSTITUTIONAL EFFECTS OF TERM LIMITS

Leadership

Term limits have dramatically reshaped legislative institutions. The changes are much more substantial than those regarding representation. In the wake of term limits, legislators have remade leadership roles, changed committee structures, and revamped the staff's role. In Arkansas, leadership has been weakened and dispersed. In Maine, leadership turnover is higher. It now follows a quick "leadership ladder" sequence of roles. And in term-unlimited Kansas, changes have been much less dramatic—indicating that in the other states, term limits are indeed a causal factor behind these changes.

Arkansas's legislature has been revolutionized by term limits. Before the change, the entire legislature was dominated by a few leaders—particularly the senate president, who was said to be more powerful than even many governors. A few leaders close to the senate president dominated committees. In fact, it was not unusual for the same person to chair multiple committees. Those days are gone. In the wake of term limits, Arkansans have seen their house speaker empowered. In addition, several new leadership positions have been created in both chambers. The house once featured one speaker pro-tempore; today it features four of them. Both chambers have added the position of floor leader, and that of party whip. Most of this dispersion of power has come at the expense of the senate president. The phenomenon of one person chairing multiple committees is a thing of the past. Astonishingly, even some members of the minority party are now chairing a few house committees! Since term limits came about, Arkansas legislators have implemented a subcommittee system for the first time in the state's history—further dispersing power.

The impact of term limits has not been quite as revolutionary in Maine, but it has still been very substantial. Leadership turnover is now higher, and those rising to leadership positions in the house now do so in a nearly lockstep "leadership ladder" pattern. The pattern begins with election as party whip for a term. The next term, one moves on to the position of floor leader. After one term of that, the leader-designate rises to the speakership. Overall, leaders' control has been weakened over what happens on the house and senate floor—those interviewed for this study said that the house, in particular, is now more fractious. These changes interrupted a pre-term-limits pattern of professionalization. Before 1993, a pattern was developing in which Maine's legislative leaders were more experienced than their forerunners. Maine leaders were serving longer as rank-and-file legislators before taking leadership roles. Term limits reversed this pattern.

The job of a Maine legislative leader has also changed due to term limits. These leaders now spend more time educating their freshman members about legislative institutions and procedures. Given their shorter time horizons, legislators are spending less time building institutional capacity and more time pursuing policy-based outcomes. The latter have a more immediate, tangible payoff. Even in this citizen legislature state, election to a leadership position by the party caucus increasingly depends on the time, effort, and success a leadership candidate has had traveling the state fundraising and campaigning on behalf of the party's candidates for state legislature. Those elected to the legislature often vote for the ones that helped them win, in gratitude.

Once again, Kansas serves as a control due to its lack of term limits. In this case, the Kansas Legislature shows a good deal more institutional stability than its counterparts in Arkansas and Maine. Leadership is more consolidated in the Kansas House than in the Kansas Senate. In the former, the speaker is uncontested as the most powerful person in his or her chamber. S/he appoints all committee members from the majority party and is close to the majority leader. The Appropriations Committee is considered the "Speaker's Committee"—the speaker appoints his or her strongest supporters to that committee and the chair is expected to hew to the speaker's guidelines when crafting a budget. The Kansas House has not seen the weakening of leadership and dispersion of power present in Arkansas and Maine.

The Kansas Senate is remarkably different from its counterpart across the capitol. Power is divided between a senate president and a majority leader, neither of who have the power to appoint committees. All committee assignments are made by a special committee on committees. Although the senate president, the majority leader, and the minority leader all try to influence this process by lobbying the committee for their chosen assignments, this approach substantially weakens the power of leadership. This system came about and is retained in part due to the "three party state" dynamic, which creates a situation in which no single faction has a majority sufficient to consolidate power. Some interviewed legislators suggested that this approach weakens the senate as an institution, relative to the house. Overall, the Kansas House shows the kind of stability one might expect in a state that does not have term limits. However, the Kansas Senate's example shows that power may be dispersed for other reasons besides term limits.

Committees

Term limits dispersed power in the Arkansas General Assembly. The state's committee system has been adjusted accordingly. For the first time in the state's history, the legislature now uses subcommittees. Minority Republicans, having made major gains in the number of seats held, now chair some committees. Perhaps the most interesting finding regards the decreasing number of attorneys elected to the General Assembly. Subjects told researchers that the decline in attorneys has brought a remarkable decline in the legislators' ability to "screen" bills for legality and practicality. As a result, the legislature increased reliance on centralized, nonpartisan staff.

Like Arkansans, Mainers have seen their legislative staff become more important under term limits. However, unlike their counterparts in Arkansas, Maine legislators have not made significant changes in the committee structure or jurisdiction to accommodate term limits. Researchers were told by interviewees that the committee chairs in Maine now show their lack of experience. They could use more training. Maine's committees have lost some of their "gatekeeping" power: they have less control over what legislation hits the floor and what legislation does not. Floor amendments are now more common. Committee reports are less likely to be heeded.

In control-state Kansas, observers and legislators praised the committee gatekeeping system. Both chambers have evolved a subcommittee approach to the budget during the past decade—mirroring the change in Arkansas, but this time without term limits forcing the change. Relations between the Kansas House and Senate can be rocky. Researchers were told by legislators from each chamber that theirs did the better job of screening bills. Senators accused the house of under-performing its gatekeeping function and sending them bills that were not well-screened. They called this a "fix it on the floor" philosophy. House leaders denied this. However, senate leaders did concede that the state's "three party state" dynamic led to more floor amendments in the senate than in the past—this represents a weakening of gatekeeping authority. Also, the legislators' self-reporting of stable procedures may be self-serving. In fact, the Kansas Legislature's leaders always struggle to unite factions into a majority. For years, Kansas budgets have been hastily assembled in a frenzy of last minute, late-night deal-making (Loomis 1994; Smith 2003).

Once again, the control state of Kansas casts doubt on this study's findings. Studying Kansas forces researchers to question whether or not changes in the other states can be really attributed to term limits. While Arkansas developed subcommittees under term limits, Kansas developed them without term limits. While the Maine Legislature now features weakened committee "gatekeeping," the Kansas Senate does, too—even without term limits. But the relatively stable example of the Kansas House indicates that the gatekeeping system may be a little more solid in a state that does not have term limits. Still, the results are mixed.

Staff

All three of these state legislators rely heavily on staff to disseminate institutional knowledge. This is inevitable, given that the legislatures are in session only part of the year, and the fact that the legislators are paid too little to treat the job as full-time when they are not in session. The two term-limited state legislators have increased their reliance on staff since term limits took effect.

Arkansas and Maine feature no personal staff at all. In Arkansas, there are not even many interns, due to an office space shortage in the capitol. But Arkansas does have centralized, nonpartisan staff. They are crucial repositories of institutional knowledge. Observers told researchers that the staff now has a lower turnover rate than the legislators themselves. They also said that the staff now has more of a role in screening bills. Still, staffers are not making policy. Interviewees added that the new legislators treat staff with more respect than did some of the legislators' long-serving predecessors.

Maine contrasts sharply with Arkansas on this issue. In the Pine Tree State, it is the partisan staff that has gained favor since term limits took effect. Partisan staffers have become the key storehouse of institutional memory. These staffers are now the key to maintaining rules and norms, because the new legislators are less interested then their own predecessors in maintaining the institution itself.

Term-limit-free Kansas resembles Arkansas rather than Maine, in that Sunflower State legislators turn to centralized, nonpartisan staff to fill the gaps in institutional knowledge left by high legislator turnover. As in Arkansas, interviewers in Kansas were told that staffers tend to serve longer than the legislators themselves, thus making staff the storehouse of institutional memory. Kansas is more generous than the other two states in providing for personal staff. Each rank-and-file senator has one administrative assistant, and there is also one assistant for every three rank-and-file house members. Each committee chair and party leader gets an administrative assistant. Though accommodations are modest, Kansas legislators do have some modest office space which many must share. Most offices must be shared by several legislators. Maine and Arkansas have no personal space at all for the legislators, except for the desks on the chamber floors.

The Kansas Legislature features small partisan staffs for the leaders of each party in each chamber, but their resources are stretched thin. One staffer interviewed had moved to the Sunflower State from another Midwestern state with a more-professionalized legislature. She was astonished to discover how much smaller her staff was, compared to the other state.

She had to stretch resources as far as she could, for example, by cutting photocopying so as not to hand out hard copies of bills in caucus unless they were almost sure to be debated that same day. This small partisan staff augments its meager resources with unpaid college and graduate school interns, and some Kansas party caucuses even fundraise for the express purpose of supplementing staff pay. Overall, it is the centralized, nonpartisan staff that secures institutional knowledge in Kansas. Legislators and staffers in both chambers and both parties praised these staffers effusively, arguing that they were well chosen, that morale was high, and that the legislature could not function without them.

Once again, the causal effects of term limits become muddled due to the inclusion of control-state Kansas. All three states feature heavy reliance on staff to hold institutional knowledge and screen legislation. However, in Maine this refers to the partisan staff. By contrast, centralized, nonpartisan staff takes that role in the other two citizen-legislature states. It appears that all three citizen legislatures rely heavily on staff due to high turnover among the legislators themselves, though the imposition of term limits in Maine and Arkansas may have accelerated this trend. The most startling contrast is not between the states with term limits and the state without them, but rather between Arkansas and Kansas, on one hand, and Maine, on the other. Why do the first two states' legislators turn to centralized, nonpartisan staff while the latter prefer to empower the partisan staffers? One plausible answer deserves further study: Maine features many independent voters and a long tradition of close party competition. Kansas and Arkansas have traditionally been bastions of one-party control. Kansas is usually in the hands of Republicans, while conservative southern Democrats have dominated Arkansas for over a century, though their grip is loosening.

Lobbyists

The role of lobbyists proved difficult to study in these states. This may be due in part to the fact that few legislators are willing to admit that lobbyists may sway their votes. Nor do lobbyists themselves wish to cultivate such an image. The legislators and lobbyists were nearly universal in their insistence that the lobbyist's role is to provide information. However, researchers were able to pinpoint some changes in Arkansas and Maine. Since the role of lobbyists appears to be remarkably stable in Kansas, changes in the other states may well be due to term limits.

In Arkansas, several interviewees suggested that lobbyists' influence has declined under term limits. The reason given for this is the removal of a well-connected "old guard" from legislative leadership. Longtime, powerful leaders have been removed from office (again—the senate president is most notable). These leaders had long, well-cultivated ties with certain lobbyists, which term limits swept away. Furthermore, the dispersion of power in the Arkansas General Assembly has also changed lobbying relationships. Once, the key task of an Arkansas lobbyist was to be in the good graces of the few that held most of the power. Today, many more legislators, even members of the minority party, hold power. Ties to each must be cultivated. These ties must be renewed frequently due to the much higher turnover. Sweeping away the "old boys' networks" was a well-known goal of term limits proponents—they are bound to be gratified by the Arkansas experience.

In Maine, as in Arkansas, few people argued that lobbyists had gained power under term limits. However, the dynamics are different. Maine's situation is complicated by the state's Clean Elections Law, which provides public financing for candidates that meet certain criteria and agree to certain restrictions. New legislators interviewed were very skeptical of lobbyists, perhaps due to the climate created by this law. Another possible explanation is the fact that many of Maine's candidates opt for public financing instead of developing fundraising ties to the groups the lobbyists represent.

In control-state Kansas, as elsewhere, legislators, staffers, and lobbyists were adamant in rejecting the suggestion that lobbyists had undue influence over legislation. One partisan staffer said, "I've never seen a vote swayed based on taking someone out to dinner." Lobbyists said that their primary task is simply tracking where a bill is within the committee system at any given time. Another lobbyist argued that his ranks have grown due to the government's increasing complexity. One lobbyist had to rack his brain to recall any changes during the past ten years. Finally he thought of one: there are more female lobbyists today. The lobbyists' situation seems more stable in Kansas than in the other states, suggesting that the changes elsewhere may indeed be due to term limits. Proponents of the limits will be gratified to hear that lobbyists appear to have lost power as a result. Most notably, term limits have indeed swept away the "old boys' network" in Arkansas.

The Legislative Process

There is no one-size-fits-all answer to how term limits have changed the legislative process. Republicans have clearly gained ground in Arkansas, but this may not be due to term limits. Civility and respect for rules and norms have declined in Arkansas and Maine, but experience in control-state Kansas has been mixed, suggesting that term limits may not be the sole cause in the other states. The Arkansas and Maine Legislatures are more partisan, while Kansas is dominated by a deeply split GOP whose factions spend more time fighting each other than they do fighting Democrats. In Arkansas, term limits empower the house relative to the senate, but the same phenomenon is happening in Kansas, without term limits. And in Maine, term limits empower not one chamber over another, but rather the governor over the legislature. Arkansas has responded to term limits with a new committee system, but Kansas has done the same (though less dramatically) even without term limits. Maine legislators have kept the committee system as-is but put more emphasis on training new legislators.

Partisanship

In Arkansas, perennial-minority Republicans have gained many seats, though not the majority. This pattern reflects a larger trend throughout the southern states, though it may have been hastened by term limits and the resulting higher turnover. Republicans now chair some committees in the Natural State, but paradoxically, observers also said that there is more partisan polarization than before.

In Maine, there is also some evidence of increasing partisanship—most notably the aforementioned reliance on partisan staff to hold institutional knowledge. Researchers were told that the biggest change is shorter time horizons, which lead to less regard for institutional norms and more focus on getting things done quickly.

In Kansas, the partisan dynamic is complicated by the "three party state" dynamic. Republicans function as two parties-within-a-party, making caucuses lively affairs. Traditionally outnumbered by moderate Republicans (but gaining steadily), dissident Sunflower State conservatives have pushed for minority-friendly rules in both chambers, thus making the process more open to Democrats than one might guess from the state's long history of Republican domination. Kansas Democrats told interviewers that they can be effective at stopping legislation or amending bills if they are experts on rules and procedure. Overall, Arkansas and Maine feature higher partisan divisions between Democrats and Republicans, while in Kansas, internal divisions within the GOP are the driving factor in state politics. How many of these differences are due to term limits? The answer is difficult to ascertain. Arkansas seems the easiest case—there, Republicans have grown from near-nonexistence as a legislative force to a powerful minority, and they also hold the governorship. Term limits probably hastened an inevitable change in this realigning southern state.

Civility

Arkansas and Maine have experienced declines in legislative civility. These may be due to term limits. In Kansas, most observers rated civility fairly well, though there is some evidence of strained relations, particularly in the senate.

In Arkansas, interviewees saw a clear decline in civility on the floors of both chambers. They attributed this to the decreased time legislators have for apprenticeship. Shorter time horizons lead to less time spent learning the rules and expectations of the game and socializing with one's colleagues. This appears to be the reason for declining civility. The knowledgeable observer survey confirms this—it shows that Arkansas legislators are now less likely to know and observe the unwritten rules of the process.

In Maine, civility is also on the decline. But the cause seems to be different. Maine legislators and observers fingered the rush to get legislation passed caused by shorter time horizons. This rush disrupts the process of building friendships and observing niceties. Furthermore, the committees' weakened powers of gatekeeping are leading to more floor disputes, again disrupting civility.

In Kansas, many interviewees defended the legislature's record of civility. One longtime staffer argued that civility was still very good in Kansas. He said, "We have a saying: you can disagree, but don't have to be disagreeable." However, some rough spots on the Senate floor regarding social issues like gay marriage put a few stains on this record. Overall, Kansas legislators seemed to maintain civility well on the chamber floors, but there was much cursing and muttering behind the scenes, particularly when divisive "culture war" issues or crucial decisions like redistricting were on the agenda. Several Kansas House leaders proudly noted that civility was better in their chamber than in the state senate.

It is interesting to note that turnover in the Kansas Senate, as in both chambers of each term-limited state, is high. It may be that the impact of term limits on civility are indirect—that they are in fact the result of high turnover, which in turn is hastened by term limits. The Kansas Senate features very high turnover even without term limits, which may be why it more closely resembles the performance of term-limited bodies than does the Kansas House with its lower turnover.

Balance of Power

The Arkansas Governor has several advantages over the legislature, but these are not the result of term limits. Arkansas governors are in office year-round and they have the powerful item veto. Still, governors struggle with the legislature: a recent power struggle involved the governor's push to consolidate small school districts. Legislators, defending local control and hometown pride, resisted this. Interestingly, a conservative Republican governor has also tussled with Democratic legislative leaders over the governor's tax increase proposals. In sum, interviewees saw little evidence for the claim that term limits actually empower the governor relative to the legislature. Those studied agreed that term limits empowered the house relative to the senate, mainly by dispersing power once held by the senate president.

Maine's results contrasted sharply with those in Arkansas. Maine observers agreed that term limits empowered the governor and the executive branch, relative to the legislature. Some attributed this to the state's governor, a popular independent, during the initial years under term limits, but the trend continued under his successor, a less charismatic Democrat. However, observers noted that the entire executive branch, including agency heads, had gained power. Executive leaders possessed the institutional knowledge being lost among the term-limited legislators. Observers were more divided when discussing Maine's other power shifts. Most notably, there was no consensus regarding how term limits affected the house-senate balance of power.

Kansas appears to be much more stable regarding the balance of power. This gives credence to the claim that term limits are causing the above-mentioned shifts in the other states. Observers agreed that there was no overall shift in power between the executive and legislative. They argued that the governor's power depended heavily on the political skills of whoever held the office. Though a Democrat, the current governor received high marks from legislators and observers—many Republican leaders preferred her style of working with the legislature to that of her predecessor, a fellow Republican. But governors can also squander power—one observer told stories of a governor facing bulk roll-call veto overrides. As mentioned previously, the Kansas Senate's very high turnover weakens any institutional advantage it would otherwise have over the house. Overall, the Kansas experience features only incremental change. Kansas suggests that the more dramatic balance of power shifts in Arkansas and Maine may indeed be due to term limits. In Arkansas, the big story has been a shift from senate to house, while in Maine, it has been from the legislative to the executive branch.

Adaptations

In Arkansas, influence has been dispersed to more leadership positions and a new subcommittee system. In Maine, leaders responded to term limits by emphasizing training and mentoring for new members. Maine leadership has expanded training programs already in existence before term limits took effect. There has been talk of a per-member bill introduction cap for each session, but this has not been implemented. Instead, leaders have personally asked members to limit bill introductions. It may be working: Maine's bill introductions rose dramatically right after term limits took effect, but more recently they have fallen. Still, they have not returned to pre-term-limit levels.

Maine has also created a new office to cope with the loss of institutional knowledge legislators now face. The new Office of Program Evaluation and Governmental Accountability (OPEGA) is based on a similar model used in

Florida. It was created to help with oversight of the executive branch by delivering reports to the legislature. It is accountable directly to the legislature, not the executive branch.

Control-state Kansas features a good deal of stability regarding legislator training and institutional adaptations. One longtime, high-ranking staffer had to think long and hard to recall any major institutional adaptations. However, he did suggest one: the legislature has greatly increased its reliance in information technology. Some members now research legislation using the World Wide Web, thus they no longer rely exclusively on staff for this function. A few committees are even experimenting with going "paperless." Kansas staffers did tell researchers that there are training and mentoring programs in place for new members, but these have been around for some time and have not been altered substantially in recent years. As mentioned before, Kansas has also evolved a subcommittee system to handle the budget. Legislators told interviewers that this was needed largely because of the increasing complexity of government in modern times.

CONCLUSION

Proponents of term limits did not say much about citizen legislatures. The reform was directly mainly at what were seen to be the bad effects of professionalization in other states and Congress. But term limits have indeed had some far-ranging effects in these citizen legislatures. Some of the changes are stark, while many others have been more muddled.

The most robust impact of term limits regards leadership and balance of power. While these things appear relatively stable in control-state Kansas (particularly in the house), in Arkansas the changes have been revolutionary, while in Maine, they have been substantial. Though term-limits proponents were not targeting citizen legislatures, they may still point to Arkansas as a success story. This state was clearly ruled by an "old boys' network" and a few powerful senate leaders before term limits took effect. The key to effectively lobbying was to cozy up to these powerful leaders. Term limits have weakened the senate president's iron grip on power. They have led to the creation of new leadership positions and a subcommittee system. They have opened up the once all-male state senate to a few women. And they appear to have hastened the increase in seats held by Republicans, as well as their power. Interestingly, term limits have empowered the house relative to the senate. Although it is true that many term-limited house members later run for senate, increasing the latter's institutional knowledge, the dispersion of power has been more than enough to negate any resulting power shift. Instead, the speaker and those holding the newly created leadership positions in both chambers now hold a good deal more power than before.

Centralized, nonpartisan staff has been empowered as the storehouses of institutional knowledge and procedure.

Maine's example gives more pause. The Pine Tree state has seen the legislature weakened, partisan staff empowered, and civility decline under term limits. But there has been no corresponding increase in representation for women or racial minorities. Nor have committee structures been forced to adapt. This is due in large part to the fact that Maine already had higher turnover than Arkansas, plus a more modern legislature, even before term limits took effect. Maine's term limits have resulted in a shift of power from the legislative to the executive. Partisan staff, not centralized staff, has been the ones empowered by the legislature's high turnover and loss of institutional knowledge. This may be due to the fact that partisan competition is closer and has a longer tradition in Maine than in the other states studied. Would-be party leaders in the Maine House now follow a "leadership ladder" pattern, serving in a different office every two years and becoming speaker within three terms. Overall, leaders in both chambers are less experienced than their predecessors, reversing a pattern of more-experienced leadership that had taken hold before 1993. Maine legislators have created a fledgling new office to help with oversight, and leaders not dedicate more resources to training.

The inclusion of term-unlimited Kansas is crucial to this study. Lacking term limits, the Sunflower State's example shows that other factors may lie behind some of the observed changes. It is true that the Kansas Legislature shows stability with regards to the legislative-executive balance of power, the role of lobbyists, and the role of staff. This suggests that corresponding changes in the other two states may indeed be due to term limits. But Kansas, like the other states, has seen a decline in legislators' time spent on home-district concerns. It has also seen a decline in civility. Like Maine, Kansas features recent increases in the volume of mail sent to constituents. And like Arkansas, Kansas has recently developed a subcommittee system to cope with the increasingly complex state budget. Thus none of these latter phenomena in the other states can necessarily be attributed to term limits.

Throughout this discussion, it has been clear that the Kansas Senate more closely resembles the term-limited chambers of Arkansas and Maine than does the Kansas House. This is no mystery. Average turnover in the Kansas is substantially higher than in the Kansas House. In the other states, the whole point of term limits was to force higher turnover. Thus instead of attributing changes in those state directly to term limits, it makes more sense to say that these changes are due to high turnover. Term limits are one way of forcing high turnover but they are not the only way: The Kansas Legislature, especially the Senate, features high turnover due to internal state politics and possibly to low pay. To represent the argument graphically:

Term limits	→	Increased reliance on staff, less
and/or Higher turnover	→	civility, changing balance of power
Other factors	→	relationships, more training, possible
		changes in leadership and/or
		committee structure

Finally, it should be noted that term limits have suppressed the outliers in the study. On most measures, the outlier in this group was Arkansas. The state had much more concentrated power, much less representation of women, and much more turnover than the others. Term limits have forced higher turnover and masked many of these differences.

NOTE

1. Special thanks to Brenda Erickson, Art English, Richard Powell and Rich Jones for contributing to this chapter.

11

Living With Term Limits

Alan Rosenthal

Michael V. Saxl, Speaker of the House, admits to being one of the greatest beneficiaries of term limits in Maine, and perhaps in the nation. In just five years, he went from being the lowest-ranking to the highest-ranking member of the house. Like the three legislators who preceded him in the top leadership position, his first term as speaker was also his last. Despite a rapid ascent up the leadership ladder, Saxl was of the opinion that the few positives were outweighed by the many negatives that resulted from term limits in Maine (Saxl 2001, 27).

Legislators in Maine and the other term-limited states that have been studied (Arizona, Arkansas, California, Colorado, and Ohio) largely agree with Saxl's assessment that the negative consequences of term limits trump the positive ones. Knowledgeable observers, who include legislative staff, lobbyists, and members of the state house press corps, also agree that the legislative process and legislative institutions have suffered as a result of term limits.

Since the period of legislative modernization and capacity building, which ran for about twenty years, from the mid-1960s into the 1980s, the legislative process and institution have been undergoing some erosion and decline (Rosenthal 1998). This had occurred in the non-term-limited states as well as in the twelve where term limits had had impact by 2000. Thus, some of the negative effects undergone by state legislatures are not attributable to term limits per se. But term limits probably enhanced these effects and produced others. At the very least, the changes taking place in term-limited states are more pronounced than those happening elsewhere.

However, term limits effects have differed somewhat in the six legislatures examined in this volume. California and Maine, where term limits impacted as early as 1996, appear to have undergone the greatest change. Ohio, where term limits impacted in 2000, appears to have undergone the least. In each state, and indeed in each chamber, change plays out somewhat differently.

COMPOSITIONAL EFFECTS

The most immediate and most visible effect of term limits has been the altered composition of the legislature. Limited terms means just that—newly elected members can serve only six, eight, or in a few cases twelve years in the house and eight or twelve in the senate. This results in higher turnover, a principal objective of term limits advocates. High turnover is not restricted to term-limited states, however, and it existed in some of the states studied here before term limits were imposed. Overall there has been a slight decline in turnover in non-term-limited states and an increase in turnover in term-limited states, a moderate increase in senates and a steeper increase in houses.

Thus, the tenure of term-limited legislators is shorter, and the proportion of freshmen at the start of each session is higher. This is much more the pattern in state houses than in state senates, since the tendency is for term-limited house members to run for the senate, while many fewer term-limited senators run for the house. Really missing in term-limited legislative bodies are veteran members, those with fifteen, twenty, or twenty-five years experience. Such legislators have been around long enough to learn the procedural ropes, familiarize themselves with many issues, specialize in one or two policy domains, and earn reputations as skillful legislators. They are gone, having been replaced by lawmakers who leave long before they can gain comparable experience.

While they obviously differ from non-term-limited legislators in their tenure and experience, term-limited legislators do not differ in the characteristics they bring to legislative service. Term limits may have tended to increase electoral competition in a few places, such as Arizona, or it may have hastened minority party opportunities to win some seats, as in Arkansas. But there is no evidence overall that term limits have increased competition or benefited one political party or the other. Nor would one expect either to be the case.

What proponents of term limits did expect and desire was the creation of opportunities for a new breed of legislators. They wanted amateur, citizen legislators, who would cycle in and out of public office, replacing the professionals who had been taking over legislative bodies since the 1960s. These expectations and desires have not been met. The people who run for the legislature in states with term limits are not different from their predecessors. Nor are they very different than their counterparts in non-term-limited states. Like longer tenured legislators, they like politics and are interested in carving out careers in politics for themselves. Term limits did create more opportunities, but the same types of people as before take advantage of these opportunities. If anything, the pool of political careerists has expanded, not contracted, as a result of term limits.

In California, where the contemporary term limits movement began, new legislators have been drawn from the same occupational backgrounds as previously. They had been and they continue to be professional politicians. As John Carey and his colleagues found in the nationwide survey conducted as part of this project, legislators in term-limited states were more likely than those in non term-limited states to have held elective public office prior to their election to the legislature (Carey, Niemi and Powell 1998, 271–300).[1]

In evidence of the continued professionalization of legislative politics is the fact that even before their terms expire, legislators in California, Ohio, and other term-limited states begin working toward securing their next public office. House members, reaching their limits, aspire to the senate—and many run successfully, while others settle for county or local office. Senate members, reaching their limits, also try to remain in public life. But many legislators also call it quits once their terms run out, in part because no offices are readily available.

Not only has there been little or no change in the political backgrounds or foregrounds of legislators in term-limited states, there has also been rather little change in their demographic characteristics. With greater turnover and consequently more open seats, some observers hoped that more women and more minority candidates would be elected. Yet, in the states under study there have been no discernible changes along these lines, and certainly none that can be attributed to term limits. In California, while more women and Latinos have been elected, the churning from term limits did not create the trend, but rather allowed it to be expressed somewhat earlier than otherwise. Generally speaking, as the national survey evidences, there are no differences between term-limited and non-term-limited states in members' gender, minority status, religious affiliation, age, family income, or ideology.

BEHAVIORAL EFFECTS

Because their time in office is fixed, term-limited legislators approach their jobs differently than legislators whose horizons extend farther. Because their tenure is brief, term-limited legislators also develop differently than legislators whose experience keeps accruing.

Anyone going into politics, and facing elections every two or four years, is not likely to think ahead very far. The future pretty much is now and not years ahead. Such short sightedness is even greater for legislators who face specified limits on their terms. They approach their legislative careers with a special sense of urgency. They do not have long, and they are thus impatient to get their agendas accomplished. As a legislative leader in Michigan commented, "Members must beat the clock to deliver on their campaign promises" (Perricone 2001, 30). Some lawmakers are strategic enough to choose issues and bills that promise more immediate payoffs. And if they aspire to leadership positions, they have to begin their campaigns quickly and need to get on the leadership ladder as soon as possible.

The notion if apprenticeship has not meant much in state legislatures for many years. It means even less in term-limited legislatures, where it is not unusual to find freshman members chairing standing committees. There is obviously no time for an apprenticeship of any kind before members have to dive right into the thick of lawmaking.

Nor are term-limited legislators disposed to specialize, since insufficient time is available to them to become expert in one policy domain or another. Committee members, and committee chairs in particular, do not serve long enough or gain enough experience to develop expertise in the jurisdictional areas of specific committees. During their limited tenures in the house or senate, they are more apt to move up the ladder, from leadership on a less important committee to leadership on a more important one or to a party leadership position. The survey of knowledgeable observers, which was conducted as part of this study project, shows that legislators in non-term-limited bodies were believed to specialize more than those in term-limited bodies and also to be more knowledgeable about both statewide issues and how the legislature operates. All of this is to be expected, if time on task in the legislature is equivalent to time on task in other endeavors.

It is believed by some observers that term limits not only help make legislators impatient but also keep them from the mellowing that comes along with aging. The longer people serve, the more they realize that they cannot always win and that accommodation is required. In Arizona, for instance, years of service have tended to make ideologically-driven legislators more pragmatic. That cannot happen anymore.

ORGANIZATIONAL CHANGE

Democratization is not new to state legislatures. For the past twenty-five years or so, resource disparities between leaders on the one hand and rank and file on the other and among members generally have been narrowing (Rosenthal 1998). That narrowing has been accelerated by term limits, largely because no member possesses the advantages of experience and expertise that normally accompany longer tenure. Thus, all members of the senate and all members of the house, thanks to short and equal terms, are more equal than they otherwise would be. However, the leveling of members is very different in each of the chambers. In the house, it is a dramatic leveling down, while in the senate the leveling has less of a downward slope.

When their terms expire, many house members will run for the senate. Substantially fewer senators, upon the expiration of their terms, run for the house. There are even those, like Ohio's Louis Blessing, who go back and forth. Blessing served fourteen years in the house before term limits, then term-limited out of the senate, and thereafter was again elected to the house. The result of the largely one-way migration is that many members of the senate, and nearly all of those in California, previously served in the house.

As a consequence, members of the senate, many who have served previously in the house, are more experienced than their counterparts on the other side of the capitol. In Maine, for example, senators may have lost respect for their inexperienced house colleagues; and conflict has increased between members of the two bodies. Disparities in experience tend to make the senate more influential vis-à-vis the house. In California, since term limits, the senate has been the dominant legislative body in the lawmaking process. It may still be too early to say definitively, but it appears that term limits contributes to an imbalance in the lawmaking influence of the two chambers.

Organizationally, what counts about as much as anything else is the condition of legislative leadership. When term limits were first being enacted, both proponents and opponents anticipated that legislative leaders—in particular, the presiding officers and majority party leaders—would suffer as a consequence. They were on the mark; as expected, the effectiveness of the legislature's top leadership has declined. There are individual exceptions, but the overall pattern is clear.

The job of leadership is not fundamentally different in term-limited legislatures, as compared to non-term-limited ones. Leaders have responsibility for appointments to standing committees, scheduling legislative sessions and the floor consideration of bills, developing strategies, negotiating, getting party members elected and reelected, and so forth. Certainly the leadership job is no less than it used to be; it may be somewhat more because of term limits. In a number of states, legislative leaders have started to play a role in candidate recruitment. In those with term-limited legislatures, due to higher turnover the need for candidate recruitment may be greater and the burden on leaders heavier. Once candidates are recruited and members elected, leadership has the additional task of spending time educating newcomers on the process and the issues. Some member education can be delegated to staff, but not all of it.

Leaders in term-limited legislatures are less likely to be equipped for the job than leaders in non-term-limited legislatures. They have less time to prepare, perhaps four to six years of service in the case of the house and about the same in the senate (although here leaders probably have also had six, eight, or possibly twelve years service in the house as well). Occasionally, members force a good deal of experience into a relatively short period, as in the case of the Maine house. Here members climb a leadership ladder, ascending first to whip, then to floor leader, and finally to speaker over three successive terms.

While learning the ropes on their way to leadership, competition intensifies. Legislators have to decide early and begin their quest for leadership almost as soon as they are sworn in for the first time. They cannot be expected to win over colleagues by dint of ability demonstrated over time. They have to launch their campaign for leadership, and that usually includes raising funds for the reelection of their legislative party colleagues. The campaign continues until the election of leadership takes place.

Elections of new leadership are frequent in term-limited states, fundamentally because of the limited amount of time that members have left to serve in their chamber. Sometimes, and more likely in a senate than a house, a member will retain top leadership for more than a term. For example, Larry Householder held the speakership for two terms in Ohio. Two terms would appear to be the limit for speakers and senate presidents, while one term is becoming the norm. In Colorado, for instance, following every state election new people are being selected as speaker and majority leader in the house and president and majority leaders in the senate.

How long does it take to learn the job of top leadership? No doubt, it takes longer than leaders in term-limited situations have to spend in such office. Therefore, leaders in term-limited legislatures cannot be expected to have the experience necessary to hone their skills. Furthermore, leaders are lame ducks practically as soon as they are sworn in, and certainly once they hand out committee appointments. Members tend to have less allegiance when they know that leaders will soon be gone. As reported by Berman in chapter 5 of this volume, a house member in Arizona regarded term limits as liberation for dissidents, pointing out that the speaker will be gone in a year and, "He can't put me in the doghouse for the next ten years." A member, who does not have to look forward to the probability or possibility of having to deal with a leader for the foreseeable future, has less incentive to go along with that leader today.

The national survey of legislators shows that in term-limited states the power of majority party leadership has declined. Power is more dispersed, incoming classes of members have solidified, and leadership finds it more difficult to build and manage consensus. With only occasional exceptions, leaders in term-limited legislatures are considered to be weaker than leaders in other legislatures.

Like top leaders, committee chairs have also lost influence as a consequence of term limits, according to the national survey of legislators. Yet, knowledgeable observers, who were surveyed in selected states, reported no difference in the influence of standing committees in term-limited and non-term-limited states. Yet, the case studies included in this volume suggest some marked differences. The California study concludes that:

> The committee system in the California Legislature is not working to develop the necessary expertise and institutional memory. Committee chairs and senior staff have significantly lower levels of experience and do not stay with committees for more than one term on average. This pattern has weakened gatekeeping especially in the Assembly. Legislators have not taken their budget subcommittees seriously in recent years.

Committee members and, most important, committee chairs have less experience, knowledge, and expertise in term-limited legislatures, and the differences between them and non-term-limited legislatures are substantial, according to the knowledgeable observer survey. This is understandable, since members serve only briefly on specific committees and have no incentives to specialize. Before term limits, committees knew the issues within their jurisdiction. That is no longer the case. Before term limits, committee members had incentives to work out compromises and bring a consensus recommendation to the floor. Not anymore. Before term limits committees were serious about their responsibility as gatekeepers, screening out many bills. Less screening is done today. Before term limits, the focus of legislators was on the committees to which they were assigned. The focus has shifted.[2]

To some extent, the business of committees has shifted to the majority party caucus. While on major issues the committee process has become more of a formality, the real work has been going on in the caucus room. In Maine, for example, leaders do not give committees enough time to work bills over and build consensus, even if committees wanted to do so. They pull bills out of committee and let disagreements be resolved in a partisan, not a bipartisan, setting. Furthermore, with only a brief time to serve, leaders have a sense of urgency about their legacy. Major policy initiatives, therefore, are more likely to come from them than from the committees and the committee chairs.

Legislators in term-limited states pay less attention to reports and recommendations of standing committees on which they do not serve. A committee's work is apt to be revised in caucus, challenged on the floor, or modified by amendments, although it may not be rejected absolutely. Legislator deference to standing committees has declined significantly because of term limits.

With leaders and members no longer as experienced as they used to be, their loss of power could be assumed to be someone else's gain. Political scientists generally predicted that the legislative staff, on the one hand, and lobbyists, on the other, would have additional power under term limits.

However, the evidence for either prediction is mixed and less than persuasive.

Certainly, the job of professional staff in term-limited states has changed, and perhaps the need for staff services has increased. Staff faces the challenge of educating new members, probably more on process matters than on substantive issues. Neither the national survey of legislators nor the survey of knowledgeable observers in selected states evidenced greater staff influence because of term limits. New members do turn to both nonpartisan and partisan staff for information; and staff, of course, is responsive. Nonpartisan staff—which still dominates in most states including Arizona, Arkansas, Colorado, Maine, and Ohio—is careful not to overstep its bounds by offering policy advice rather than simply information and options. Partisan staff—which dominates in California (and Michigan among term-limited states)—is more likely to offer both policy and process advice. But that is as common in non-term-limited states as in those with term limits.

One of Thad Kousser's conclusions is that members of nonpartisan staff have lost the close relationship they once had with veteran members (Kousser 2005). If this is true, it is a real loss for the legislature. Probably the most productive staffers have been those who worked with legislators who were policy experts, usually at the committee level. There was no question in these relationships of who had primary influence, but legislator and staffer together playing their respective roles were able to craft important legislation. With veteran legislators and experienced committee chairs generally extinct in term-limited states, this type of working relationship can no longer be found.

The job of lobbyists, and especially contract or independent lobbyists, has also been affected by term limits. Most obviously, the more rapid turnover of legislators requires lobbyists to devote greater effort to the education of members on subjects they are promoting. Unlike in non-term-limited states, lobbyists nowadays cannot count on legislators having much familiarity with the organizations, clients, and issues they represent.

The relationships that develop between lobbyist and legislator over the course of years have no opportunity to develop under term limits. Lobbyists try to make up the ground, building relationships as quickly as they can do so. But it is not the same. Relationship building necessitates that lobbyists and legislators spend substantial time or high quality time together. Neither is any longer an option. And newer members, who are by no means confined to term-limited legislatures, view lobbyists with some suspicion. Given the anti-lobbyist climate outside the legislature, it is not surprising that freshman legislators would be standoffish. With experience in office, these new legislators would gain confidence and figure out how to make the most of lobbyists, their information, and their support. Having learned the procedural ropes and having acquired familiarity with the substance of policy, they would not have to resist lobbyists out of fear of relying too heavily on them for information or being taken advantage of by them. The required time is not available. Still, it should be noted that, according to the authors of the California study, nine out of ten bills that freshmen legislators introduce come from lobbyists.

Although the job of the lobbyist is probably tougher under term limits, there is disagreement as to whether lobbyists are more or less powerful than they used to be or than they are in other states. The national survey of legislators suggests that term limits has had no measurable effect on the influence of interest groups and the knowledgeable observer survey reports no difference in the influence of lobbyists in term-limited and non-term-limited states. In some states, such as California and Colorado, there seems to be a greater reliance on lobbyists; in other states, such as Arizona, Arkansas, and Maine, this is not the case.

If the overall influence of lobbyists has not shifted much, influence within the lobbying profession may have leveled at least somewhat. With relationships no longer as important as they used to be, the influence among contract or independent lobbyists who relied more on a relationship game may be somewhat diminished. Meanwhile, in-house lobbyists, representing associations, corporations, and labor have been less affected, because for them their organization and its standing were more important than the relationships they forged. Under term limits, moreover, veteran lobbyists have suffered more than newer ones, because of the leveling of the playing field. While relationships may have lost some clout, the importance of political support—for the most part campaign contributions—is undiminished with or without term limits. In Maine, it is true, the adoption of a "clean election" law a few years ago decreased the reliance of legislators on lobbyists for campaign contributions; but that change had little to do with term limits.

LEGISLATIVE PERFORMANCE

Although the effects of term limits on legislative composition, behavior, and organization are important, of greatest concern are effects on legislative performance. Does the legislature do a better or a worse job as a consequence of term limits?

The job of the legislature is not that of producing one policy or another or that of helping to improve the state economy or reforming elementary and secondary education. The products of the legislature are, of course, critical; but whether specific products—that is bills and revenue and expenditures enacted into law—are more or less worthwhile varies according to the values and interests of the observer. Furthermore, it should be realized that the legislature is not only a means to an end; it is an end in itself. The legislature and the legislative process as an end furnish the means by which the states and their citizens examine various options and decide on just what public policy should be (Rosenthal 2004). The legislature's major value is that it is the driving engine of representative democracy in the states.

The job of the legislature is essentially fourfold: first, representing constituents and constituencies, by means of serving their interests and expressing their views; second, lawmaking, which includes study and deliberation, negotiation and compromise, and putting together a succession of majorities to pass budgets and enact bills; third, balancing the power of the executive, especially on matters of revenues and expenditures and decisions on public policy for the state; and fourth, providing for the maintenance and wellbeing of the legislature as an institution. How, then, have term limits affected the performance of these aspects of the legislature's job?

The effects of term limits on representation remain unclear. Surveys show one thing, case studies another. The national survey of legislators suggests that term-limited legislators alter their behavior in a Burkean direction. As reported by Carey, Niemi and Powell (2003):

> Legislators in term limits states seem no less interested in getting reelected as long as they are eligible, and spend equal amounts of time campaigning and fundraising. Yet their interest in reelection does not manifest itself in an exclusive focus on district matters. Rather, by their self-reports they pay less attention to their constituents—whether judged by constituency service or by attention to pork—and are more inclined to favor their own conscience and the interests of the state in contrast to those of the district.

This diminished district orientation is especially apparent in legislators' last terms. The knowledgeable observers survey, conducted in selected states, produced similar results. Legislators in term-limited states tended to spend less time talking to their constituents, solving constituents' problems, seeking funds for projects in their districts, and sending newsletters and other mailings to the district.

The case studies presented here, however, reveal no disconnect between term-limited legislators and their districts. In Arkansas, Arizona, Colorado, Maine, and Ohio the effects are nil. Lawmakers deal with constituents, respond to district concerns, and do case work just as was done before and currently is done elsewhere. In fact, an examination of legislator's requests of the Legislative Council for help from the constituent service staff shows no lessening after term limits kicked in. Larry Householder, Ohio's former speaker of the house suggests a heightened district orientation, observing that new legislators were even more attuned to constituent service (Householder 2001, 31). And Chuck Perricone, Michigan's former speaker of the house, points out that more members commuted home and grassroots re-

lationships in the district had become more important than the influence
of colleagues and lobbyists in the capitol (Perricone 2001, 30).

There is doubt, then, as to whether term limits have impacted on representatives serving their districts' interests. There is even greater doubt as to
whether term limits have changed how representatives express their constituencies' views (Rosenthal 2004, 35–36). Generally speaking, on very few
issues do constituency views exist. On even fewer are the views clearly on one
side of an issue rather than the other. On issues where the constituency has
a position, representatives and constituents usually see eye to eye. Rarely
does a representative have to choose between conscience and constituency.
In such instances, and depending on the issue, the representative is slightly
more inclined to choose conscience. Term limits does not appear to make
any difference regarding this mode of representation. Certainly, no support
is furnished for George Will's contention that term limits would increase the
independence of legislators and allow them to think more about the collective good (Will 1993).

Lawmaking in the legislature has also been impacted by term limits, although no dominant pattern has yet to emerge. There is no real difference
between knowledgeable observers in term-limited and non-term-limited
states in their assessments of deliberation, negotiation, and compromise by
the legislature. Although they report more partisanship generally, its inci-
dence is about the same in both types of states.

Nevertheless, the case studies report effects. In Arizona, it is noted, inexperienced legislators are more apt to make mistakes. Maine has witnessed a
larger number of bills introduced. Ohio, in particular, has suffered from a
decrease in civility because legislators have little time or incentive to build
relationships with one another. Colorado's "policy champions," members
who stayed with an issue for years, no longer exist. And according to
Kousser, term-limited legislators, whose perspective is extremely short-
range, produce less innovative policies (Kousser 2005, 338). Most notably,
in California the legislative budget process appears to have broken down.
Legislators know less about the budget as a whole; relatively little work gets
done by the subcommittees; and fiscal accountability is reduced.

The major impacts of term limits on the lawmaking function probably
stem from a weakening of both leadership and committees. As mentioned
earlier, inexperienced and transitional leaders exercise less influence over
members and face greater difficulty in building consensus. They are probably more inclined to try to put together the votes they need in their own
majority party caucus rather than by working with the minority party.

The weakening of committees and the committee process, however, may
in the long run do the greatest damage to the legislature. With standing committees regarded by members as less expert and less authoritative, the work
of shaping legislation now is being done elsewhere. Usually that elsewhere

is the majority party caucus. This accounts in part for the observation that partisanship is on the rise in states like California, Colorado, and Ohio, even though it may not be directly linked to term limits. A shift from committee to caucus entails subtle, albeit significant, changes in the legislature's performance of its lawmaking function.

It is in the committee stage that most study and deliberation takes place. And it is here that the focus is largely, although not entirely, on the substantive merits of bills, alternatives, and amendments. Such study and deliberation seldom takes place on the floor of the chamber or in a caucus room. Indeed, scrutiny within the caucus may have its deliberative aspects, but it is apt to focus more on political merits than on substantive ones.[3] How will a measure help or hurt caucus members with their constituents and how will it play out politically at the next election? In caucus, of course, expert knowledge is less relevant than it is in committee.

When the locus of scrutiny and decision shifts to the majority party caucus, members of only one party participate in the process. By contrast, standing committees consist of members of both parties. Although the majority party controls the committee, minority party members seldom are denied a role. A knowledgeable and respected member of the minority can influence the crafting of legislation in the processes of deliberation and negotiation that take place in committee. So, when the committee is replaced by the caucus, minority party members lose their lawmaking role. Thus, the bipartisan, substantive nature of the enterprise is eroded, while the partisan, political nature is strengthened. And this development reinforces the rise in partisanship that stems mainly from the competitiveness of politics today and the fact that the legislature is presently an arena which election campaigns are conducted.

The third major part of the legislative job is that of balancing the power of the executive. In nearly all the states the governor has the upper hand in relationship to the legislature, primarily because the governor is one and the legislature is many. The governor alone decides what legislation to propose and what budget to present, albeit after consultation within and outside of the executive branch. The legislature, by contrast, consists of two houses, two or more parties, and anywhere from 60 to 424 legislators. Decisions in the legislature are reached by a succession of majority votes. Because the governor is one, and because he or she is elected statewide, the governor commands the "bully pulpit" and, through the media or otherwise, can get the administration's message across to the public.

In a system of separated powers and checks and balances, the legislative branch ought to maintain parity with the executive. This is difficult for it to do; and, in the judgment of members themselves, legislatures do not perform the balancing function as well as they do the functions of representation and lawmaking (Rosenthal 2004, 232–43).

The evidence is clear and consistent that, as a result of term limits, the legislature has been losing ground to the governor and executive branch. The national survey found the increased influence of governors in term-limited states as opposed to non-term-limited states, according to the perceptions of legislators. The knowledgeable observer survey, which focused on Arizona, Arkansas, California, Colorado, Maine, and Ohio, among term-limited states, and Illinois, Indiana, and Kansas among non-term-limited ones, also shows that term limits has weakened the legislature. The perceived influence of the governor has grown, compared to a decade ago, to the greatest extent in Colorado and Maine, to a somewhat lesser extent in Arkansas, California, and Arizona among the term-limited states, and even less in Kansas, Illinois, and Indiana. Only in term-limited Ohio is the governor perceived to be weaker vis-à-vis the legislature today; and this is largely attributable to the problems faced by the administration of Governor Bob Taft and the fact that Ohio's Republican senate and house even after term limits have both continued to assert themselves in a traditional way for the legislature. Similarly, the influence of administrative agencies has grown markedly in term-limited states but less so in others.

Kousser's examination of budgets reinforces the point. His conclusion is that term-limited legislatures are weaker in dealing with governors: "Every state with term limits," he writes, "shows a substantial decline over the past decade in how much legislatures are able to alter the governor's requests." Legislatures do worse in bargaining over budget items, controlling budget lines, and shaping policy (Kousser 2005, 25, 176, 339).

The study of California details the legislature's decline in the number of requests for administrative agencies in connection with the budget, the drop in the number of audits to investigate agency activities, and the decline in legislative requests for information from the executive in connection with the budget. It is not surprising, since newer legislators do not know what questions to ask and have little incentive to ask questions at all. Their main concern as budgeters is with their own districts.

The sapping of the strength of legislative leadership is felt in the relationship of the legislature and the governor. In dealing with the governor, inexperienced and transient legislative leaders are unable to represent their members and negotiate from positions of strength. It is difficult enough for seasoned leaders, who have the full support of their caucuses. It is even tougher for the term-limited leaders whose power is on the wane almost as soon as they assume office. It is little wonder that the upper hand of governors' vis-à-vis legislatures is higher in term-limited states than it is elsewhere.

The fourth function performed by legislatures is less concrete than the other three. The care and maintenance of the legislature as an institution requires concern and commitment on the part of both leaders and members.

Even before the advent of term limits, relatively few legislators truly had an institutional orientation. The large majority were consumed by other, more immediate tasks.

The development of an institutional orientation takes time, and there is no guarantee that it will develop at all. Newly elected members come to the legislature with their own constituencies, beliefs, and agendas clearly in mind. Until given responsibility as subcommittee or committee chairs or as party leaders, they think and operate mainly as individual entrepreneurs, while also having to act as team players. It is only when they have to build consensus within a committee or round up the votes for a bill wanted by members of the caucus that members see the legislative process and the legislature from a collective perspective. This experience appears necessary for members to become concerned about the strength and well being of the legislature. Historically, for example, it had been the most experienced members of the Colorado legislature who served as preservers and enforcers of institutional norms and defenders of the legislative branch in separation-of-powers conflicts. These members are no longer around.

Institutional orientations are rarer today than they used to be. In both the term-limited and non-term-limited states included in the knowledgeable observers survey, the perception was that current legislators were less apt to defend and support their institution. The only exception was Indiana, where the institutional commitment was perceived to be high. Term-limited legislators, however, were seen to be even less committed than others.

Members have few incentives to bother much with the legislature as an institution. They do not expect to be there very long and their experience in leadership positions is necessarily brief. Their perspective almost has to be short term, while the institution is long term. Leaders generally share the perspective of immediacy, although they have a larger institutional role. Take Maine, for example. For leaders as well as members here process matter less than results. Looking to achieve some legacy, leaders focus on their agendas, which they have to achieve quickly. They focus on their policy proposals, not on the well being of their institution. They are generally unconcerned with how well the legislature works. Since Maine's leaders no longer come from committee leadership positions, they have limited understanding of how committees develop consensus and how much effort it takes. So, they are not reluctant to bypass committees. They are in a hurry; they have to be.

Perhaps today more than ever, legislatures are under siege. The media are critical, and often unfairly so. Interest groups are relentless in their demands. People in general are cynical, even distrustful. Legislatures need appreciation, understanding, and support. But if legislative leaders and members do not rally round their institution, the public cannot be expected to change its attitudes and provide any support. Term limits has done considerable harm here.

CONCLUSIONS

A decade's experience with term limits leads to several conclusions.

First, while the effects are not uniform among the states, patterns do emerge. The most notable ones are as follows:

On the composition of legislatures:
1. Higher turnover
2. Less experienced members
3. No veterans
4. Acceleration of political ambition

On the behavior of legislators:
5. Short-term orientations
6. Decline in specialization and expertise

On organizational matters:
7. Further democratization
8. Weakening of house vis-à-vis senate
9. Weakening of top leadership
10. Weakening of standing committees
11. More difficult job for legislative staff
12. More difficult job for lobbyists

On legislative performance:
13. Deterioration of lawmaking process
14. Less study and deliberation
15. Decreased role for minority party members
16. Weaker legislature vis-à-vis governor and executive departments and agencies
17. Diminished commitment by leaders and members to the legislature as an institution

Second, the stated objectives of the proponents of term limits have not been met. Although more opportunities for legislative office have been created, the same kinds of people run for office. The non-political citizen legislator has not emerged in states dominated by politicos, nor has the nature of the membership changed in the so-called citizen legislatures with term limits. Nor has the legislature become more independent, as some of the proponents hoped. If anything, term-limited legislatures are more dependent.

Third, arguments made by opponents of term limits, in large part, have been borne out. The lack of experience, knowledge, and tenure potential has had harmful effects. And in a zero-sum power game, the governor and executive have come out ahead. The legislature, as opponents feared, is a weaker institution because of term limits.

Fourth, the effects appear to be greater in the more professionalized legislatures, such as California, Michigan, and Ohio. The less-professionalized legislatures already had a mild form of term limits because of relatively high voluntary turnover. According to Kousser, the consequence is a narrowing of the gap between professional legislatures, on the one hand, and citizen legislatures, on the other. Thus, some of the changes wrought by the legislative modernization movement of the late 1960s, 1970s, and early 1980s have been undermined by term limits (Kousser 2005, 332, 346).

Fifth, the legislature as an institution and the legislative process are diminished. The good news is that, despite adverse effects, nobody will die from the imposition of term limits in the sixteen states where they have had impact or are about to have impact. That is to say, legislatures in these states are still working, performing their functions of representation, lawmaking, and balancing the power of the executive. Bills are introduced and enacted, budgets are adopted. Even with term limits, some like Ohio, appear to be doing pretty well at their job.

The bad news is also that nobody will ever die from term limits. The negative effects are barely perceptible to the naked eye; it takes investigators with more powerful lenses to discern the damage being done. This means that without the equivalent of catastrophe or scandal that in some way can be tied to term limits, the odds are that public support for term limits will not erode much. However, the odds can be overcome and they have been in several instances. Term-limits initiatives have been beaten on the ballot in Mississippi and North Dakota. In 2003, the Idaho legislature repealed the statute that had been adopted through an initiative. Proponents of term limits rounded up the required number of signatures to put it on the ballot again. But the voters rejected the proposition, and the Idaho Legislature was successful in throwing off the shackles of term limits. On the other hand, efforts in California to extend the limits of legislators' terms have thus far been unsuccessful.

It would seem that as far as adoptions are concerned term limits have run the course. Just about every state that allows for the initiative to bypass the legislature has adopted or rejected term limits (or has had it thrown out by the courts). In only one state, Louisiana, did the legislature itself adopt term limits, even though there was no possible threat of an initiative. Other legislatures are not likely to do so of their own accord.

Nevertheless, repeal at least in a few states is still possible, albeit not probable. Persuading the electorate to allow public officials to serve longer will be a hard sell in the current climate of cynicism toward and distrust of political people, political institutions, and political processes. A campaign to win the public over will require energetic leadership, a broad-based coalition of interest groups, bipartisan support, and a message and approach that delivers genuine public education. And, then, there is still no guarantee. But, for those who regard the legislature as a vital institution to democracy and are concerned about its weakening, the effort is worthwhile; indeed, it is imperative.

NOTES

1. John M. Carey, Richard G. Niemi, and Lynda W. Powell, "The Effects of Term Limits on State Legislatures: Results from a New Survey of the Fifty States" (2003), will be referred to as the "national survey" in the text.

2. It should be noted that term-limited legislatures are not the only ones with weak committee systems. In Illinois, for instance, committees have been weak for many years without ever having to endure term limits.

3. This may be one of the reasons why Richard Brake characterized the legislative process in Maine and Michigan as being less deliberative. See his, "Who's in Charge? The Impact of Term Limits on State Legislative Budgeting," Ph.D. dissertation, Temple University, May 2003.

Bibliography

Abrams, Matt. 2003. "Increased Amendments in California Make a Case For—or Against—Term Limits" *Institute of Governmental Studies Public Affairs Report*, vol. 44, no.1, Spring 2003.

Anderson, Mark. 1995. "Changes on the Way: Preliminary Effects of Term Limits in Arizona," *U.S. Term Limits Foundation Outlook Series*, IV (November 1995): 4.

Anonymous. 2003. "GOP bloc may swing budget vote," *The Arizona Republic* (June 9, 2003), A1, A2.

Arkansas Democrat Gazette. 1999. "Top 10 most influential lobbyists in Arkansas." January 11, 1999, 2A.

———. 2003. "Key Lobbyists 84th General Assembly." January 12, 2003, 14A.

Bailey, Eric. 2004. "Age Before Duty," *Los Angeles Times*, June 8, 2004, A1.

Barber, James D. 1962. *The Lawmakers: Recruitment and Adaptation to Legislative Life*. New Haven, CT: Yale University Press.

Barge, Liz. 2001. "Term Limits Affect Legislative Career Paths," *Institute of Governmental Studies Public Affairs Report*, vol. 42, no.3, Fall 2001.

Barth, Jay. 2003. "Arkansas: More Signs of Momentum for Republicanism in Post-"Big Three" Arkansas." *The American Review of Politics* 24: 111–126.

Bell, Charles G. and Charles M. Price. 1980. *California Government Today: Politics of Reform*. Homewood, IL: The Dorsey Press.

Berman, David R. 1998. *Arizona Politics and Government: The Quest for Autonomy, Democracy, and Development*. Lincoln, NE: University of Nebraska Press.

———. 2001. "Arizona Government Over Time: The Good, The Bad, and the Ugly." In *Pieces of Power: Governance in Arizona*, ed. Brent Brown and Jeffrey Chapman. Phoenix, AZ: Arizona Town Hall, 17–32.

Beyle, Thad L. 1992. "Term Limits in the State Executive Branch," in *Limiting Legislative Terms*. Gerald Benjamin and Michael J. Malbin, eds. Washington, D.C.: CQ Press.

———. 2004. "Governors." In *Politics in the American States*, eds. Virginia Gray and Russell L. Hanson. Washington, D.C: CQ Press.

Blair, Diane D. 1988. *Arkansas Politics and Government: Do the People Rule?* Lincoln: University of Nebraska Press.

Bowman, Ann O'M., and Richard C. Kearney. 1986. *The Resurgence of the States*. Englewood Cliffs, NJ: Prentice-Hall.

Brady, David and Brian Gaines. 1995. "A House Divided? Evaluating the Case for a Unicameral California Legislature," in *Constitutional Reform in California: Making State Government More Effective and Responsive*, ed. Bruce E. Cain and Roger G. Noll. Berkeley, CA: Institute of Governmental Studies Press.

Brake, Richard. 2003. "Who's in Charge? The Impact of Term Limits on State Legislative Budgeting." Ph.D. dissertation, Temple University, May 2003.

Bratton, Kathleen A. and Haynie, Kerry L. 2001a. "When the Seniority Ladder Collapses: The Determinants of Leadership in Term Limited and Non-Term Limited States Legislatures." [Paper presented at the Annual Meeting of the American Political Science Association, San Francisco, California, August 30–September 1, 2001.]

———. 2001b. "The Determinants of Leadership in Term-Limited and Non-Term-Limited State Legislatures." Presented at the Annual Meeting of the American Political Science Association, San Francisco, CA.

Brokaw, Brian, Keith Jobson, and Paul Vercruyssen. 2001. "Knowledge and Power in the Post Term Limits Era: The Effects of Term Limits on Committee Chief Consultants in the California Legislature." Paper completed for UC Berkeley's PS 171: California Politics, Prof. Bruce Cain, Spring 2001.

Brummett, John. 2007 "Time to Pay the Speaker." *Arkansas Times*, 24 May, 23.

Burchell, Joe. 1998. "There's no fun in legislative run, Arizonans say term limits and lack of civility are cited," *The Arizona Daily Star* (July 5, 1998), 1A.

Burns, John. 1971. *The Sometimes Governments*. New York: Bantam.

Cain, Bruce E. and Marc Levin. 1999. "Term Limits." *Annual Review of Political Science*. 2: 163–88.

Cain, Bruce E. and Thad Kousser. 2004. *Adapting to Term Limits: Recent Experiences and New Directions*. San Francisco, CA: Public Policy Institute of California.

Cain, Bruce, John Hanley, and Thad Kousser. 2006. "Term Limits: A Recipe for More Competition?" In *The Marketplace of Democracy: Electoral Competition and American Politics*, eds. Michael P. McDonald and John Samples. Washington, DC: Brookings Institution.

California Journal Press. 1997. *California Political Almanac, 1997–98, Sixth Edition*. Sacramento, CA: California Journal Press, and earlier editions.

———. 2004. *Roster and Government Guide*. Sacramento, CA: Statenet, and earlier editions.

California Legislature. 2001. *Assembly Final History, 1999–2000 Session*. Sacramento, CA: California Legislature, and earlier editions.

———. 2001. *Senate Final History, 1999–2000 Session*. Sacramento, CA: California Legislature, and earlier editions.

Capell, Elizabeth. 1993. "The Impact of Term Limits on the California Legislature: An Interest Group Perspective." Paper presented at the annual meeting of the Western Political Science Association, Pasadena, CA.

——. 2001. "Ten Years Into Term Limits: Academic Findings and the View from the Legislature," Institute of Governmental Studies Conference, Sacramento, California, May 17, 2001.

Caress, Stanley M. 1999. "The Influence of Term Limits on the Electoral Success of Women." *Women & Politics* 20: 45–63.

——. 2001. "Term Limit's Impact on the Election of Minority State Legislators: Evidence from the California State Assembly and Michigan State House." [Paper presented at the Annual Meeting of the American Political Science Association, San Francisco, California, August 30–September 1, 2001.]

Carey, John M., Gary F. Moncrief, Richard G. Niemi, and Lynda W. Powell. 2003. "Term Limits in the State Legislatures: Results from a New Survey of the 50 States." Presented at the Annual Meeting of the American Political Science Association, Philadelphia, PA.

Carey, John M., Richard G. Niemi, and Lynda W. Powell. 1998. "The Effects of Term Limits on State Legislatures," *Legislative Studies Quarterly* 23 (May 1998), 271–300.

——. 2000. *Term Limits in the State Legislatures.* Ann Arbor, MI: University of Michigan Press.

——. 2003. "The Effects of Term Limits on State Legislatures Results from a New Survey of the Fifty States" (2003),

Carroll, Susan J., and K. Jenkins. 2001. "Unrealized Opportunity? Term Limits and the Representation of Women in State Legislatures." *Women & Politics* 23: 1–30.

Citizens Conference on State Legislatures. 1971. *The Sometime Governments: A Critical Study of the 50 American Legislatures.* Kansas City, MO: The Citizens Conference on State Legislatures.

Citizens for Term Limits. 2002. "Citizens for Term Limits Position Statement." http://www.termlimits.com/position.htm (March 12, 2003).

Clucas, Richard A. 1994. "Stability in Change: Assessing the First Post–Term Limit Election in California." Paper presented at the annual meeting of the Western Political Science Association, Albuquerque, NM.

——. 2001. "Principal–Agent Theory and the Power of State House Speakers." *Legislative Studies Quarterly,* 26: 319–38.

Cohen, Linda R., and Matthew L. Spitzer. 1996. "Term Limits and Representation." In *Legislative Term Limits: Public Choice Perspectives,* ed. Bernard Grofman. Boston, MA: Kluwer.

Colorado General Assembly Legislative Council. 1990. "An Analysis of 1990 Ballot Proposals." Denver, CO: State of Colorado.

Constitution of the State of Arkansas of 1874. 1996. Published by Sharon Priest, Secretary of State.

Copeland, Gary W. 1992. "Term Limitations and Political Careers in Oklahoma: In, Out, Up, or Down." In *Limiting Legislative Terms,* eds. Gerald Benjamin and Michael J. Malbin. Washington, D.C: CQ Press.

Davenport, Paul. 2004. "More legislators included in closed-door talks on budget," *Associated Press State and Local Wire,* February 24, 2004.

Ehrenhalt, Alan. 1991. *The United States of Ambition.* New York: Times Books.

Elhauge, E., J.R. Lott, and R.L. Manning. 1997. "How Term Limits Enhance the Expression of Democratic Preferences." *Supreme Court Economic Review* 5: 59–80.

Emanuels, Ken. 2001. "Ten Years Into Term Limits: Academic Findings and the View from the Legislature," Institute of Governmental Studies Conference, Sacramento, California, May 17, 2001.

Enemark, Dan and John Cross. 2002. "Term Limits Have Changed California's Legislative Behavior," *Institute of Governmental Studies Public Affairs Report*, vol. 43. no.2, Summer 2002.

English, Art. 1991. "Work Styles in the Arkansas General Assembly." Paper delivered at the annual meeting of the Arkansas Political Science Association, Henderson State University, Arkadelphia, Arkansas.

———. 2003. "Term Limits in Arkansas: Opportunities and Consequences." *Spectrum: The Journal of State Government*. 76: 30–33.

English, Art, and John. J. Carroll. 1983. *Citizens' Manual to the Arkansas General Assembly.* Institute of Politics and Government, Little Rock, Arkansas.

———. 1992. "Arkansas: The Politics of Inequality," in Ronald J. Hrebenar and Clive S. Thomas, eds. *Interest Group Politics in the Southern States.* Tuscaloosa, AL. University of Alabama Press.

English, Art and Linda Goss. 1986. "Follow the Leader: Leadership Structure in the Arkansas General Assembly." Paper delivered at the annual meeting of the Arkansas Political Science Association, North Little Rock Hilton, North Little Rock, February 1986.

Everson, David H. 1992. "The Impact of Term Limitations on the States: Cutting the Underbrush or Chopping Down the Tall Timber?" In *Limiting Legislative Terms*, eds. Gerald Benjamin and Michael J. Malbin. Washington, DC: CQ Press.

Everson, David H., Joan A. Parker, William L. Day, Rita A. Harmony, and Kent D. Redfield. 1982. *Illinois Issues Special Report: The Cutback Amendment.* Springfield, IL: Illinois Issues.

Farmer, Rick. 1993. "Alienation and Term Limits." Paper presented at the Southwestern Political Science Meeting, New Orleans, LA.

———. 2002. "The Future of Political Parties in Term Limited State Legislatures." *Spectrum* 75(4): 14–8.

Farmer, Rick, John David Rausch, Jr. and John C. Green. 2003. *The Test of Time: Coping with Legislative Term Limits.* Lanham, MD: Lexington Books.

Fenno, Richard F., Jr. 1978. *Home Style: House Members in Their Districts.* Ontario, CA: Scott, Foresman and Company.

Francis, Wayne L. 1989. *The Legislative Committee Game.* Columbus, OH: The Ohio State University Press.

Francis, Wayne L., and L. W. Kenny. 1997. "Equilibrium Projections of the Consequences of Term Limits upon Expected Tenure, Institutional Turnover, and Membership Experience." *Journal of Politics* 59: 240–52.

Frank, Thomas. 2004. *What's the Matter With Kansas: How Conservatives Won the Heart of America.* New York: Metropolitan.

Fund, John H. 1992. "Term Limitation: An Idea Whose Time Has Come." In *Limiting Legislative Terms*, eds. Gerald Benjamin and Michael J. Malbin. Washington, DC: Congressional Quarterly.

Garrett, E. 1996. "Term Limitations and the Myth of the Citizen-Legislator." *Cornell Law Review* 81: 623–97.

General Accounting Office. 2003. *Campaign Finance Reform: Early Experience of Two States That Offer Full Public Funding for Political Candidates,* (Washington, D.C., Government Printing Office, May 9, 2003).

Gove, Samuel K. 2001. "Origins, Mechanics, and Politics." In *Redistricting Illinois, 2001.* Urbana-Champaign, IL: Institute for Government and Public Affairs.

Gove, Samuel K., and James D. Nowlan. 1996. *Illinois Politics and Government: The Expanding Metropolitan Frontier.* Lincoln, NE: University of Nebraska Press.

Grofman, Bernard, ed. 1996. *Legislative Term Limits: Public Choice Perspectives.* Boston, MA: Kluwer Academic Publishers.

Harris, Don. 1992. "Calling it quits at the Capitol, Record 19 leaving legislative posts," *The Arizona Republic* (May 10, 1992), B1, B6.

Herzberg, Donald G., and Alan Rosenthal, eds. 1972. *Strengthening the States: Essays on Legislative Reform.* New York: Anchor.

Hibbing, John R. 1991. *Congressional Careers: Contours of Life in the U.S. House of Representatives.* Chapel Hill: University of North Carolina Press.

Householder, Larry. 2001. "Term Limits and a Model for Governance" *Spectrum* (Fall 2001): 31.

Hyneman, Charles S. 1938. "Tenure and Turnover in Legislative Personnel." *Annals of the American Academy of Political and Social Science* 195: 21–31.

Jacobson, Gary C. 2000. *The Politics of Congressional Elections.* 5th ed. New York: Addison-Wesley.

Jarvis, Matthew. 2004. "Knowledgeable Observer Survey." Data analyzed at the University of California at Los Angeles.

Jewell, Malcolm E., and Sarah M. Morehouse. 2001. *Political Parties and Elections in American States.* 4th ed. Washington, DC: CQ Press.

Jewell, Malcolm E., and Marcia Lynn Whicker. 1994. *Legislative Leadership in the American States.* Ann Arbor, MI: University of Michigan Press.

Karp, Jeffrey A. 1995. "Examining Public Support for Term Limits." *Public Opinion Quarterly* 59: 373–91.

Kiefer, Michael, 1998. "The work of Art Hamilton," *New Times* (October 1, 1998).

King, James D. 2000. "Changes in Professionalism in U.S. State Legislatures." *Legislative Studies Quarterly* 25: 327–44.

Kousser, Thad. 2005. *Term Limits and the Dismantling of Legislative Professionalism* (New York: Cambridge University Press, 2005).

———. 2006. "The Limited Effect of Term Limits: Contingent Effects on the Complexity and Breadth of Laws." *State Politics and Policy Quarterly* 6: 410–29.

Kullman, Joe. 2001. "Lawmakers urge more commitment to environment," *East Valley Tribune* (June 29, 2001), np.

Kurfirst, Robert. 1996. "Term-Limit Logic: Paradigms and Paradoxes." *Polity* 29: 119–40.

Lazarus, Jeffery. 2006. "Term Limits' Multiple Effects on State Legislators' Career Decisions." *State Policy and Politics Quarterly* 6: 357–83.

Ledbetter, Cal Jr. and Beadle Moore and Glen W. Sparrow. 1979. *The Arkansas Plan: A Case Study in Public Policy. University of Arkansas at Little Rock Monograph Series.*

Little, Thomas H. and Rick Farmer. 2007. "Legislative Leadership." In *Institutional Change in American Politics,* Karl T. Kurtz, Bruce Cain, Richard G. Niemi, eds. Ann Arbor: University of Michigan Press.

Loomis, Burdett R. 1994. *Time, Politics, and Policies: A Legislative Year*. Lawrence: University Press of Kansas.

Lopez, E.J. 2003. "Tem Limits: Causes and Consequences." *Public Choice* 114: 1–56.

Lucas, Beth. 2000. "Term limits arrive: What's next," *Arizona Capital Times* (May 5, 2000), 1, 13, and 14.

———. 2001. "Sen. Smith won't seek reelection, blames Senate atmosphere," *Arizona Capitol Times* (November 23, 2001), 20.

Lucas, Donna and Porter Novelli. 2001. "Ten Years Into Term Limits: Academic Findings and the View from the Legislature," Institute of Governmental Studies Conference, Sacramento, California, May 17, 2001.

Malbin, Michael J. 1992. "Federalists v. Antifederalists: The Term-Limitation Debate at the Founding." In *Limiting Legislative Terms*, eds. Gerald Benjamin and Michael J. Malbin. Washington, DC: CQ Press.

Malbin, Michael J., and Gerald Benjamin. 1992. "Legislatures after Term Limits." In *Limiting Legislative Terms*, eds. Gerald Benjamin and Michael J. Malbin. Washington, DC: CQ Press.

Man of the Year. 2006. Los Angeles: Universal Studios.

Meinke, Scott R., and Edward B. Hasecke. 2003. "Term Limits, Professionalization, and Partisan Control in U.S. State Legislatures." *Journal of Politics* 65: 898–908.

Miller, James Nathan. 1965. "Hamstrung Legislatures." *National Civic Review* 54: 178–87.

Moen, Matthew C. and Kenneth T. Palmer. 2003. "Maine: The Cutting Edge of Term Limits," in *The Test of Time: Coping with Legislative Term Limits*, ed. Rick Farmer, John David Rausch, Jr., and John C. Green (Lanham, Maryland: Lexington Books, 2003), 48–50.

Moeser, Chris. 1999. "'Mushrooms' fight for education," *The Arizona Republic* (April 4, 1999), A6.

Moncrief, Gary, Richard G. Niemi, and Linda W. Powell. Nd. "Time, Term Limits, and Turnover: Trends in Membership Turnover in U.S. State Legislatures." 2004 in *Legislative Studies Quarterly*.

Moncrief, Gary F. and Joel A. Thompson. 1993. *Changing Patterns in State Legislative Careers*. Ann Arbor, Mi.: University of Michigan Press.

———. 2001. "On the Outside Looking in: Lobbyists' Perspectives on the Effects of State Legislative Term Limits." *State Politics and Policy Quarterly* 1: 394–411.

Moncrief, Gary F., Joel A. Thompson and William Cassie. 1996. "Revisiting the State of U.S. State Legislative Research." *Legislative Studies Quarterly* 21: 301–35.

Moncrief, Gary F., Joel A. Thompson, and Karl T. Kurtz. 1996. "The Old Statehouse, It Ain't What It Used to Be." *Legislative Studies Quarterly* 21: 57–72.

Moncrief, Gary F., Joel A. Thompson, Michael Haddon, and Robert Hoyer. 1992. "For Whom the Bell Tolls: Term Limits and State Legislatures." *Legislative Studies Quarterly* 17: 37–47.

Mondak, Jeffrey J. 1995. "Elections as Filters: Term Limits and the Composition of the U.S. House." *Political Research Quarterly* 48: 701–27.

Mooney, Christopher Z. 1994. "Measuring U.S. State Legislative Professionalism: An Evaluation of Five Indices." *State and Local Government Review* 26: 70–78.

———. 1995. "Citizens, Structures, and Sister States: Influences on State Legislative Reform." *Legislative Studies Quarterly* 20: 47–68.

Morehouse, Sarah McCally and Malcom E. Jewell. 2003. *State Politics, Parties and Policy.* New York: Roman and Littlefield.

National Conference of State Legislatures. 1999. Members Termed Out 1996–2000. Denver, CO: National Conference of State Legislatures.

National Governors Association. 2007. "Governors' Political Affiliations and Terms of Office, 2007." http://www.nga.org/Files/pdf/GOVLIST2007.PDF.

Olson, David J. 1992. "Term Limits Fail in Washington: The 1991 Battleground." In *Limiting Legislative Terms,* eds. Gerald Benjamin and Michael J. Malbin. Washington, DC: CQ Press.

Opheim, Cynthia. 1994. "The Effect of United States State Legislative Term Limits Revisited." *Legislative Studies Quarterly* 19: 49–59.

Osborne, Nathan. 2004. "California's Termed-Out Legislators—Where Do They Go?" Paper completed for Political Science 102G: The Laws of Politics, UC San Diego, June 2004.

Peery, George and Thomas H. Little. 2003. "Leading When the Bell Tolls: Perceptions of Power Among Termed and Untermed Leaders" in *The Test of Time: Coping with Legislative Term Limits.* Rick Farmer, John David Rausch, Jr. and John C. Green, eds. Lanham, MD: Lexington Books.

Peirce, Neal R. and Jerry Hagstrom. 1984. *The Book of America: Inside Fifty States Today.* New York: Norton.

Perricone, Chuck. 2001. "A New Paradigm Under Term Limits," *Spectrum* 74 (Fall 2001): 30.

Petracca, Mark. 1991a. "The Poison of Professional Politics." *Policy Analysis* 151: online edition.

—— 1991b. "Pro: It's Time to Return to 'Citizen-Legislators.'" *San Francisco Chronicle,* 26 March 1991.

——. 1992. "Rotation in Office: The History of an Idea." In *Limiting Legislative Terms,* eds. Gerald Benjamin and Michael J. Malbin. Washington, DC: CQ Press.

Pitzl, Mary Jo, Chip Scutari and Ashley Bach. 2002. "Candidate fillings hit state record," *The Arizona Republic* (June 13, 2002), 1, 16.

Polsby, Nelson W. 1991. "Some Arguments against Congressional Term Limitations." *Harvard Journal of Law and Public Policy* 16: 1516–26.

Powell, Richard J. 2000. "The Impact of Term Limits on the Candidacy Decisions of State Legislators in U.S. House Elections." *Legislative Studies Quarterly* 25: 645–61.

Price, Charles M. 1992. "The Guillotine Comes to California: Term-Limit Politics in the Golden State." In *Limiting Legislative Terms,* eds. Gerald Benjamin and Michael J. Malbin. Washington, DC: CQ Press.

Rausch, John David. 1998. "Legislative Term Limits and Electoral Competition in Oklahoma: A Preliminary Assessment." *Oklahoma Politics* 7: 39–58.

Reinhart, Mary K. 1993. "Lawmakers open session tomorrow aiming to fit priorities into 100 days," *The Arizona Daily Star* (January 10, 1993).

Riske, Phil. 2006. "Bee Fires 4 Top Senate Aides, Says Their Longevity Was a Detriment," *Arizona Capitol Times* (November 17, 2006): 1, 6.

Robb, Robert. 2000. "Term limits work, and lawmakers hate that," *The Arizona Republic* June 16, 2000, B11.

Rosenthal, Alan. 1981. *Legislative Life: People, Processes, and Performance in the States.* New York: Harper and Row.

———. 1992. "The Effects of Term Limits on Legislatures: A Comment." In *Limiting Legislative Terms*, eds. Gerald Benjamin and Michael J. Malbin. Washington, DC: CQ Press.

———. 1993. *The Third House: Lobbyists and Lobbying in the States*. Washington, DC: CQ Press.

———. 1996. "The Legislature: Unraveling of Institutional Fabric." In *The State of the States*, ed. Carl E. Van Horn. 3rd ed. Washington, DC: CQ Press.

———. 1998. *The Decline of Representative Democracy*. Washington, DC: CQ Press.

———. 2004. *Heavy Lifting: The Job of the American Legislature* (Washington, DC: CQ Press, 2004).

Rosenthal, Alan, Burdett A. Loomis, John R. Hibbing, and Karl T. Kurtz. 2003. *Republic on Trial: The Case for Representative Democracy*. Washington, DC: CQ Press.

Ruelas, Richard. 2000. "Good voters go for bad legislators," *Arizona Republic* (December 1, 2000), B1.

Saxl, Michael V. 2001. "Term Limits and Diminished Returns," *Spectrum* 74 (Fall 2001): 27.

Schreckhise, William D., and Janine A. Parry and Todd G. Shields. 2001. "Rising Republicanism in the Arkansas Electorate? A Characterization of Arkansas' Political Attitudes and Participation Rates." *The MidSouth Political Science Review.* 5. 1–20.

Scutari, Chip, and Robbie Sherwood. 2002. "New legislature has fewer women," *The Arizona Republic* (December 16, 2002), A1.

Smith, Michael A. October/November 2003. "Kansas: The Three Party State." *Campaigns and Elections* v. 24, no 10: 36–37.

Squire, Peverill. 1992. "Legislative Professionalization and Membership Diversity in State Legislatures." *Legislative Studies Quarterly* 17: 69–79.

State of California, Department of Finance. 1999. *Race/Ethnic Population Estimates: Components of Change for California Counties, July 1970–July 1990*. Sacramento, CA: Department of Finance.

———. 2003. *Race/Ethnic Population Estimates: Components of Change for California Counties, April 1990 to April 2000*. Sacramento, CA: Department of Finance.

State Politics and Policy Quarterly. 2006. Winter. Champaign, IL: University of Illinois Press, vol. 6, no. 4.

Steen, Jennifer A. 2006. "The Impact of State Legislative Term Limits on the Supply of Congressional Candidates." *State Politics and Policy Quarterly* 6: 430–47.

Straayer, John A. 2000. *The Colorado General Assembly*. Boulder, CO: University Press of Colorado.

———. 2003. "Colorado: Lots of Commotion, Limited Consequences," in Rick Farmer, John David Rausch Jr., and John C. Green, eds. *The Test of Time: Coping with Legislative Term Limits*. Lanham, New York, Boulder and Oxford: Lexington Books.

Straayer, John A., and Jennie Drage Bowser. 2004. *Colorado Legislative Term Limits*. Joint Project on Term Limits, National Conference of State Legislatures, Council of State Governments, State Legislative Leaders Foundation, http://www.ncsl.org/jptl/Case Studies/Case Studies Contents.htm. 36, Table 21.

Thomas, Clive S., and Ronald J. Hrebenar. 2004. "Interest Groups in the States." In *Politics in the American States*, eds. Virginia Gray and Russell L. Hanson. 8th ed. Washington, DC: CQ Press.

Thompson, Joel, and Gary Moncrief. 2003. "Lobbying under Limits: Interest Group Perspectives" in Rick Farmer, John David Rausch Jr. and John C. Green, eds, *The Test of Time: Coping with Legislative Term Limits.* Lanham, Boulder, New York and Oxford: Lexington Books.

Tothero, Rebecca A. 2003. "The Impact of Term Limits on State Legislators' Ambition for Local Office: The Case of the Michigan House." *Publius* 33: 111–22.

University of Akron. 2007. "2007 Ohio Politics Survey." http://www.uakron.edu/ bliss/docs /Springpollreport.pdf

U.S. Term Limits, Inc. 2003. "About USTL–Mission." http://www.termlimits.org/ About/about. html (March 12, 2003).

Van der Slik, Jack R., and Kent D. Redfield. 1989. *Lawmaking in Illinois: Legislative Politics, People and Processes.* Springfield, IL: Sangamon State University.

Wheeler, Charles N., III. 2000. "It's the 20th Anniversary of the Regrettable Cutback Amendment." *Illinois Issues,* November, 42–43.

White, John K., and Daniel M. Shea. 2000. *New Party Politics: From Jefferson and Hamilton to the Information Age.* New York: Palgrave McMillan.

Will, George F. 1993. *Restoration: Congress, Term Limits, and the Recovery of Deliberative Democracy.* New York: Free Press.

Wong, Christina, 2003. "In California, the Governor has Become the Legislative Gatekeeper." *Institute of Governmental Studies Public Affairs Report,* vol. 44, no.1, Spring 2003.

Yang, Kelly. 2002a. *Percentage of Termed-Out Members Who Run for Other Office.* Institute of Governmental Studies Research Brief, April 9, 2002.

———. 2002b. "Term Limits Get Too Much Credit for Boosting Female and Minority Representation," *Institute of Governmental Studies Public Affairs Report,* vol. 43, no.2, Summer 2002.

York, Anthony. 1999. "Bedlam by the Bay," posted on Salon.com on August 5, 1999.

Yozwiak, Steve. 1991. "Politicians' Standing Plummets," *The Arizona Republic,* February 13, 1991, A1, A7.

Index

About the Contributors

Art English is a professor of political science at the University of Arkansas at Little Rock. He has authored and coauthored numerous articles on Arkansas Government.

David R. Berman is a professor emeritus of political science and a senior research fellow at the Morrison Institute at Arizona State University. Among his books are *State and Local Politics*, *Arizona Politics and Government*, and *Local Government and the States*.

Bruce Cain is Robson Professor of Political Science and the director of the Institute of Governmental Studies at the University of California, Berkeley. He is co-author or coeditor of *The Reapportionment Puzzle*, *The Personal Vote*, *Congressional Redistricting*, and *Voting at the Political Fault Line: California's Experiment with the Blanket Primary*. He has served widely as a redistricting consultant.

Rick Farmer is director of committee staff at the Oklahoma House of Representatives and a fellow at the Ray C. Bliss Institute of Applied Politics at the University of Akron. He is coeditor of *The Test of Time: Coping with Legislative Term Limits*.

John C. Green is director of the Ray C. Bliss Institute of Applied Politics and distinguished professor of political science at the University of Akron. He has written works on political parties, interest groups, and social movements, with a special emphasis on the role of religion in politics and campaign finance.

Rich Jones is the director of policy and research at the Bell Policy Center in Denver, Colorado where he advocates for policies that promote opportunity for all Coloradans. Previously he was the director of legislative programs for the National Conference of State Legislatures and worked in the Pennsylvania General Assembly.

Thad Kousser is an assistant professor of political science at the University of California, San Diego and the author of *Term Limits and the Dismantling of State Legislative Professionalism* and coauthor of *Adapting to Term Limits: Recent Experiences and New Directions*.

Karl T. Kurtz is director of the Trust for Representative Democracy at the National Conference of State Legislatures and has been working with and studying American legislatures for over thirty-five years. He is coauthor of *Republic on Trial: The Case for Representative Democracy* and coeditor of *Institutional Change in American Politics: The Case of Term Limits*.

Thomas H. Little is the director of curriculum development and research for the State Legislative Leaders Foundation. A former associate professor at the University of Texas at Arlington, he has published numerous book chapters and articles on state legislatures and legislative leadership.

Christopher Z. Mooney is a professor of political science with the Institute of Government and Public Affairs at the University of Illinois at Springfield. He is the founding editor of *State Politics and Policy Quarterly* and conducts research on state legislatures and morality policy.

Richard J. Powell is an associate professor of political science at the University of Maine. He is a coauthor of *Changing Members: The Maine Legislature in the Era of Term Limits* as well as numerous journal articles and book chapters on term limits, state politics, the presidency, Congress, and elections.

Alan Rosenthal is a professor of public policy and political science at the Eagleton Institute of Politics, Rutgers University. He has written extensively about state legislatures, most recently *Heavy Lifting: The Job Of The American Legislature*.

Michael A. Smith is associate chair of political science at Emporia State University. His publications include several journal articles and a book, *Bringing Representation Home*, in which he studied U.S. state representatives' "home styles."

John A. Straayer is professor of political science at Colorado State University. He directs the department's legislative internship program. His publications include *The Colorado General Assembly*.

Brian Weberg is director of the Legislative Management Program at the National Conference of State Legislatures. He is an expert on legislative staffing systems, organization and management and regularly consults with state legislatures on these and related topics.

Jason Wood has worked as a consultant on numerous state legislative and local election campaigns, and in the administration of two mayors of the City of Cleveland.

Gerald C. Wright is professor of political science at Indiana University. He is currently involved in a study of coalitions and representation in Congress and the state legislatures.